Magic Guidebooks

Disneyland

2024

The BEST Disneyland Tips, Virtual Queue Tips, Disney Genie+, Disney California Adventure, Star Wars Galaxy's Edge, Avengers Campus, Disneyland Dining, Hidden Mickeys, and more!

ISBN: 979-8-9889768-3-7

Magic Guidebooks

Disneyland 2024

- Covers the entire Disneyland Resort including Disneyland Park, Disney California Adventure Park, Downtown Disney, and beyond
- Fast and useful insider tips and recommendations
- Money and time-saving tactics for worry-free planning
- Line-skipping strategies without the need to purchase Disney Genie+ or Lightning Lanes
- Discover the best food with unbiased restaurant reviews and fan-favorite menu choices
- Dedicated chapters for Star Wars: Galaxy's Edge and the Marvel-themed Avengers Campus
- Explore secrets, histories, and magical details found around the Disneyland Resort—including lists of Hidden Mickeys!

BONUS: Guides to Universal Studios Hollywood, Los Angeles attractions, the San Diego Zoo, and Legoland

Table of Contents

ABOUT THIS GUIDE

When developing and writing this book, we had *you* in mind. Maybe you're a first-time visitor to the Disneyland Resort, or perhaps, you've frequented it over the decades. Wherever you come from and whatever your experience, we wanted to provide a complete guide from start to finish, while giving a critique of the Disneyland Resort. The purpose of this guide is to give real advice covering the many attractions, restaurants, and hotels at the Disneyland Resort and beyond.

Who are we? Well, we're theme park enthusiasts who spend a lot of time gathering first-hand knowledge and experiences from all around the world. In fact, we've visited every Disney Resort, including the new Shanghai Disneyland, because we love them so much. Advice in this guide is crafted from trial and error—and we're passing the fruits of our hard work on to you!

Keep in mind that this guide is an "unofficial edition," meaning that we are in no way affiliated with the Walt Disney Company, the Disneyland Resort, the Walt Disney World Resort, nor have we ever been. We are simply fans of the Disneyland Resort who are giving an honest opinion on what it has to offer. Though we call ourselves fans and do our best to keep a fun feel, we're also critical of the Resort when needed. It's more important to us that you have a great vacation by skipping out on some of the less-than-exciting attractions than for us to make Disney look good.

If you're planning a longer stay in Southern California, we've added more exciting attractions to our guide. Get information on visiting Universal Studios Hollywood (including details on the Wizarding World of Harry Potter), LEGOLAND, the San Diego Zoo, and more! There's so much to cover, but we've managed to fit everything into this guide—so don't forget to pack your Magic Guidebook for your trip!

FOR DISNEYLAND NEWBIES

If you've never been to the Disneyland Resort before, this book is perfect for you! We've crammed our guide with tidbits about the best food, attraction recommendations based on interest, hotel pros/cons, and so much more. We'll fill you in on Disneyland lingo and history as well as what's coming next. In the end, you'll have the knowledge of a pro!

FOR RETURN VISITORS

The Disneyland Resort is a constantly changing place. From exciting themed dining to limited-time thrilling attractions, sometimes we can't imagine what would come next! If you haven't been to Disneyland in ten years, this guide is a great fit.

However, if you go every week, you probably won't learn much. That, of course, doesn't mean that you won't learn *anything*, but you're likely already a pro, and a guide to a park that's basically your second home won't be much use. Still, if you're curious, we welcome you along for the ride! Even as often as we go, we still learned *a lot* from researching for this book.

A WORD FOR ALL

Since Walt Disney World Resort updates its experiences so frequently, some of the items in this guide will change even weeks after its publication. For example, restaurants in Disney Springs might close, attractions may be re-themed, and popular food items could become discontinued. To cover this, we send updates via our free e-mail newsletter to our readers.

If you'd like updates about future guidebook releases, visit our website and sign up today for our free e-mail list: www.magicguidebooks.com/list (don't worry, we won't spam you).

THE HAPPIEST PLACE ON EARTH

The Disneyland Resort in California is home to virtually countless attractions and experiences designed for guests of all ages. With two breathtaking theme parks, three stylish hotels, and a dazzling Downtown Disney for shopping and eating, it's no wonder that millions of people flock to Disneyland from all over the world! In fact, 18 million annual visitors come to Disneyland, making it the second-most visited theme park in the world (behind the Magic Kingdom in Walt Disney World). Disney California Adventure has just over half as many guests with about 9.8 million annual visitors.

So, why is it "The Happiest Place on Earth"? The truth is, no matter our age, Disneyland brings us back to feeling like a kid again! There are streets that emulate a turn-of-the-century American town, lands of yesterday and tomorrow, and even an alien planet straight out of the Star Wars universe! With world-class rides, stunning fireworks over a castle, delicious gourmet food, wondrous lands, and themed bars for adults—the Disneyland Resort has it all!

In short, whether you enjoy thrilling attractions like roller coasters or scenic views over a river, you will be floored by the magic of Disneyland. Walt Disney's dream park has lasted all of these years due to inventive thinking and daring moves designed by folks who love to entertain. To this day, the Cast Members of Disneyland join together to create unforgettable experiences for their guests. No matter who you are or where you come from, the Disneyland Resort welcomes you with open arms.

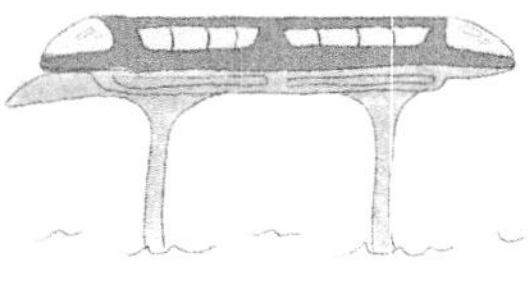

THE DISNEY WAY

The Disneyland Resort prides itself for being "show ready"—meaning that the attractions and experiences are all part of a believable, functioning show. Every piece of Disneyland is treated like an on-going theatrical production and run like a well-oiled machine. The idea is that the storytelling is convincing and surprising to all guests. After all, you're paying a ticket price to visit a place that feels like magic.

Another facet of Disney's "show ready" concept is a spotless stage. The Disneyland Resort is immaculately clean. This means that you're never too far from a trash or recycle bin (they're practically everywhere). These receptacles are decorated to fit within the lands and are frequently emptied by custodial staff. Even the janitors of Disneyland are part of the show. You might catch them greeting guests and painting Disney characters on sidewalks with their brooms and a bucket of water!

In the event that an attraction doesn't feel show ready, Disney will pull the plug. A single, flickering lightbulb on a ride could force the attraction to close until it's show ready again. If you've ever visited another theme park and spotted dirty restrooms, piles of trash, and graffiti, Disneyland will feel like a breath of fresh air.

WHY DO I NEED A GUIDE?

While you can visit the Disneyland Resort any time and attempt to experience it on your own, having invaluable tips from insiders will make all the difference. This guide will save you time waiting in lines, money, and give you the best options to fit your mood. We visit the Disneyland Resort more times in a year than we can count and we know all the ins and outs of the parks.

Whether you are looking to ride all of the thrilling attractions in one day, or don't like rides at all, this book will be your guide. Since the idea is to save you time, we've decided not to drone on and on about every little detail and thought about visiting the park. However, that doesn't mean we're not thorough. The point of this guide is to give you the most important information and travel tips to make planning your trip easy and your experience at Disneyland a lot of fun (after all, fun is the reason you're visiting)!

We detail ideas for trips with kids, other adults, and even just yourself! Packed with insider secrets—we call them "Magic Tips" — we answer questions you didn't think to ask! These include delicious secret menu items, little-known experiences, hidden adventures, and more. Our guidebook is your ultimate planning tactic to visiting the Disneyland Resort!

COMPARED TO DISNEY WORLD

As native Southern Californians, Disneyland has a special place in our hearts. Truthfully, we believe that there is a magic in the Disneyland Resort that doesn't exist at any other Disney theme park. While we *love* Disney World, Walt Disney created Disneyland (he unfortunately passed before Walt Disney World was completed) and the magic residing in the Disneyland Park comes from Walt himself.

The Cast Members (Disney employees) are always helpful and friendly and the parks are impeccably clean! Sure, many of the rides are similarly themed at both Resorts, like Pirates of the Caribbean and Big Thunder Mountain Railroad (though you'll notice plenty of differences in these rides), but the Disneyland Resort has more details in the parks that create a magic unlike anywhere else.

We will add that Disney World's castle is much larger (over 100 feet taller than the Sleeping Beauty Castle in California), and many Disney World fanatics notice this first. Disneyland and Disney California Adventure have unique attractions like the Matterhorn Bobsleds, Cars Land, Indiana Jones Adventure, and the seasonal Haunted Mansion Holiday starring the characters from Tim Burton's *The Nightmare Before Christmas*, to name a few. Disneyland and Disney California Adventure are located right across from one another, so you won't have to ride on busses from park to park like at Walt Disney World.

HOW LONG SHOULD I STAY?

To best answer this question, we must first address Disney's approach to creating this vacation destination. The Disneyland Resort is broken into four main areas: Disneyland Park, Disney California Adventure Park, Downtown Disney, and the Disneyland Resort Hotels. Each of these areas provides unique entertainment and accommodations for visiting guests. Disneyland Park focuses on Disney Princesses, Star Wars, and Mickey Mouse and his friends (Minnie Mouse, Donald Duck, Goofy, and Pluto). Disney California Adventure Park offers attractions based on the Pixar and Marvel franchises. While both theme parks reach beyond those center focuses, those are the major appeals for visiting each destination.

Downtown Disney and the Resort hotels offer unique entertainment without a paid ticket. These include world-class themed dining, pool lounges, virtual reality experiences, and shopping. To do it all, you'll need at least 3-4 days at the Resort. We recommend dedicating an entire day to each theme park and then a separate day to either complete what you missed or experience again what you liked most.

Keep in mind that most visitors of Disneyland aren't staying on property or even at a nearby hotel. Many guests visit just for the day and are still able to experience much of what the Resort has to offer—if they have a great plan of action. Our guide gives all of the recommendations, tips, tricks, and action plans you'll need to cover everything—no matter how long you're planning to stay. Be sure to check out our pre-planned attraction lists at the end of this guide to discover the easiest methods for skipping the lines and doing it all.

WHY IS DISNEYLAND SO EXPENSIVE?

It's no secret that Disneyland tickets, hotel rooms, dining, and merchandise cost a pretty penny. All right, it's more than a pretty penny; Disneyland is expensive! A bottle of soda costs around $4 and one meal for a family of four can easily exceed $100. The least expensive hotel room on the Disneyland Resort's website is listed at over $300 a night!

Disney claims that it raises prices to help with guest flow. Popular dates, like weekends, have higher prices than a Tuesday or Wednesday. We've been a little skeptical of this claim in the past (is Disney just being greedy?), but recently the crowds have thinned on typically popular days. Even traditionally busy summer months like June, July, and August have dwindled in attendance. Instead, guests are visiting during the fall and spring to save money. Families can often save *hundreds* of dollars just by booking on less expensive dates versus a holiday weekend.

Parents who want to experience Disney magic with their kids often save for years before booking. We understand the worry that your trip could break the bank—or become a total bust with a high price tag. Thus, we created this guide to help plan your Disneyland trip with ease—and save some money along the way. Keep in mind that Disneyland isn't just any amusement park. This is a world-class, premium experience. However, there are several tricks, discounts, and tips you'll want to pick up from this guide before you go.

DISNEYLAND LINGO

If you are new to the Disney theme parks or just haven't been in some time, you'll instantly notice a new lingo at the parks. Whether you're talking to a fellow guest or Cast Member, or reading signs by rides, it helps to know the terms first. Secondly, we have our own phrases that we use frequently throughout this book. Most of these phrases are fairly intuitive, but, so that we are all on the same page, we invite you to familiarize yourself with the section to help with reading this guide.

THE LINGO

The Disneyland Resort - The area that encompasses both theme parks (Disneyland and Disney California Adventure), Downtown Disney, the three hotels, and the parking lots.

Cast Member - A term for all Disney employees. We find that the Disneyland Resort Cast Members are the friendliest of them all!

Park Hopper - A ticket that allows you to visit both Disneyland and Disney California Adventure in a single day.

Magic Key - Disneyland's annual pass program. Guests who purchase these passes are called "Magic Key holders" and they can visit the parks several times a year for one price.

"Dark Ride" - An indoor ride where the vehicle is guided along a track. Typically, these are family-friendly rides like "it's a small world" —and they also have air conditioning!

Virtual Queue - A virtual line where a guest is called back to the attraction once their "boarding group" time is called. Guests often use the Disneyland app to secure a boarding group within the virtual queue to select attractions.

Lightning Lane - Skip the lines through a

dedicated queue at dozens of attractions. Lightning Lane is accessible as an extra-paid feature guests can access using the Disneyland mobile app.

Disney Genie – An in-app planning tool for building your daily itinerary. Guests can manage their plans day-of and get forecasts about lower wait times. An upgradeable feature called Disney Genie+ allows guests to pay in bulk for access to most Lightning Lanes.

Single Rider Line - A fast way to get on the rides as long as you don't mind traveling by yourself.

Walt Disney Imagineer - Simply known as "Imagineers," these are the creatives behind the attraction designs of the parks.

Closed for Refurbishment - No one likes seeing this sign as it means that the ride is closed for restoration. Some refurbishments can last a couple of days, while others have lasted years. Refurbishment scheduling occurs most often in the off-season months like January through March.

MAGICBAND+

This amazing (and stylish) piece of technology allows you to do it all with a wearable bracelet! The updated MagicBand+ works as your theme park ticket, lights up during special moments around the parks and during select shows, plays interactive games, and more. The new MagicBand+ starts around $35. Find them for sale on ShopDisney.com and inside several stores within the parks, hotels, and Downtown Disney.

Only MagicBand+ currently works at Disneyland (this could update later in 2024). If you have an older MagicBand model from Walt Disney World, you likely won't be able to use it at Disneyland. If you've purchased a MagicBand+ or already have one, you can link it by following the directions on the Disneyland app, just tap "menu "followed by "MagicBand+."

Keeping in mind that MagicBand+ may not have tap-to-pay features or unlock hotel rooms at the resort. Nonetheless, guests using Lightning Lanes and watching nighttime shows may find that this these high-tech bracelets make their vacation a breeze. MagicBand+ is not required and guests may use their mobile phones to access theme park tickets and Lightning Lane reservations. However, tapping your MagicBand+ to access the park and Lightning Lanes is much faster than using your phone. A MagicBand can only be linked to one person, so each person in your party will need their own if they'd like to use its features.

LINGO FOR THIS GUIDEBOOK

Top Choice! - Our most-recommended hot spots and eateries.

· **Magic Tips** ·
We post some of our best tips in boxes that look like this! Magic Tips are designed to help you save time waiting in lines, get the best viewing areas for shows and parades, and save money while booking! They might also provide some extra context and recommendations for experiencing a certain attraction.

RIDE LEVELS

- **Thrill Riders** - Those looking for themed rollercoasters, drop rides, and other thrills will enjoy these attractions.
- **Everyone** - Great for riders of all ages—even many Thrill Riders will likely enjoy these attractions.
- **Family** - Suited for kids and adults, but these attractions may not interest Thrill Riders.
- **Kids** - Designed for kids ages 6-10.
- **Young Kids** - Designed for young kids ages 2-5.

RESOURCES

DISCOUNT BOOKING WEBSITES

DisneyRewards.com

Getting a Disney Visa credit card comes with many benefits for your stay. In fact, many infrequent visitors love the Disney Visa Card because it offers additional discounts they can use when booking and visiting the parks. Perks may include discounted hotel rooms, exclusive character greets, free items for your visit, and a sign-up offer with a statement credit. Disney Visa cardholders also receive 10% off select merchandise and dining around the Disneyland Resort as well as 15% off select guided tours. Not only does Disney Visa work at the Disneyland Resort, but its benefits work at Walt Disney World and the Disney Cruise Line, too!

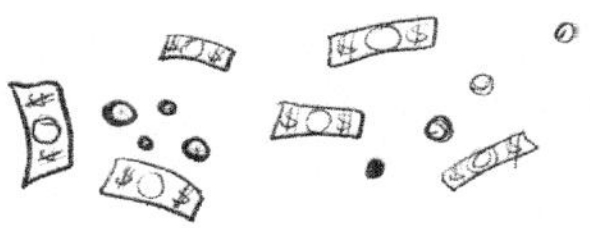

Orbitz.com/deals

For special promotions (look for codes for up to 15% off hotels). These often work at the Disneyland Resort hotels as well as neighboring accommodations.

Bookit.com/coupon-codes

Search here for discounts on flights, hotels, and ticket bundles.

Amextravel.com

If you have an American Express card, this can save you money, plus earn you more rewards.

Costcotravel.com

If you have a Costco Membership, you might save big on vacation packages and tickets.

CONTACT INFORMATION

Disneyland.com
Visit for booking and up-to-date information.

Hotel Reservations (714) 781-6425
https://disneyland.disney.go.com/hotels

Disney Dining (714) 781-DINE
Book your restaurant reservations in advance.
https://disneyland.disney.go.com/dining

Tickets (714) 781-4565
Book your tickets in advance.
https://disneyland.disney.go.com/tickets

RESORT MAP

For navigating the parks, we recommend using the maps found on disneyland.com or the Disneyland app in conjunction with this guide. Once you arrive, don't forget to pick up a free park map when you enter the parks.

INTRODUCTION

On April 30, 2021, Disneyland reopened its parks after an unprecedented 412-day closure due to the Covid-19 pandemic. Initially, capacity was capped at 25%, and every guest needed a park ticket and a theme park reservation.

While the world has seemingly moved on from pandemic-era restrictions, it's still apparent that the Disneyland theme parks are forever changed. Required theme park reservations, mobile ordering, and the use of virtual queues expanded as a result of the guidelines for reopening. While it's unclear whether or not Disneyland will keep its reservation system, it's apparent that managing crowd sizes is the Resort's priority. As new attractions debut in 2024, some experiences may use a Virtual Queue to manage demand to keep the physical lines at a minimum.

NEW 2024 ATTRACTIONS

TIANA'S BAYOU ADVENTURE

Disneyland Park

Opening Date: Late 2024

Tiana's Bayou Adventure reimagines the previous Splash Mountain ride into an attraction based on Disney's 2009 animated film, *The Princess and the Frog*. Set in the Louisiana bayou, guests follow the tale of Princess Tiana after the film's events. Tiana now owns a booming restaurant business, but there's an important missing ingredient! Dozens of new animatronics, effects, music, and even the smell of beignets bring this story to life for all ages! Experience this new attraction later in the year.

STAR TOURS UPDATES

Disneyland Park

Opening Date: Spring 2024

New destinations are coming to Star Tours from the Disney+ series *Ahsoka*! It's unclear if the attraction will shut down before these changes are added to the ride. However, Disneyland has set an opening timeline for Spring 2024.

FANTASMIC!

Disneyland Park

Reopening Date: Spring 2024

After the Maleficent dragon animatronic caught fire in 2023, Disneyland hasn't taken any chances reopening its *Fantasmic!* nighttime spectacular. Instead, the Resort decided to bring new additions to the show at a later time. *Fantasmic!* is scheduled to reopen in Spring 2024 at Disneyland Park.

HAUNTED MANSION EXPANSION

Disneyland Park

Opening Date: Sometime in 2024

Disneyland plans to expand its Haunted Mansion attraction with a new queue and shop. The queue will have nods to some of the fictional characters in the ride, and the shop will be based on Madam Leota. Disneyland may keep the ride open while these changes are being made to the outside.

MORE EXPERIENCES

D23 CONVENTION

Anaheim, CA

Reopening Date: August 9-11, 2024

D23 is the biggest Disney fan event ever! Previously known at the D23 Expo, D23: The Ultimate Disney Fan Event announces the latest news and product releases—including the theme parks! In the past, updates for both Disneyland and Disney+ have debuted at D23. In addition, there are special celebrity guests, company executives, and plenty of free exclusives that only those visiting can snag. D23 takes place at the Anaheim Convention Center (about a 15-minute walk from Disneyland). In addition, the Honda Center in Anaheim will host some of the most significant parts of the Expo for attendees to see. Dates are subject to change. For more information, visit: www.d23.com.

DOWNTOWN DISNEY TRANSFORMATION

Downtown Disney

Reopening Date: Throughout 2024

Downtown Disney began its transformation in 2022 but will continue into 2024. New dining, shopping, and entertainment additions will include Din Tai Fung, Porto's, a stage, and more restaurants, including Centrico and Paseo. Downtown Disney takes on a mid-century modern feel with its reimagining that could feel more like Disneyland of the past!

PLANNING WHEN TO VISIT

Wanting to go to Disneyland is easy—planning it can be a whole other animal! The good news is, we're here to help. We've been to the Disneyland Resort more times than we can count and we've picked up hundreds of useful tips for you. In this part of the guide, we will walk you through the choices of travel and our recommendations for saving time and money.

It's true that some months at Disneyland are less crowded than others. Visiting during holidays when school is out will be much more packed than visiting a weekday in mid-September. That may seem obvious, but there are several other dates that you might assume won't be busy, but are indeed very popular—and vice versa.

Choosing a time for your vacation may not be entirely up to you. It could depend on allowed time off from work, your travel schedule, or your children's vacation days from school. Whether you have flexible travel days or not, we have laid out a month-by-month breakdown of what to expect when you visit the Disneyland Resort. We also give you tips on how to avoid the long lines, save time planning, and make your stay a very enjoyable one!

MOST RECOMMENDED MONTHS

Disneyland draws much of its crowds from locals who have a tradition of visiting the theme parks. These can be families living anywhere in Southern California who visit for the day. For this reason, we recommend visiting when kids are in school during the week or away from typical spring, summer, and winter breaks.

We usually rank September as the best time to visit as hotels and ticket prices will be lower than in other months. Families with kids will be back in school after Labor Day. The weather will also be warm, and if you enjoy Halloween decorations, those begin early this month at both theme parks.

January (after the holidays) is also one of the least-busy months at the Disneyland Resorts! Ticket prices will be the lowest during the weekdays and special multi-day ticket promotions may be available. The weather will also be much cooler and chances of rare Southern Californian rain increase drastically during January. Ride refurbishments—especially for water-based attractions like Grizzly River Run—are often scheduled during off-season months like January and February.

November also makes a great traveling month to visit Disneyland. Like January, this is a cooler month with a few chances of rain, but also with better ticket prices and hotel discounts. Since the week of Thanksgiving can become crowded, we recommend planning a trip the week before or after the holiday. Best of all, the Christmas decorations and speciality treats arrive at both parks beginning in early November!

· **Magic Tips** ·

Disneyland staffs more employees on crowded days. This means that there will be more roller coaster trains running and restaurant availability may increase during these times. For this reason, you may also see more Cast Members on busier dates like the weekend. In addition, Disneyland could also allow for more reservations on a weekend date.

Why doesn't Disneyland just fully staff each day? Well, it's to save on cost. Like most businesses, larger revenue means more money for hourly employees. Some of Disneyland's attractions are quite old and running them at full capacity could cause them to breakdown more frequently. This also means that attractions will undergo routine maintenance as needed. When some popular attractions are down, this increases lines for other rides and experiences during the off season. Maintaining a balance during peak and non-peak times keeps the theme parks in a well-oiled state.

LEAST RECOMMENDED MONTHS

2024 is expected to be a fairly busy year for families planning their vacations. For this reason, we expect to see the summer and holiday seasons explode with eager guests at the Disneyland Resort. Of course, there's no way to fully predict future crowds in these often uncertain times. Still, it's very common that once schools are out, the crowds increase at places like the Disneyland Resort.

Summer months including June, July, and August, are by far some of the most crowded times. Traditionally, crowd sizes appear to be busier from July 4th through August 15th.

If you're craving a visit during the Halloween season, try planning a visit during the week. In October, Disneyland stays open late, so you'll be able to enjoy extended spooky hours at the parks. If you can, avoid weekends in October as these can be some of the most crowded days.

The absolute worst time to visit Disneyland is around the holidays. We recommend avoiding December visits after the first week and into the new year. Holiday crowds can be uncomfortably busy and difficult to plan around! Ticket prices will also be the highest during these times.

May can be another busy month, especially on the weekends. A discounted ticket deal for Southern Californian residents often ends during this time, so guests usually visit to get in the final days of the promotion.

Note: Are you planning your visit during one of our least recommended travel dates? Don't worry! This guide will help you avoid those long lines. Be sure to follow one of our pre-planned attraction lists—we use them ourselves and they can save you hours of time waiting in lines, or help you avoid them altogether. Tips for beating the crowds are at the end of this chapter.

DAYS BY POPULARITY

For the most part, the Disneyland Resort is the most popular on the weekends. However, Mondays are surprisingly busy as many guests will take off an additional day to create a 3-day weekend (most assume that Mondays will be far less busy than Sundays, which isn't always true).

Ranking the Days (most popular to least popular):

1. Saturday
2. Sunday
3. Monday
4. Friday
5. Thursday
6. Wednesday
7. Tuesday*

*Holidays can impact how the weeks work and make Tuesday as popular as Monday. For example, the Tuesday after Labor Day is often just as busy as a typical Monday at the parks. In general, it's best to avoid the busy holidays and three-day weekends (Friday through Tuesday) as they get very busy.

Ranking the Holidays (most popular to least popular):

1. Christmas Day (and week)
2. New Year's Eve/Day
3. Presidents' Day week
4. Thanksgiving week
5. Veterans Day
6. Fourth of July
7. Memorial Day weekend
8. Labor Day weekend

· **Magic Tips** ·

We gathered our crowd information from inside sources, our own observations, and by using certain calculations. Some crowd measurements can be seen via the Disneyland mobile app when looking at ride wait times. However, this data can be faulty as the app isn't always accurate. Also, hourly ride capacity can change depending on how many vehicles Disney runs at a time.

A better way to check for crowds is via Disneyland's tier pricing. Daily ticket costs will be higher (Tier 4 or 5 pricing) on more crowded days and lower (Tier 0 or Tier 1 pricing) on less crowded days. Visit the Disneyland ticketing website to check these dates: **disneyland.disney.go.com/tickets**

MONTH BREAKDOWN

JANUARY

Overview: January is busy in the first two weeks, and generally less busy after that. The first week will be crowded because of the holiday rides, treats, music, and decorations lighting the resort.
Weather: Mid-60˚F (15˚C) during the day and chilly at night.
Least Crowded Days: The last week in January.
Most Crowded Days: The first two weeks (especially around New Year's) and Martin Luther King Jr. Weekend (Friday through Monday).

Holiday Rides and Attractions (usually end by early January):

1. Holidays on Main Street (Disneyland)
2. Haunted Mansion Holiday (Disneyland)
3. "it's a small world" Holiday (Disneyland)
4. A Christmas Fantasy Parade (Disneyland)
5. Holiday Fireworks (Disneyland)
6. Holidays on Buena Vista Street (Disney California Adventure)
7. Cars Land Christmas (Disney California Adventure)
8. Festival of Holidays food event (Disney California Adventure)
9. World of Color: Season of Light (Disney California Adventure)
10. Meet Santa Claus (Disney California Adventure)

NEW YEAR'S EVE

If you're brave enough to face the crowds, you can celebrate the New Year by visiting the Disneyland Resort on December 31st. This can be one of the most popular events of the year! Both parks stay open late (Disneyland usually until 2am and California Adventure until 1am) and Disneyland hosts the New Year countdown and fireworks display at midnight.

SPECIAL EVENT: RUNDISNEY

January 11-14 2024

The Disneyland Half Marathon series takes place over this weekend with several different runs. It is sold out for 2024 so the event could make these weekends busier.

FEBRUARY

Overview: An increasingly popular time to visit the Disneyland Resort. Like January, the weather is cooler. February is subject to attraction closures for refurbishment.

Weather: Low-70°F (21°C) during the day and chilly at night. February has been known to have sudden heatwaves, bringing the weather above 90°F (32°C).

Least Crowded Days: Any week except near Presidents' Day Weekend (Friday through Monday).

Most Crowded Days: Presidents' Day Weekend.

SPECIAL EVENT: LUNAR NEW YEAR

Early 2024

Celebrate Lunar New Year at Disney California Adventure. Watch a spectacular nighttime show before World of Color, sample delicious food, and meet characters like Mulan and Mushu!

For dates, visit: https://disneyland.disney.go.com/events-tours/lunar-new-year/

SPECIAL EVENT: VALENTINE'S DAY

Around February 14th

Valentine's Day has a short run at Disneyland with special treats and sweets available around the park. Also look for romantic photo booths around Main Street on February 14th!

MARCH

Overview: March's popularity has increased recently as spring breaks spread throughout the month. If you visit in March, be sure to do so during the week, Tuesday through Thursday. March is also subject to attraction closures for refurbishment.

Weather: Mid-70°F (21°C) during the day and chilly at night, but March has been known to have occasional heatwaves, bringing the weather above 90°F (32°C).

Least Crowded Days: the first Tuesday, Wednesday, and Thursday of March.

Most Crowded Days: Last two weeks of the month.

Deals: Disneyland Resort hotels may have have discounted multi-day tickets during this time for Southern California residents.

SPECIAL EVENT: FOOD & WINE FESTIVAL

Mid-March to Mid-April

Every spring, California Adventure lines the street between Buena Vista and Paradise Gardens Park with tasty seasonal food and adult beverages. You can sip and savor at several booths from creamy mac 'n' cheese to California-grown wines. The menu changes from year to year, and we highly recommend tasting your way through the most delicious snacks!

APRIL

Overview: With spring breaks continuing through April, the end of the month tends to be the least crowded.

Weather: Mid-70°F (21°C) during the day and chilly at night.

Least Crowded Days: The last two weeks of the month.

Most Crowded Days: First two weeks of the month

Special Days: Dapper Day (Spring) – See guests dressed in their "Sunday Best" on this unofficial, yet widely celebrated day. If you are interested in participating, visit: **DapperDay.com** for more details and event dates (usually in April or May). This semi-annual day also occurs in the fall.

SPECIAL EVENT: EGGSTRAVAGANZA

Early April through Easter Sunday

Search for Easter eggs designed with Disney and Pixar characters throughout the Resort! These eggs can be found in both theme parks and Downtown Disney. Special Eggstravaganza maps are usually available for purchase in the World of Disney and select theme park stores. Kids love participating in this annual Easter egg hunt!

MAY

Overview: Disneyland literally blooms during the spring with plenty of flowers around the Resort! Toward the end of the month, the resort will already feel like summer. May is subject to attraction closures for refurbishment, but these are often completed by Memorial Day.
Weather: Mid-70°F (21°C) during the day and sometimes chilly after sunset.
Least Crowded Days: The first two weeks of the month.
Most Crowded Days: Memorial Day weekend (Friday through Tuesday).
Mother's Day (May 12, 2024): Disneyland often gives complimentary flowers at the park entrance to mothers visiting on this day.

· **Magic Tips** ·
Weekends in May are especially busy due to the conclusion of promotions before summer. We recommend weekday visits for fewer crowds.

GRAD NITE
Disneyland and Disney California Adventure host special celebrations for graduating high school seniors in May and June These events typically lead to larger crowds, especially in the evening. Most Grad Nite tickets are sold for Disney California Adventure though some packages include access to Disneyland. Disney California Adventure also hosts a private Grad Nite party from 9:00pm-2:00pm with a special feature of World of Color for graduates.

2024 Grad Nite Dates:
May 10, 14, 15, 17, 19, 22, 23, 28 & 31
June 2, 5, 7, 9, 12 & 14
All dates and times are subject to change.
More info: www.disneycampus.com

JUNE

Overview: This month is known for "June Gloom" in Southern California. A thick, gray blanket of clouds will block out the sun until the afternoon on most days, though the temperature may be warm.
Weather: Mid-80°F (27°C) during the day. Typically cools at night.
Least Crowded Days: Tuesdays, Wednesdays, and Thursdays, and the first week of the month.
Most Crowded Days: The last week of the month.

· **Magic Tips** ·
The Disneyland Resort often debuts new attractions in the summer months of June and July. If you are planning a visit for the opening weekend of a new attraction, plan to get to the parks well ahead of park opening. Virtual queues also may be available, depending on the attraction.

JULY

Overview: The weather heats up (sometimes unbearably so) and crowds from all over the world venture into the Disneyland Resort during July. If you are planning to visit in July, we highly recommend our tips for beating the crowds at the end of this chapter.
Weather: High-80°F (27°C) during the day. Typically keeps warm at night.
Least Crowded Days: Tuesday, Wednesdays, and Thursdays (unless one is July 4th).
Most Crowded Days: July 4th

FOURTH OF JULY
Catch a stunning 15-minute fireworks spectacular on July 4th. See American flag projections on the castle, red, white, and blue fireworks, with patriotic music playing throughout the Disneyland Park.

AUGUST

Overview: The weather continues to heat up even more in August as crowds continue to pour in until school begins.
Weather: Mid-90˚F (32˚C) during the day. Typically keeps very warm at night.
Least Crowded Days: Tuesdays, Wednesdays, and Thursdays and the last two weeks of the month.
Most Crowded Days: The first two weeks of the month.

SEPTEMBER

Overview: More hot weather typically all month long with Halloween rides and treats beginning in early September. See October for Disneyland Halloween details.
Weather: High-90˚F (32˚C) during the day. Typically keeps very warm at night.
Least Crowded Days: Tuesdays, Wednesdays, Thursdays, and Fridays (except for Halloween event nights—more on that next).
Most Crowded Days: Labor Day weekend.

OCTOBER

Overview: October is a favorite time of ours at the Disneyland Resort! The weather cools down as the Halloween party kicks into full gear at both parks!
Weather: Low-80˚F (27˚C) during the day, cools at night.
Least Crowded Days: Mondays, Wednesdays, and Fridays
Most Crowded Days: Halloween party on select dates and Halloween day, October 31st. Also beware of shorter hours during dates with the Oogie Boogie Bash Halloween party. Disney California Adventure will close early for daytime guests. However, Disneyland Park usually remains open and can become crowded on these Halloween party nights. Once the party starts, guests flock to Disneyland Park and it often feels a lot more crowded.

SPECIAL EVENT: HALLOWEEN
Select Nights Mid-September – October 31, 2024
Halloween is one of the most exciting times to visit the Disneyland Resort! From thrilling autumn decorations like Mickey-shaped pumpkins and characters in costume, it's fun both day and night to visit Disneyland from mid-September through Halloween! Both parks are covered in decorations and some rides like Guardians of the Galaxy and Haunted Mansion have spooky re-themes! On select nights, Disney California Adventure hosts Oogie Boogie Bash, a special ticketed event where guests can trick-or-treat, meet Disney villains, and see stunning Halloween shows!

OOGIE BOOGIE BASH

Join villains and characters from *The Nightmare Before Christmas* as you trick-or-treat around Disney California Adventure, see a Halloween parade, meet rare costumed characters, and end it all with a special "Villainous!" World of Color show. Oogie Boogie Bash isn't necessarily scary, but there is a fun spookiness to it. There are treat trails, fog, and special Halloween lighting to give the park an eerie edge not found on other nights. We love these Halloween parties because it's a time when guests of all ages can dress in costume and visit the parks.

The event is popular and could sell out within days of tickets going on sale. However, Disneyland limits the guest numbers (hence the high extra cost of $100+ per person). It's nice to line up the parade just minutes before showtime, and still have a great spot. Also, popular attractions like Guardians of the Galaxy and Soarin' Over the World have very short wait times.

Other perks of Oogie Boogie Bash are unlimited PhotoPass downloads, early park admission to Disney California Adventure, and all of the premium candy (like Snickers and Reese's) are complimentary.

· Magic Tips ·
If you are staying at one of the Disneyland Resort hotels, you may be able to purchase tickets even if the party is sold out. Ask your hotel concierge for availability.

HALLOWEEN ATTRACTIONS

- **Main Street Pumpkin Festival** (Disneyland) – Snap photos near a giant-sized Mickey pumpkin and autumn decorations on Main Street, U.S.A.
- **Haunted Mansion Holiday** (Disneyland) – Jack Skellington and his friends from Tim Burton's *The Nightmare Before Christmas* take over the Haunted Mansion. The attraction features new animatronics, special effects, and music through the first week of January.
- **Guardians of the Galaxy—Monsters After Dark** (California Adventure) – Help save Groot from rampaging alien monsters that have taken over The Collector's Fortress!
- **Cars Land Haul-O-Ween Celebration** (California Adventure) – Cars Land is completely decorated for the spooky holiday. Luigi's Rollickin' Roadsters and Mater's Junkyard Jamboree get Halloween makeovers with new music and fun for the entire family.
- **Halloween Décor** (Both Parks) – See massive Mickey-shaped pumpkins, try delicious treats, and see your favorite characters dressed in their Halloween costumes in both theme parks.
- **Halloween Treats** – Spooky eats find their way into the menus at Disneyland. These are often new takes on sweets like churros, cupcakes, and candy apples. However, you can also find seasonal savory snacks at many of the restaurants.
- **Halloween Cake** – The Grand Californian Hotel displays a huge decorative Halloween cake in its lobby. Stop by to check it out!

NOVEMBER

Overview: The holidays begin mid-November at the Disneyland Resort. Expect larger crowds beginning Veterans Day onward. *See December for Disneyland Holiday details.*
Weather: Mid-70°F (21°C) in the day, cools to 50°F (10°C) at night.
Least Crowded Days: The first week of the month.

Most Crowded Days: Veterans Day weekend and Thanksgiving week.

UNOFFICIAL EVENT: DAPPER DAY (FALL) – Like in the spring, guests dressed in their "Sunday Best" visit on this unofficial, yet widely celebrated day. Visit **DapperDay.com** for more details and a date.

Thanksgiving: If you're looking for a turkey dinner in the parks on Thanksgiving, the following are great locations:
Disneyland: Carnation Cafe, Plaza Inn, Blue Bayou, and Cafe Orleans.
Disney California Adventure: Carthay Circle, Wine Country Trattoria, and Flo's V8 Cafe.
More Spots: For premium dining for Thanksgiving (with all the fixin's), we recommend the Blue Bayou at Disneyland or Carthay Circle at California Adventure—don't forget to book your reservation months ahead. For a quick-service restaurant that's more affordable, try Flo's V8 Cafe at California Adventure.

DECEMBER

Overview: The holidays are in full gear at the Disneyland Resort. See decorations all around with special treats, fun holiday-themed rides, and a chance to meet Santa Claus!
Weather: Low-60°F (15°C) during the day, can cool at night to mid-40°F (5°C).
Least Crowded Days: The first week of the month.
Most Crowded Days: The last two weeks, especially Christmas Day and New Year's Eve.

SPECIAL EVENT: CHRISTMAS
Mid-November – Early January
See the glimmering Christmas lights decorating the Disneyland Resort! From magnificent Christmas trees to endless strings of lights and ornaments, you'll be in awe of the Resort's holiday transformation!

HOLIDAY ATTRACTIONS

- **A Christmas Fantasy Parade & Holiday Fireworks** (Disneyland) – Mickey, Santa, and Disney Princesses celebrate Christmas aboard stunning floats with a fireworks display!
- **Haunted Mansion Holiday** (Disneyland) – It's the same attraction as Halloween, but continues through New Year.
- **Cars Land Christmas** (Disney California Adventure) – Cars Land gets a jolly makeover with Christmas fun. Luigi's Rollickin' Roadsters and Mater's Junkyard Jamboree get Christmas-themed attraction overlays.
- **"Jingle Cruise"** – Jungle Cruise gets a Christmas makeover with holiday humor and décor around the riverboat ride.
- **"it's a small world" Holiday** (Disneyland) – See the magnificent lights that illuminate this classic attraction on the outside. Inside, see the wondrous holidays celebrated all around the world.
- **World of Color: Season of Light** (Disney California Adventure) – Light up the night with a spectacular water show perfectly designed for the holiday season. Watch your favorite Disney characters come to life and celebrate the joy of the season with heartwarming Christmas songs.
- **Christmas Characters** – Meet Santa Claus in Critter Country (Disneyland) or Elias & Co. (Disney California Adventure) and Mickey and his friends in their holiday clothing. Don't forget to say hello to Jack Skellington and Sally near Haunted Mansion!
- **Holiday Treats** – Look for special holiday snacks around the parks. These could include specialty churros, macarons, ice cream, and limited-time menu items.
- **Festive Foods Marketplace** – Visit California Adventure and sample your way around the holidays at these unique booths. From sweet treats to adult beverages, you'll never know what you might find! The Festive Foods Marketplace booths usually line the walkways in Buena Vista Street and Paradise Gardens Park. If you're in the mood to try several items, purchase a "Tasting Passport" that gives you a bit of a discount (saves about $1-$2 per item).

DISNEY'S MERRIEST NITES

Disneyland's new holiday event, Merriest Nites, kicked off in 2021 but did not return for 2022. If Merriest Nites returns for 2024, expect smaller crowds, easier viewing of A Christmas Fantasy Parade, and special parties around the park hosted by popular characters.

BEAT THE CROWDS

1. **Get There Early** – We can't stress this tip enough. If you can, get to the park gates 30-40 minutes before opening to avoid long lines that form after the first hour.

2. **Make a Plan** – Follow one of our pre-set day plans (or make your own). We use these planners ourselves and it will save you hours of time waiting in lines (many times you'll miss the long lines altogether).

3. **Know Where to Start** – Have your pre-planned ride list ready before heading to park! We offer our recommendations at the end of this guide.

4. **Avoid Busy Lunch and Dinner** – Eat lunch before 11:15am or after 1:30pm and dinner before 5:30pm or after 7:30pm. If you want to try a Dole Whip on a busy day, order one early before 10:30am—they make great breakfast treats!

5. **Ride During Parades** – Grab a map for showtimes and plan your rides accordingly. It's easier to ride a Fantasyland attraction during a parade when the families are watching the floats.

6. **Splash Early** – Water rides like Grizzly River Run become super busy on hot days. To avoid the long lines, ride them before 11am. At least you'll be able to dry off in the afternoon sun that follows!

7. **Book Dining Beforehand** – Reservations can be made at Disneyland.com 60 days in advance. If you don't see the time slot you want, keep checking a few times a day for cancellations.

8. **Switch Sides** – Disneyland can have much larger crowds than Disney California Adventure. If you have a Park Hopper and the crowds are too much at Disneyland, head to the opposite park and see what you can ride or see there.

9. **Use the Extra Magic Hour** – Those staying at a Disneyland Resort Hotel or that purchased a 3-day ticket or higher have access to the theme parks an hour before opening. The calendar on Disneyland's website and app lists these special times. Guests with Extra Magic Hour in the morning have access to a special line to cut the rest of the guests. The lines are so short during this hour that you can often ride 4-5 attractions before other guests enter the park. However, not all rides are always open. California Adventure has most of its attractions available, but Disneyland keeps just Tomorrowland and Fantasyland open.

10. **Accept the Wait** – Waiting in line isn't the end of the world. Sometimes we all have to do it for the best attractions. The trick is to wait the *shortest* amount of time for the *fewest* rides possible. You can avoid the longest lines by following our planned-out ride lists.

11. **Take a Break** – The worst thing you can do on your vacation is exhaust yourself. If you are feeling worn out, take a break at your hotel or visit Downtown Disney. The resort offers so many surprises that you might have a blast drinking a cup of coffee while you listen to music near Starbucks rather than surrounded by a swarm of people. After you and your group have recharged, head back into the parks to complete your ride list.

· **Magic Tips** ·
If you can't get to the theme parks early, plan to stay late! Just like the morning hours, late nights often have shorter wait times.

WHEN DISNEYLAND HITS CAPACITY

On rare occasion, Disneyland will hit capacity and stop selling tickets. This only happens a few times a year and usually between

Christmas and New Year's. When this happens, tickets to Disney California Adventure are usually still available. In this case, Disneyland can switch your ticket to the other park, if you so desire. Additionally, guests may be offered discounted park hopper tickets for when other guests leave. We've also seen Disneyland extend park hours in the evening to give late-arriving guests the opportunity to enjoy the park for another hour or two after its scheduled closing.

· **Magic Tips** ·
When Disneyland uses a reservation system for its park, you likely won't have to worry about the parks hitting capacity in this way. Reservations are designed to ensure a positive guest experience by managing crowd sizes. After all, no one wants to visit a theme park when all of the lines are hours long and they can't find a place to sit for lunch.

WHAT TO WEAR & BRING

Disneyland forbids certain everyday items, but also permits other items you may assume are banned. For instance, you can bring your own water into the park. This can be extremely helpful because a bottle of water at the Disneyland Parks costs about $4! Be aware that the Disneyland Resort security inspects your bags before you enter the parks. There also may be a metal detector. In this section, we review tips and tricks for a comfortable and cost-effective stay at the Resort.

1. **Comfortable Clothing** – Shorts, t-shirts, sneakers (trainers), and tank tops are seen all around the parks for a good reason: they are comfortable. You'll be standing in the warm California sun all day, so we recommend that you dress comfortably.

2. **Hats and Sunglasses** – Again, the California sun! It's a wonderful thing, but you don't want to get burned. Be careful of hats and sunglasses on rides (most

high-speed attractions will have a compartment to store your items).

3. **Sunscreen** – Even on a cloudy day the ultraviolet rays from the sun can give you an uncomfortable burn. Be careful and stay protected.

4. **Stroller** – Kids can get tired and Disneyland has zones to park strollers with attendants that watch them while you ride. All strollers must be within the limits of 31" (79cm) wide and 52" (132cm) long.

5. **Jacket or Sweater** – A hot day at the Disneyland Resort can still become chilly at night. We highly recommend having a jacket or sweater to keep you warm.

6. **Water Bottles** – Disneyland will allow you to bring sealed bottles of water into the parks. Save yourself money and bring your own. If you don't mind fountain water, you can refill it at water fountains near any restroom for free.

7. **Snacks** – You can save money (or help any picky eaters in your party) by bringing your own snacks.

8. **Waterproof Bag** – If you plan on riding the water attractions, like Grizzly River Run, you're likely to get soaked. The last thing you want is to accidentally drench your cellphone, keys, and/or wallet! Either purchase a waterproof carrying bag or bring a sandwich baggie.

9. **Money** – The Disneyland Resort accepts all major credit cards and cash. For currency exchange, visit City Hall (Disneyland), Chamber of Commerce (California Adventure), or any Resort Hotel front desk.

10. **School-Sized Backpack** – Carry your items in one of these. Make sure it's not too large to fit on the rides. Also, keep in mind that your bag will be checked by security before entering the park area.

11. **Identification** – For adults, make sure you plan on bringing your government-issued ID if you plan to drink alcoholic beverages.

12. **Simple Rain Gear** – It doesn't rain much at the Disneyland Resort (only around 12 inches of rainfall in a year), but just in case it does, compact umbrellas and ponchos are great ways to stay dry.

WHAT *NOT* TO WEAR AND BRING

1. **Ice** – Loose ice isn't permitted, as it is a safety hazard, though ice packs are allowed. If you need ice, ask quick-service restaurants for a cupful.

2. **Adult Costumes and Masks** – Children under 14 are allowed to wear costumes, but, so as not to trick people into thinking a non-Cast Member is a character, Disneyland bans these for adults (unless allowed for special events).

3. **Remote Control Toys and Drones** – Disneyland bans these for safety reasons. Even those skates that slide out from kids' shoes are banned. If you need a vehicle, you may rent a scooter or wheelchair from Guest Services.

4. **Your Pet** – The Disneyland Resort Kennel Club offers daily service for $20 per pet. Keep in mind that you will need to feed your pet during the day and they don't provide overnight stays. Call (714) 781-7662 for details. If you need overnight accommodations for your dog, Camp Bow Wow is about 15 minutes from the Resort: campbowwow.com/anaheim.

5. **Alcoholic Beverages** – These are not allowed in the parks (though you may purchase alcoholic drinks in the theme parks and Downtown Disney).

6. **Lawn Chairs** – You might be tempted to bring these to watch a parade, but Disneyland bans them. We assume it's to keep the resort's aesthetics from looking like a 4th of July picnic.

7. **Glass Bottles** – Another safety precaution, but small glass containers of baby food are allowed.

8. **Wrapped Gifts** – For inspection reasons, you cannot bring wrapped gifts into the park—though gifts may be wrapped once you enter the park.

9. **Cigarettes** – Disneyland has banned smoking around the theme parks. You'll need to exit security to smoke.

BACKUP PLANS

RENT A LOCKER

Lockers are an affordable way to store your belongings and purchase merchandise. Lockers start at $7 for a day rental. Disneyland's are located on Main Street and California Adventure's are located on Buena Vista Street. Lockers are also available outside of each park.

PLAN A RETURN

If you don't want to rent a locker, make a plan to return to your hotel midday. There, you can eat, refill on drinks, and maybe take a power nap before heading back to the parks.

REPLACEMENT ITEMS

If you forget any items, Disneyland likely sells them. Check the Main Street, U.S.A., Buena Vista Street, and Downtown Disney shops for any items that you may need.

IN CASE OF BAD WEATHER

Outdoor theme parks can be a nightmare in extreme weather. Hot summer days and unexpected Southern Californian rainstorms can close rides, pause parades, and stop the mobility of your party. There are some great spots to hide out in around the Resort in case of these rare weather patterns.

SEE A SHOW

Great Moments with Mr. Lincoln (Main Street, U.S.A. in Disneyland) and the Animation Academy (Hollywood Land in Disney California Adventure) have large galleries set in indoor spaces. These are both shielded from the weather, and have comfortable seating, and experiences for all age groups. The Enchanted Tiki Room, Royal Theatre, and Tomorrowland Theater in Disneyland and Hyperion Theatre in DCA also make great spaces to avoid extreme weather for long periods of time.

GO ON A LONG RIDE

The Disneyland Railroad, Pirates of the Caribbean, Indiana Jones Adventure, Finding Nemo Submarine Voyage, and "it's a small world" are also great ways to avoid the weather. These attractions range from 10-20 minutes in length, thus giving you ample breaks when needed. Keep in mind that some of these rides have queues that may not have much covering.

TAKE A BREAK

If the weather is too severe, head back to your hotel room or plan a table-service meal. Last-minute dining reservations can be made for the theme parks and Downtown Disney via the Disneyland mobile app. Most restaurants have indoor seating with air conditioning. If you know that the weather will be hot, plan a midday break and book ahead of your visit.

Play Disney is a free mobile application to play games around the theme park. This app is available to download on the Apple and Android mobile market places as a complimentary entertainment piece. Simply download, create an account, and start playing! The app works especially well with features in Star Wars: Galaxy's Edge.

PLAY DISNEY APP

It was inevitable that guests would stare at their phones while waiting in lines, so Disney designed a free mobile app to use for this specific purpose. Play Disney immerses visitors in games and other added magic designed for all ages. Some of these fun experiences include trivia, music, and collectables!

Overall, Play Disney will score better with kids and tweens as the cartoonish appearance of the app seems catered to them. Teens and adults might enjoy the trivia which can be challenging at times. Play Disney is also better in small groups as the competition can heat up to see who scores the highest.

If you're planning on trying Play Disney, we recommend downloading the app before you leave home, that way you don't have to worry about poor connectivity or waiting to download a large file. The application is also a bit of a battery drainer, so make sure to pack a portable charger!

Some of the experiences can only be played while physically in the queue for a ride. For example, Space Mountain Rocket Race is a competitive mini game designed for 2-5 players, and will only open once your phone recognizes that you are near Space Mountain in Tomorrowland. However, some other experiences, like listening to music from around the park and Disney Parks Trivia, can be played anywhere—including home! Getting acquainted with the application and its features before you arrive will help with the fun of using it at the theme parks.

· Magic Tips ·

The Play Disney app also accesses free collectables like cards at the Penny Arcade on Main Street, U.S.A. You can get a free printout prophecy from Esmeralda the Fortune Teller located at the front of the store!

BOOKING YOUR TRIP

TIPS BEFORE YOU BOOK

The earlier you can begin planning your Disneyland vacation, the better. We recommend 6-8 months ahead of time at least. However, we also offer tips for last-minute booking deals.

PRE-BOOK YOUR HOTEL

During popular dates, Disneyland area hotels often sell out or have very limited availability. So if you're planning a trip on a weekend, during the holidays, or in the middle of summer, we highly recommend booking in advance. Refer to our hotels chapter for more details on the best places to stay within your budget.

FLY INTO LAX OR JOHN WAYNE

If you are planning to fly, we recommend LAX (Los Angeles International Airport) because it tends to be the least expensive and easiest to travel out of. LAX is located right next to highways that will take you to Disneyland. However, John Wayne Airport is even closer to Disneyland! We recommend comparing prices for both airports and including transport cost to your hotel. We go into more detail about transportation in the next chapter.

BUNDLE FOR BIGGER SAVINGS

Sometimes you can save money by purchasing a flight, hotel, and car bundled package from Disneyland.com or a third-party travel site. However, the best way to save on theme park tickets is usually to buy multi-day passes.

KNOW THE TICKET PRICING STRUCTURE

Disneyland uses a multi-tier ticket pricing structure. Tickets are typically the least expensive Tuesday through Thursdays outside of the holidays, spring break, and summer. Most weekends require a Tier 5 or the most-expensive Tier 6 ticket. In addition, you can use a higher tier ticket on any of the lower tier dates. For example, if you purchase a Tier 6 ticket, it can be used any date, including weekends and holidays.

However, if you purchase a Tier 4 ticket, you may be excluded from using it most Saturdays and holidays. Tier 1 tickets—the least expensive—are typically only valid on select weekdays during less-busy months like September and February. Unfortunately, if you use a Tier 6 ticket on a less-expensive date, Disneyland will not refund you the difference.

1-DAY DISNEYLAND RESORT TICKET PRICING

TICKET TIER	ADULT (10+)	CHILD (3-9)
Tier 0	$104	$98
Tier 1	$114	$108
Tier 2	$129	$122
Tier 3	$144	$136
Tier 4	$159	$150
Tier 5	$160	$159
Tier 6	$179	$169

PARK HOPPER TICKET

If you want to visit both Disneyland and Disney California Adventure in a single day, you'll need to purchase a Park Hopper ticket. For an extra $65, you'll be able to visit both parks in a single day.

· Magic Tips ·

In 2021, Disneyland introduced new Park Hopper restrictions. Guests must make a reservation for their starting theme park and can only hop after a certain time. However, once you're allowed to hop, you may go back and forth between the parks as long as capacity allows (which is most dates). Usually this time is 11am.

THEME PARK RESERVATIONS

Once you've purchased your theme park ticket, you may be required to make a reservation for your choice of theme park. The standard Disneyland tickets work at both parks, so the reservation secures your spot at either Disneyland or Disney California Adventure on a specific date. Those with park hopper tickets may also need to reserve their starting park.

Disneyland implemented reservations when it reopened back in 2021 as a method to manage crowd sizes. If you purchased tickets directly through Disneyland.com, you'll likely make your reservation during the ordering process by selecting your date and park. We highly recommend that you check the Disneyland reservation calendar first before visiting at the following link: https://disneyland.disney.go.com/experience-updates/park-reservations.

MULTI-DAY TICKET

Since Disneyland does not discount single-day tickets, the best deals come with multi-day purchases. These ticket prices are the same no matter which day you visit (all multi-day tickets are essentially Tier 6). Multi-day tickets are also great for vacations as they usually expire 13 days after the first use. Park Hoppers also are a better deal when you buy multiple days.

MAGIC MORNING & EXTRA MAGIC HOUR

Some multi-day tickets may come with extended park hours called "Magic Morning." These are often 3-day (or more) tickets that allow guests to visit Disneyland or Disney California Adventure an hour before park opening. Disneyland Resort Hotel guests can also take advantage of these same hours (they are called "Extra Magic Hour" for hotel guests). During other times, Disneyland will offer the early morning benefit to guests staying at surrounding hotels. You'll know if this benefit comes with your ticket or stay at the time of purchase.

DISNEY GENIE+

This paid add-on feature allows you to book Lightning Lane reservations to skip the bulk of many lines. Genie+ works with the Disneyland mobile app and also gives you unlimited downloads of photos taken during your trip. Disney Genie+ costs $25 and up per person, per day. We outline this in better detail later in this guide.

DISCOUNTED MULTI-DAY TICKET DEALS

Each year, Disneyland rolls out discounted ticket packages for those visiting on multiple dates. These are often similar to purchasing two days and getting the third free or at a discounted rate. Special ticket offers can be booked via disneyland.com and sometimes third-party sites.

DISCOUNT HOTELS

There are many ways to save on booking your stay at the Disneyland Resort. Some are better than others depending on the offer.

DISNEYLAND.COM

When Disneyland.com has hotel sales, usually the third-party websites will as well—but not always. Disneyland.com often has the most variety of room choice and sometimes offers discounted multi-day passes. In the spring, Southern California residents typically get a discount on multi-day tickets.

PROS

1. A larger selection of rooms than offered by third-party sites.
2. You can add flights, transportation, character dining, and tickets to other theme parks.
3. Disneyland.com often has flexible cancellation policies for full refunds, including park tickets.

CONS

1. The travel insurance is a lot pricier than most other sites.
2. Hotel rooms are often cheaper through third party sites.
3. Rarely offers discounted bundles that include park tickets.

MORE DISCOUNTS

DISNEYLAND

(714) 520-5060 / www.disneyland.com

- Get individual and multi-day tickets.
- Comes with early admission "Magic Morning" on certain days with a 3-Day ticket purchase.
- Allows you to print tickets, have them mailed, or use your mobile device for e-tickets.
- Tickets are nonrefundable but if you bundle them with a hotel, they may be refundable.

MILITARY DISCOUNTS

The Disneyland Resort now offers discounted "salute" tickets for active and retired U.S. military. These discounts are found on military bases and include fantastic deals on multi-day tickets.

SALUTE TICKET OFFER	ADULT (10+)
3-Day Military Park Hopper Ticket	$245
4-Day Military Park Hopper Ticket	$280

Tickets are for ages 3 and older. Tickets may be used on non-consecutive dates. Blockout dates may apply. Terms subject to change; read full details at place of purchase before buying. We also recommend checking for discounts at Disney-owned hotels.

MAGIC KEY ANNUAL PASSES

In 2021, the Disneyland Resort revamped its annual passport program with new tiers, benefits, and required park reservations. The Magic Keys—Disneyland's name for its annual passes—allow guests to visit both Disneyland and Disney California Adventure. All passes have "blockouts" during busy dates, meaning that the pass will not be valid on that day.

MAGIC KEY BENEFITS

1. Visit Multiple Dates – Magic Key holders can visit the Disneyland Resort parks multiple times throughout the year!

2. Park Hopper – A Magic Key allows access to both Disneyland and Disney California Adventure!

3. Easy Reservations – Magic Key holders can easily make reservations on the Disneyland app!

4. Discounts – Get discounts on select food, drink, parking, and merchandise around the Disneyland Resort.

· **Magic Tips** ·
Magic Key holders also receive 20% off Disney Genie+ services for themselves. The discount cannot be used for guests without Magic Keys. Unfortunately, there is not advance purchase so Magic Key holders may buy Genie+ within the Disneyland app after entering the park.

5. Advanced Event Purchase – Magic Key holders get first access to special event tickets and merchandise opportunities.

6. Exclusives – Throughout the year, Disneyland hosts special experiences just for those with a Magic Key. These often include free merchandise like buttons, photo ops, and more! In addition, Disneyland holds a "Magic Key Holder Month" filled with more surprises and giveaways!

7. Member Lounge – The Magic Key Terrace in Disney California Adventure is just for those with an annual pass. Dine on exclusive food and drink in this reservations-only terrace.

8. Payment Plan – California residents can pay monthly for their Magic Key. A down payment may be required.

CONS

1. Price – Disneyland Magic Key annual passes are very expensive. Prices can be over $1,000 per pass.

2. Required Reservations – Even those with the highest level Magic Key must make a reservation before visiting the parks. Reservations can be made 90 days ahead of your visit. Those who do not show up for 3 reservations within a 90-day period may be blocked from making a reservation for 30 days.

3. Parking Cost – Only the highest Magic Key comes with included parking. All others must pay during their visit (though lower pass types receive some parking discounts).

PRICING & BENEFITS

IMAGINE KEY

$449

Discounts: 10% off select dining and merchandise

Reservations: Allows for 2 park reservations at a time

Exclusive to residents of Southern California (zip codes 90000 to 93599), the Imagine Key allows access to Disneyland and Disney California Adventure on select weekdays only. Imagine Key holders are blocked from visiting the parks most summer dates and during the holidays.

ENCHANT KEY
$699
Discounts: 10% off select merchandise and dining
Parking: 25% off parking at the Toy Story Lot
Reservations: Can hold 4 park reservations at a time
Get access to both parks with blockout dates. The Enchant Key works most weekdays and has several weekend dates. However, this pass type is blocked most Saturdays, about half of the summer (including all of July), and most holidays.

BELIEVE KEY
$1099
Discounts: 10% off select merchandise and dining
Parking: 50% off parking in the parking structures and Toy Story lot
Reservations: Can hold 6 park reservations at a time
Get access to both parks throughout the year with far fewer blockout dates than the Enchant Key. While this pass works most weekends and weekdays, holidays and some Saturdays in July and October may be unavailable.

INSPIRE KEY
$1,599
Discounts: 20% off select merchandise and dining
Reservations: Can hold 6 park reservations at a time
Admission to both parks most says of the year. The Inspire Key is blocked for two weeks during the winter holiday season. This pass also includes complimentary parking in the structures and the Toy Story lot.

· **Magic Tips** ·
Disneyland stops selling Magic Keys from time to time. However, there could be new "drops" of these annual passes as other guests don't renew. Disneyland typically announces these drops on their social media.

For blockout dates and more details: disneyland.com/magickey

SPECIAL EVENT TICKETS

The Disneyland Resort will often throw limited-time special events with separate ticket prices. Some of these events are privately held by companies while others are on sale for the general public.

The popular Disneyland After Dark series has hosted themed parties dedicated to Star Wars, Marvel, Disney in the '90s, and more! These incredibly fun nighttime events typically have minimal crowds, shorter wait times, rare characters to meet, and specialty food! However, events run late into the evening after park hours and are often $120 and up per ticket. Guests may also have early access to the park before their visit.

We review these special experiences in a later chapter. To see updates about 2024 Disneyland After Dark events, visit: https://disneyland.disney.go.com/events-tours/after-dark/

CHAPTER FOUR

TRAVELING TO DISNEYLAND

INTRODUCTION

With the planning out of the way, it's time to begin your vacation to the Disneyland Resort. Getting there doesn't have to be tricky, but if you don't plan correctly, it might feel like a complicated mess. Again, we're here to help and simplify! Contrary to what many believe, Disneyland is not in Los Angeles. The Resort is located in Anaheim, California, which is about 25-30 miles south of Los Angeles (a 45-minute drive from the LAX Airport). However, it is easy to travel from Los Angeles to Disneyland and back in a day. In this chapter, we review the different methods of getting to the Resort. How you get there is entirely up to you, but if you're feeling indecisive (or just need more information), read thoroughly to get the best choices.

BY AIRLINE

If you aren't planning a road trip and live far away from the Disneyland Resort, flying will likely be your best option. While airlines can be expensive at times, there are several ways to save money:

- Compare airlines to see the best pricing.
- Check baggage fees and allowed carry-on items. We prefer Southwest because they give you two free checked bags and the pricing is usually very competitive.
- Book during promotions and travel deals.
- Book early to get the best discounts.

LAX (Los Angeles International)

We recommend LAX because it tends to be the least expensive and easiest to travel from. LAX is located right next to highways that will take you to Disneyland.

JOHN WAYNE AIRPORT

The John Wayne Airport is much smaller and more accessible than the busy, often crowded, LAX. If you can find an inexpensive flight into John Wayne, you'll have a much faster connection to the Disneyland Resort.

BY CAR

Whether you're taking a road trip, staying in a neighboring city, or you live close enough to drive to the Resort, this can be a great method to take in the beautiful sights of California before you head to "The Happiest Place on Earth!"

CAR RENTAL

We recommend Enterprise.com or Dollar.com for car rentals as they typically have a great selection and the best pricing. Pre-booking before you arrive at the airport is advised. Here are some popular car rental companies near LAX, John Wayne, and Disneyland:

- www.enterprise.com – You can visit the company's website or see typically better deals on Priceline.com (or bundle with your airfare and hotel booking).
- www.dollar.com – Click the "specials" tab for deals.
- www.budget.com – Click the "deals" tab for offers.

DRIVING TO DISNEYLAND

We recommend using a GPS navigation app to easily navigate to Disneyland. However, finding parking at the Disneyland Resort can sometimes be a bit confusing. We recommend following the road signs that direct traffic to the parking areas (typically written "theme park parking"). If you've chosen another airport, follow the steps above but I-5 will be your ticket to entering the Disneyland Resort. From San Diego, the northbound carpool lane also empties straight onto Disneyland Drive.

Once on Disneyland Drive, follow the signs to available parking (the time of day you get to the Resort will also determine which parking is still available).

PARKING AT DISNEYLAND

Disneyland has three main parking areas: the Mickey and Friends parking structure, the Pixar Pals parking structure, and the Toy Story parking lot. We recommend the Pixar Pals structure for families, especially for ones with strollers. This lot has easy access to the trams and an easy pedestrian bridge into Downtown Disney. While the walk to the parks can take between 15-20 minutes from the structure, its security checkpoint is usually much faster than the ones near the tram.

Parking is $30 at each of these lots though this could increase again in 2024. Furthermore, oversized vehicles should park in the Toy Story Parking lot as the garages can't accommodate many of them.

Discounted Parking: Some neighboring hotels and parking lots offer less-expensive parking. To find these spaces, we use the free SpotHero mobile application. This app shows available parking around the Disneyland Resort (and other places you might travel) with distances and daily cost. You might save $10 a day and park within walking distance of Disneyland.

· **Magic Tips** ·

To avoid a surprise parking fee increase, you can pre-purchase a parking voucher on the website: https://disneyland.disney.go.com/tickets/parking.

Take note of where you parked so that you can easily find your spot again when you leave!

On busier days, Disneyland parking structures may reach capacity. If you are arriving later in the day, check @DisneylandToday on Twitter to see up-to-the-moment posts about parking availability.

BY RIDESHARE APP

Unfortunately, the Disneyland Resort no longer offers a shuttle from the airports to the Resort. If your hotel offers this, we highly recommend using that as a less-expensive option for your visit. However, with the growing popularity of ride-sharing apps like Uber and Lyft, it's likely your top choice. Both of these services offer private drivers in clean cars (these are not cabs) and larger vehicles for big groups. Here are a few ways you can book:

UBER / LYFT MOBILE DEVICE APPS

Before your trip, setup your rideshare application with an account and link a payment method. To download one of these apps, open the App Store (Apple Devices) or Play Store (Android Devices) and search the application by its name. You'll call a car once you've arrived and collected your luggage.

Rideshare Pricing to the Disneyland Resort (each way):

John Wayne Airport – $25-$35 (standard car) / $40-$50 (XL car)
LAX Airport – $50-$60 (standard car) / $75-$95 (XL car)

Keep in mind that our ride-share prices are just estimates. The time of day and traffic will influence these costs. Unlike taxis, the drivers don't expect tips. Sometimes there is a price difference between Lyft and Uber, so if you're price-conscious, you may want to check both apps as your arrive.

BY TRAIN

Taking the train can a be relaxing and beautiful way to travel to the Disneyland Resort. Trains let out at the Anaheim train station about 2.5 miles from the Disneyland Resort. You will need a second transport from the train station to the Resort (we recommend a rideshare service like Uber).

AMTRAK

www.amtrak.com

Perfect for longer distances on a budget (and if you have the time to travel). Check the "Deals" tab for discounts on Amtrak's website.

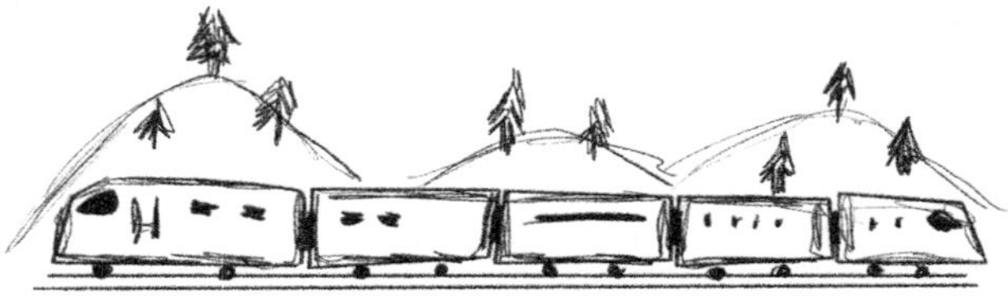

METROLINK
www.metrolinktrains.com
Better pricing than a train or plane for shorter distances (from the south of Anaheim).

PACIFIC SURFLINER
http://www.pacificsurfliner.com
This train is great for traveling within Southern California. The Pacific Surfliner, run by Amtrak, has local service from San Luis Obispo down to San Diego. Many guests use this train for travel to San Diego from the Disneyland Resort. These rates start as low as $30 each way. The Surfliner also has options to upgrade seats and areas for storing bicycles.

DISCOUNT CODES
The Pacific Surfliner often runs bundled discounts for Disneyland tickets. If you are traveling by this train, check out their deals: https://www.amtrak.com/promotions/deals.html

BY TAXI

Taxis are available outside of the airport terminals. If you'd like to pre-book a car, Taxi.com is a well-known solution. If you hail a taxi, ask for a flat rate to Disneyland.

These are the typical flat-rate prices:

- LAX: $100 each way
- Burbank Airport: $100 each way
- Ontario Airport: $100 each way

- John Wayne Airport: $45 each way
- Long Beach Airport: $45 each way

Note: It's customary to tip your cab driver 15–20%, depending on your experience with the drive.

ANAHEIM SHUTTLE

ART (Anaheim Resort Transportation) moves guests around Anaheim and surrounding Orange County stops. You can ride between Disneyland, the Honda Center for concerts, Costa Mesa for shopping, and more. Many of the hotels around Disneyland also use ART for their guests.

One-way fares start at $4.00 for adults (10+) and $1.50 for kids (3-9) and seniors (65+). Day passes start at $6.00 for adults and $2.50 for children and seniors. 3, 5, and 15-day passes are also available. However, some hotels may offer complimentary ART transportation. To purchase passes and to view the schedule, visit https://rideart.org.

INTRODUCTION

As you near the property of the Disneyland Resort, one of the first things you'll notice are the collections of hotels near the entrance. The City of Anaheim has a bit of a mid-century charm set in suburbia —and is heavily influenced by the parks. Many of the surrounding hotels also reflect this mid-century aesthetic. Since there are so many hotels, inns, and motels, it may be very difficult for you to choose where to book. Ultimately, the choice comes down to what your party needs in terms of amenities and proximity within your budget.

In this chapter, we outline the pros and cons of our many recommended hotels both on and off the Disneyland Resort property. We give our reviews, hotel details, and money-saving tips to help book your accommodations.

WHERE TO STAY

The Disneyland Resort offers three amazing hotels, each with a different theme. The Disney's Grand Californian Hotel and Spa is the most luxurious, followed by the classic Disneyland Hotel, and the slightly more affordable Pixar Place Hotel. Keep in mind that none of these properties run cheap. Since these hotels have exclusive access to the theme parks, extended park hours, and many more amenities, we recommend reviewing these properties carefully to help decide where to book.

However, it's not necessary to stay at the Disneyland Resort property for a great time. Many affordable hotels are within walking distance of the Resort. These properties may offer clean rooms, pools, breakfast, and sometimes a view of Disneyland from your room. Best of all, you might save hundreds of dollars per night!

BOOKING DISCOUNTED DISNEY ROOMS

- **Find the Best Price** – Always check third party travel websites for better deals (i.e. Priceline.com, Orbitz.com, Expedia.com) and compare them to the Disneyland website. Sometimes you can save quite a bit per night with third-party websites. Click on their "deals" or "promotions" tab to find discount coupons.
- **Get Packaged** – Though many websites offer packaged deals, sometimes these are not the lowest cost. We recommend checking the pricing of hotels and flights separately before you commit to a vacation package.
- **Cancellation Policies** – Depending on the room you book, you may have some flexibility with your hotel booking. Many times, guests can cancel or change their reservation up to a couple of weeks before their trip. However, some discounted deals many not offer any cancellation at all.
- **Direct Deals** – Seasonally, Disneyland.com will offer discounted hotel pricing (usually 20-30% off). We recommended booking early when you see these deals! When you book online at Disneyland.com or over the phone, you can often just put $200 down on a reservation (this includes any bundled park tickets and added items) and pay the remaining balance closer to your arrival date.

DISNEYLAND RESORT HOTELS

As we said before, the Disneyland Resort Hotels each have a unique sense of style and theme. Though all of the Disney hotels offer similar amenities, it's a general rule that the closer you stay to the parks, the more you'll spend per night.

BENEFITS OF STAYING AT A DISNEY HOTEL

- Closest proximity to the parks (save on walking time).
- Private entrance for guests of all three hotels through the Grand Californian Hotel to Disney California Adventure, and one dedicated entrance for the Pixar Place Hotel.
- Walking distance to the restaurants, shops, and fun of Downtown Disney.
- "Early Entry" gets hotel guests in the parks 30 minutes before opening to one of the two theme parks (it rotates daily). Guests must have a park ticket and reservation. Most rides in Fantasyland and Tomorrowland are open during this time.
- Free merchandise delivery to your hotel from any of the Disney shops in the parks. The following day you can pick them up from the bell services in your hotel.
- Gorgeous pools with waterslides.
- Disney Character Wake-Up Calls from one of your favorites—kids love this!
- Free Wi-Fi.

· Magic Tips ·
Hotel benefits aren't always guaranteed and will be offered when available. Also, social distancing measures could effect amenities like merchandise room delivery, entrance through Disney California Adventure, and Extra Magic Hour.

THE DISNEY DIFFERENCE

Disneyland Resort hotels welcome families with children as they would any other guest. If there's an accident or issue caused by a child, Disney is accommodating, understanding, and friendly. That doesn't mean they allow children to run screaming through the lobbies, but instead they may help redirect their energy. This might be through a visiting character, offered coloring book, or other activity to keep kids entertained (and other hotel guests unbothered).

Most of the rooms are large enough that four adults can stay in a single room with enough space—as long as you're okay with sharing a bathroom. If you need more beds, ask for a room with a twin-sized trundle bed. These beds are stiffer than the queen- and king-sized beds, but work well for children and average-sized adults.

· **Magic Tips** ·

If you arrive before your hotel reservation time, ask to check in early. Disney doesn't guarantee that rooms will be ready before your arrival, but it's always worth asking! You can also leave your things with bell services and visit the parks or shop in Downtown Disney until your room is ready.

MORE BENEFITS

EXCLUSIVE RESERVATIONS (When Available)

If you're staying at a Disneyland Resort hotel, you may have exclusive access to reserve at some of the most popular dining and entertainment spots. This includes the Blue Bayou Restaurant, Carthay Circle, Napa Rose, Lamplight Lounge, and Bibbidi Bobbidi Boutique, and more. Even if the restaurant no longer has available reservations, call (714) 781-DINE before your stay to ask for a hotel guest reservation.

HOTEL PARKING

You still have to pay for this but the parking is much closer than the rest of the Resort and you can leave your vehicle overnight (check Disneyland.com for details on cars and oversized vehicles as they are subject to change). Valet is also available at an additional cost.

- Self-Parking: $35 / vehicle
- Oversized Vehicles: $40 / vehicle
- Valet Parking: $65 / vehicle

DISNEY POWER WALKS (When Available)

Walks through Disneyland are offered to hotel guests beginning at 6am. Check with the Guest Services desk at your Resort Hotel for details.

LAUNDRY

You may have your clothes dry cleaned or laundered Monday through Saturday. Perfect for those traveling long distances, staying extendedly, or stopping by during a business trip. The Grand Californian has its own self-service laundry room.

IS CLUB LEVEL WORTH THE COST?

The three Disneyland Resort hotels each have their own club level access rooms. These can be standard or premium views with special access to snacks, desserts, and complimentary alcohol for adults. Club level is also about double the cost of other rooms. But is it worth the higher price tag? It really comes down to your needs. If you're planning on staying at the hotel for much of the day, having a dedicated quiet space with complimentary dining options is a great idea. The food here is mostly light bites, but is delicious nonetheless. Club level is also a great idea for those needing to grab food and a bottle of water on the way to the theme parks.

The Craftsman Club in Grand Californian, the E-Ticket Club at the Disneyland Hotel, and one in the Pixar Place Hotel each have sweeping views of the Resort with nightly displays of the Disneyland fireworks. The music in the room also syncs with the fireworks each night!

Continental breakfast runs from 6:30am-10:00am and includes pastries, cereal, juices, coffee, tea, and fruit. After an hour or so break, new lunchtime finger foods and sodas are served from 11:00am-4:00pm. In the evening, hors d'oeuvres with beer and wine for adults of age are served from 5:00pm-7:00pm. In the late evening, 8:00pm-10:00pm, gourmet desserts and specialty drinks are served for all club guests. These times and items may vary depending on the day.

SIGNATURE SUITES

If you're looking for a room with extra Disney magic, book one of the Signature Suites at the Disneyland Hotel or Disney's Grand Californian. These rooms have specially designed decor like the Big Thunder Mountain suite with paintings of the ride and other Frontierland-themed touches including a rustic bath and special sound effects. There's also a Mickey Mouse Penthouse with themed colors and a Mickey-shaped LED overhead light. More signature suites at the Disneyland Hotel include a Pirates of the Caribbean, Adventureland, and a Fairytale suite fit for a princess.

The Grand Californian has several signature suites modeled after famous Californian Mountains. These include several large connected rooms with unique decor and sweeping views of the DCA theme park or wooded areas.

While all of these suites are sure to offer unforgettable experiences, they also book quickly. Rooms also cost $5,000 or more a night!

· Magic Tips ·
Even if you're not staying at one of the Disneyland Resort hotels, you can still tour their lobbies and dine inside their restaurants.

DISNEY'S GRAND CALIFORNIAN

1600 Disneyland Dr., Anaheim, CA 92802
www.Disneyland.com
(714) 635-2300
Star Rating: 4

A visitor favorite, Disney's Grand Californian brings luxury to the Disneyland Resort. The hotel opened just before Disney California Adventure in 2001 and is designed after resorts in Northern California (specifically the Ahwahnee Hotel in Yosemite).

Staying in this hotel means that you'll be very close to the theme parks. It even has its own dedicated entrance to Disney California Adventure. In addition, the Disneyland Park gate is just a few minutes' walking distance through Downtown Disney.

The standard rooms of this hotel aren't particularly special. They have a simple, craftsman design with nature-themed decor. Overall, the amenities like the spa, grand lobby, top-notch dining, and close proximity to the theme parks is what makes this hotel stand out.

The Grand Californian doesn't come cheap. The lowest standard room price tag starts around $600 a night! Of course, there are off-season specials that might drop the room rate down to around $500, which we'll cover later. Still, staying at the Grand Californian—no matter how beautiful—is out of the price range for many families. If you're determined to stay at this resort hotel, here's a closer look:

PROS

- It's beautiful! Hotel guests will be stunned when entering the grand lobby of this magnificent hotel.
- The closest hotel to the theme parks with a private entrance to Disney California Adventure for its guests. This is our favorite feature, especially since the entrance is by the Grizzly River Run, so it makes a great stopping point if you need to change after getting soaked!
- Elegantly designed rooms and suites with balconies.
- Three amazing pools: the Fountain Pool, the Redwood Pool with a water slide, and the Mariposa Pool for relaxing. Poolside cabanas are available at the Mariposa Pool.
- Spa that offers massages, facials, and other treatments.
- Close to Downtown Disney attractions, restaurants, and shopping.
- Some rooms have a theme park view of Disney California Adventure.

CONS

- It's the most expensive of the three Disneyland Resort hotels.
- Simple room designs that lack Disney magic.
- The hotel can feel too spread out.
- Pricey overnight parking.

ROOM BOOKING TIPS

The Grand Californian Hotel is split into two sections: the main hotel and the Disney Vacation Club villas. The main hotel has the majority of rooms, where guests can choose from standard, special views, and Signature Suites. It may be tempting to book a premium view of the theme park, but these prices can be hundreds of dollars more than a standard-view room. Rooms with views of the theme parks, Downtown Disney, or the pool areas may also have loud noises until closing. Thankfully, the windows and balcony doors do a decent job of muffling these sounds. If you're worried about excess noise, choose a Woods-Courtyard View room.

Most of the rooms at the Grand Californian also come with a mini refrigerator for keeping items like water, soda, or baby formula cool. Also expect standing showers, so you'll need to ask for a room with a bathtub if needed. The larger rooms and Signature Suites have multiple spaces, special decorations, and beds to sleep up to twelve people. Those traveling with large parties may want to consider a 3-bedroom suite and request a theme park view or a quiet woods view.

The Disney Vacation Club villas are reserved for members of Disney's timeshare program. These villas are larger rooms with kitchenettes for light cooking and storing refrigerated items. You may book a DVC room via another member. If you don't know a member, we recommend using www.dvcrentalstore.com, though the Grand Californian Villas are limited and difficult to book even for members.

MORE TIPS

The decor is so similar throughout the entire hotel that its easy to get lost. The hallways and the restaurants all appear to blend together. After a night or two at the Grand Californian, you'll easily make your way through the property.

If you're staying on site and just want an easy meal, head to the GCH Craftsman Bar & Grill for a quick bite. This dining area serves American favorites like burgers and fries, breakfast items, nachos, and more. This restaurant also serves a special menu for guests wishing to dine by the pool.

If you're visiting with young kids, you'll likely want to check out the Storytellers Cafe for breakfast or brunch. This is a character meet and greet buffet with Mickey Mouse and his friends! Take photos while you choose from a wide variety of adult and kid-friendly dining options.

For a more upscale dining experience, head to Napa Rose, the hotel's signature restaurant. Napa Rose focuses on wine pairings and delicious meals crafted by award-winning chef, Andrew Sutton.

THE DISNEYLAND HOTEL

1150 Magic Way, Anaheim, CA 92802
www.Disneyland.com
(714) 778-6600
Star Rating: 4

A Disney classic, the Disneyland Hotel originally opened in the fall of 1955, but has since gone under several changes over the years. Today, the hotel is composed of four themed towers that circle a large central pool area. These buildings are the Fantasy Tower, the Adventure Tower, Frontier Tower, and the Discovery Tower, each decorated with memorabilia and furnishings that celebrate iconic Disney themed lands. The newest tower is the Discovery Tower which has several themed rooms and its own dedicated pool area.

The hotel has a contemporary feel with added Disney magic. The main pool area has bars for adults, Polynesian dining, and waterslides shaped like monorails! At night, the headboards of the beds light up with dazzling swirls! The bathrooms are a bit standard, but have bathtubs and Mickey hands that hold the lights on the walls. Nothing feels cheap here, but some of the lower cost items like standard toilet seats are likely for childproof reasons. Nonetheless, the beds are comfortable and kids will love the pools with waterslides.

· **Magic Tips** ·
The Discovery Tower was built for Disney Vacation Club but many of the rooms are bookable to everyone. Rooms here range from smaller 2-person studios with Murphy beds to massive Grand Villas with multiple bedrooms. All of these rooms have a full kitchen or kitchenette but also a steeper price.

Though it's located in the center of a suburban neighborhood and surrounded by busy streets, the Disneyland Hotel does a great job of keeping guests' eyes on Disney magic. There are beautiful pools, elegant walkways, and scenic paths surrounded by lush greenery. Ultimately, staying here immerses you in the magic of

Disneyland, even though the hotel is positioned at the far end of Downtown Disney.

The monorail line is a short walking distance away from the hotel and transports guests to Disneyland Park's Tomorrowland (you'll need a theme park ticket to ride). Guests can also walk about 5-10 minutes through Downtown Disney to arrive at the theme parks.

PROS

- Elegantly designed rooms and suites that bring Disney and mid-century charm seamlessly together.
- Large pool with two monorail-themed water slides and the smaller D-Ticket pool.
- Fantastic dining including Trader Sam's Enchanted Tiki Bar with top-notch cocktails and Tangaroa Terrace with delicious bites and Dole Whip.
- E-Ticket Club-Level option available with continental breakfast, sodas, snacks, desserts, evening wine and cheese, and more. You can view the fireworks display from this space if you have club access.
- Typically less expensive than the Grand Californian Hotel. We also like the design of the Disneyland Hotel standard rooms more than we do the Grand Californian standard rooms. They have a better Disney feel and theme.
- From our experience, the Disneyland Hotel has the best overall service of the three Disney-owned hotels.
- Close to Downtown Disney attractions, restaurants, and shopping.
- Discovery Tower villas have kitchens and a dedicated pool area.

CONS

- Further walking distance to the parks compared to the Grand Californian Hotel.
- Expensive when compared to other 4-star hotels outside of Disney property.
- The pool area can be very noisy during the day.
- Standard rooms are expensive and often don't have very nice views (parking lot or other buildings).
- Expensive overnight parking.

PIXAR PLACE HOTEL

1717 Disneyland Dr., Anaheim, CA 92802
www.Disneyland.com
(714) 999-0990
Star Rating: 4

The Pixar Place Hotel is 15-stories tall and located just beyond Downtown Disney. This hotel may be the least expensive on Resort property, but it's still a premium price with splendid rooms. In fact, Pixar Place generally has the largest room sizes at the Resort. Many families with children enjoy staying here because of the lower cost and extra square footage.

The hotel was once the Paradise Pier Hotel but switched over to a Pixar theme in 2023. Guests can hang out in the lobby, pool area, and roof surrounded by artworks of favorite Pixar characters.

Just keep in mind that Pixar Place is the furthest on-site hotel from the two Disneyland parks. Unfortunately, it doesn't touch Downtown Disney and you'll need to walk about 15-20 minutes before arriving at one of the theme park gates.

· **Magic Tips** ·
Guests staying a the Pixar Place Hotel have a dedicated entrance to Disneyland California Adventure. Find it across the street from the hotel near the gate to Disney's Grand Californian Resort Hotel. This special entrance is just a short walk from the hotel and empties into Paradise Gardens Park near Goofy' Sky School.

Most of the entertainment at the Pixar Place Hotel is found on the third-floor rooftop. The pool and hangout spots are found in this area. There's also a waterslide, dining options, and plenty of loungers for hotel guests. At night, the dazzling Disneyland fireworks can be viewed from here, and games for the entire family to enjoy. The hotel plays synchronized music for the fireworks as guests watch.

PROS

- Dedicated entrance to Disney California Adventure.
- Stylishly designed rooms themed after Pixar films.
- Typically, the largest rooms of the three Resort hotels.
- The lowest price of the three Disneyland hotels.
- Rooftop pools with the Finding Meno splash area and Crush water slide
- Great Maple is a fantastic dining spot located in the hotel.
- Close to Downtown Disney restaurants and shopping.
- See the fireworks from the pool deck on select nights.

CONS

- This is the furthest hotel in the Resort from the parks (it's close to the end of Downtown Disney and near the Disneyland Hotel). The walking distance from the theme parks to the hotel might be a bit of a trek. To avoid this, we recommend taking the monorail out of Tomorrowland to the Disneyland Hotel.
- The theme park view rooms here come with a premium up-charge, but may have obstructed views from trees. To avoid this, ask for a room on the highest level possible.
- Much more expensive than other within walking-distance hotels outside of the Resort.
- Most room views are of the city, roads, or the back of Disney California Adventure.
- Pricey overnight parking.

· **Magic Tips** ·

If you're on a tight budget, but would still like a nice room at a Disneyland Resort hotel property, book the lowest cost standard room at Pixar Place. Then, 5-7 days before your vacation, call (714) 999-0990 and request that your room have a theme park view. With a little luck, you could get a stunning view of Disney California Adventure at a lower price!

NEARBY HOTELS

If you're looking to save money, staying at a Disneyland Resort hotel will likely be out of the budget. Luckily, there are several less-expensive options nearby! We've marked our most-recommended off-site hotels with a star symbol (*).

Americas Best Value Inn & Suites
425 W Katella Ave, Anaheim, CA 92802
(800) 266-0511 / https://www.valueinnanaheim.com

Star Rating	Our Rating	Price	Distance	Pool
2	B+	Economic	Less than 1 mile	Yes

Pros: Very affordable, clean rooms, and a 10-15 minute walk to Disneyland. Larger family suites also available at a low cost. Shuttle service available to the Disneyland Resort for a small fee.
Cons: Simple room and hotel design.

Anaheim Camelot Inn & Suites
1520 S Harbor Blvd, Anaheim, CA 92802
(714) 635-7275 / www.camelotinn-anaheim.com

Star Rating	Our Rating	Price	Distance	Pool
3	B	Economic	Across the street	Yes

Pros: Affordable and a very close walk to Disneyland (under 5 min).
Cons: The pool is small and can become crowded very quickly. The room decor is a bit boring.

Anaheim Majestic Garden Hotel
900 South Disneyland Dr, Anaheim, CA 92802
(714) 778-1700 / www.majesticgardenhotel.com

Star Rating	Our Rating	Price	Distance	Pool
3	B+	Economic	About 1 mile	Yes

Pros: Affordable, close to Disneyland (10 min walk), shuttle to parks.
Cons: A bit outdated, smaller pool, and not easily walkable.
Deals: Free breakfast with select rooms.

⋆ Anaheim Marriott Hotel

700 West Convention Way, Anaheim, CA 92802
(714) 750-8000 / www.marriott.com

Star Rating	Our Rating	Price	Distance	Pool
4	A	Moderate	About 2 miles	Yes

Pros: Clean, affordable, very nice rooms, professional staff, shuttle to parks.
Cons: A bit of a walk to the parks, very expensive during busier dates.

Anaheim Marriott Suites

12015 Harbor Blvd, Garden Grove, CA 92840
(714) 750-1000 / www.marriott.com

Star Rating	Our Rating	Price	Distance	Pool
3	B+	Economic	About 2.5 miles	Yes

Pros: Clean, affordable, larger rooms, Starbucks on location, shuttle to parks.
Cons: Further from the parks, a bit outdated.

Anaheim Portofino Inn & Suites

1831 S Harbor Blvd, Anaheim, CA 92802
(714) 782-7600 / www.portofinoanaheim.com

Star Rating	Our Rating	Price	Distance	Pool
3	B+	Economic	About 0.5 miles	Yes

Pros: Affordable, spacious rooms, next to CVS (drugstore), short walk to Disneyland (10 min).
Cons: A bit outdated.

⋆ Best Western Plus Anaheim Inn

1630 S Harbor Blvd, Anaheim, CA 92802
(714) 774-1050 / www.anaheiminn.com

Star Rating	Our Rating	Price	Distance	Pool
2	A	Moderate	Across the street	Yes

Pros: Right across the street from the main entrance to the Disneyland Resort! Updated rooms and breakfast included with your stay. There are several restaurants within a block or two including Denny's, iHop, Tony Roma's, and a few pizza places!
Cons: A bit higher priced than other close hotels.

*** Candy Cane Inn**
1747 S Harbor Blvd, Anaheim, CA 92802
(714) 774-5284 / www.candycaneinn.net

Star Rating	Our Rating	Price	Distance	Pool
2	A	Moderate	About 0.5 miles	Yes

Pros: Breakfast included, shuttle, brief walk to Disneyland (10 min).
Cons: Popular and can sell out during busy seasons and on weekends.

*** Castle Inn & Suites**
1734 S Harbor Blvd, Anaheim, CA 92802
(714) 774-8111 / www.castleinn.com

Star Rating	Our Rating	Price	Distance	Pool
2	B	Economic	About 0.5 miles	Yes

Pros: Clean, simple rooms, close walk to Disneyland (10 min). Larger family suites available.
Cons: Campy design, simple and outdated rooms.

Clarion Hotel Anaheim Resort
616 Convention Way, Anaheim, CA 92802
(714) 750-3131 / www.clarionanaheim.com

Star Rating	Our Rating	Price	Distance	Pool
3	B-	Economic	About 1 mile	Yes

Pros: Near convention center, walkable to Disneyland (20 min).
Cons: Outdated building and rooms.

Cortona Inn & Suites
2029 S Harbor Blvd, Anaheim, CA 92802
(714) 971-5000 / www.cortonainn.com

Star Rating	Our Rating	Price	Distance	Pool
2	B	Economic	About 1 mile	Yes

Pros: Very affordable rooms, clean, near convention center, walkable to Disneyland (20 min).

Cons: Outdated building, simple rooms.

Fairfield Inn by Marriott Anaheim Resort
1460 S Harbor Blvd, Anaheim, CA 92802
(714) 772-6777 / www.marriott.com

Star Rating	Our Rating	Price	Distance	Pool
2	B+	Moderate	About 0.5 miles	Yes

Pros: Clean, updated, Disney theming in select rooms, brief walk to Disneyland (under 10 min).
Cons: Higher price than other 2-Star hotels.

Four Points by Sheraton Anaheim
1221 S Harbor Blvd, Anaheim, CA 92802
(714) 758-0900 / www.fourpointsanaheim.com

Star Rating	Our Rating	Price	Distance	Pool
3	B	Economic	About 0.5 miles	Yes

Pros: Clean, updated rooms, walkable to Disneyland (15 min).
Cons: Noisy due to "thin" walls.

Grand Legacy at the Park
1650 S Harbor Blvd, Anaheim, CA 92802
(714) 772-0440 / www.grandlegacyhotel.com

Star Rating	Our Rating	Price	Distance	Pool
2	B+	Moderate	Across the street	Yes

Pros: Right across the street from the main entrance to the Disneyland Resort! Affordable, larger rooms, clean, rooftop bar, and a convenience store. There are several restaurants within a block or two including Denny's, iHop, Tony Roma's, and a few pizza places.
Cons: A bit dated building, average rooms, rooftop bar can become noisy.

⋆ **Howard Johnson Anaheim**

1380 S Harbor Blvd, Anaheim, CA 92802
(714) 7776-6120 / www.hojoanaheim.com

Star Rating	Our Rating	Price	Distance	Pool
3	A	Economic	0.5 miles	Yes

Pros: Affordable 3-star hotel with mid-century modern vibe. It's clean with friendly service, a pool play area and is very walkable. Shuttles also available.
Cons: The pool areas can be crowded and noisy.

---

* JW Marriott, Anaheim Resort

1775 S Clementine St, Anaheim, CA 92802
(714) 294-7800 / marriott.com/hotels/travel/snajw-jw-marriott-anaheim-resort

Star Rating	Our Rating	Price	Distance	Pool
4	A	Luxury	About 1 mile	Yes

Pros: Elegant hotel with beautiful rooms, professional staff, close to dining like the Cheesecake Factory and P. F. Chang's.
Cons: Expensive, a bit longer of a walk to Disneyland, prices can be similar to staying at a Disneyland Resort hotel.

---

* Tropicana Inn & Suites

1540 S Harbor Blvd, Anaheim CA 92802
(714) 635-4082 / www.tropicanainn-anaheim.com

Star Rating	Our Rating	Price	Distance	Pool
2	B	Moderate	Across the street	Yes

Pros: Affordable, spacious rooms, very close walk to Disneyland (under 5 min).
Cons: Motel-feel, can be pricey for a 2-star hotel.

The Westin, Anaheim Resort

1030 W Katella Ave, Anaheim, CA 92802
(877) 264-9786 / marriott.com/hotels/travel/snawa-the-westin-anaheim-resort

Star Rating	Our Rating	Price	Distance	Pool
4	A	Luxury	Across the street	Yes

Pros: Luxury, walking-distance to Disneyland, great pool area, less expensive than a Disneyland Resort hotel with fantastic amenities.
Cons: Very expensive, a bit longer of a walk to Disneyland, prices can be more expensive than a Disney-owned hotel.

* **Wyndham Anaheim**

515 W Katella Ave, Anaheim, CA 92802
(714) 783-2793 / wyndhamhotels.com/wyndham/anaheim-california/wyndham-anaheim/overview

Star Rating	Our Rating	Price	Distance	Pool
3	A+	Moderate	About 0.5 miles	Yes

Pros: Simple but elegant rooms, affordable, friendly staff, free garaged parking, walking distance to Disneyland.
Cons: Small pool, rooms can book up quickly.

DISNEY VACATION CLUB

Disney Vacation Club (DVC) may be a right fit for those wishing to visit Disney properties year after year. In short, Disney Vacation Club is a non-traditional timeshare. Members purchase points to use annually for stays at the Disneyland Resort, Walt Disney World Resort, Aulani in Hawaii, Disney Cruise Line, and many other exciting destinations worldwide.

We only briefly overview DVC here because we could fill an entire new book can based on the ins and outs of this membership program. However, there are some perks for guests who purchase Disney Vacation Club. DVC members receive discounts on dining, merchandise, select tours, and other benefits at the Disneyland Resort.

The Grand Californian Hotel and the Disneyland Hotel have rooms bookable by Disney Vacation Club members. However, these rooms are often hard to book in advance as quantity is limited. If you wish to vacation at Disneyland or Walt Disney World at least every other year and stay on property, Disney Vacation Club could save you a lot of money. Nonetheless, the buy-in can be thousands of dollars, with points costing $200 or more each for many properties.

If you're interested in becoming a DVC member, we recommend contacting them: www.disneyvacationclub.com.

CHAPTER SIX

DISNEYLAND PARK

INTRODUCTION

Disneyland is the original world-class theme park that opened its gates in July of 1955. With more than sixty rides and attractions, there's something for everyone at this park. Disneyland is Walt Disney's concept for the perfect theme park. It's designed around a central hub with a charming castle and plenty of foliage. In fact, the entire Disneyland Resort is home to over 180,000 trees! From the hub, nine themed lands can be reached for exploration and amusement: Main Street, U.S.A., Adventureland, Frontierland, Fantasyland, Tomorrowland, New Orleans Square, Mickey's Toontown, Critter Country, and Star Wars: Galaxy's Edge. These lands are designed to provide unique attractions and immersive experiences to entertain guests of all ages.

Truly, Disneyland is a family-friendly park, but its storytelling appeals to travelers from every background. In fact, millions of adults travel to Disneyland each year without children to relive the charm and excitement from their childhood. How does Disneyland appeal to guests of all ages? While the theme park has a reputation for kid-friendly rides and character meets, it's much more than that. Think of Disneyland as a beautiful park with an ongoing theatrical production. No matter where you are within its gates, there's something to entertain you. Gorgeous rivers, fanciful food, thrilling rides, and wondrous architecture have been placed here by some of the world's best storytellers. Disneyland was designed to bring fantasy to life and that appeals to just about everyone.

MAIN STREET, U.S.A.

Disneyland's iconic grand entrance is filled with shops, dining, and a magnificent view of the castle. The first thing you'll notice is the train station, beautiful flower arrangements, and smiling faces. Choose the left or right side of the entrance to find yourself in a hub of horse-drawn street cars, carriages, unique shops, and Disney characters waiting to greet you. At night, Main Street U.S.A. becomes prime viewing for the Disneyland fireworks show.

Theme: Turn-of-the-century American town—specifically, Walt Disney's hometown of Marceline, Missouri in the early 20th century.

Forced Dedications

The buildings of Main Street, U.S.A. use forced perspective, a theatrical trick to make the buildings look taller. If you look closely, the second stories of these shops are much more narrow, which creates this illusion. The upper level windows also have names painted on them, many of which belong to Disney Imagineers. For example, the Palm Parlor is dedicated to Roland F. Crump, one of Walt Disney's leading Imagineers who designed popular attractions such as the Haunted Mansion!

RIDES

MAIN STREET VEHICLES

Description: Ride a horse-drawn streetcar, a horseless carriage, or a double-decker bus that will take you down to Sleeping Beauty Castle.

Level: Family

Recommendation: A nice ride for small children and guests who enjoy the classic appeal of Disney attractions. However, thrill riders

might rather skip this and head straight to a ride like Space Mountain.
Lightning Lane: None

> **· Magic Tips ·**
> Main Street makes for a prime viewing area for many of the parades and nighttime fireworks displays. Crowds line up along the streets sometimes hours before each show to get a great view. If you'd like to avoid the parades and shows, it's best to stay clear of Main Street around these show times.

DISNEYLAND RAILROAD

Description: A railroad that moves around the perimeter of the park and makes stops in New Orleans Square, Fantasyland/Toontown, and Tomorrowland. The Grand Circle Tour is completing the railroad trip all the way around the park without getting off on stops!
Level: Everyone
Recommendation: Fun if you'd like an easy way to ride from land to land. If you take the railroad all the way around the perimeter of the park, you will see surprises like volcanoes and dinosaurs!
Lightning Lane: None

SHOWS AND ATTRACTIONS

GREAT MOMENTS WITH MR. LINCOLN

Description: A classic animatronic show starring the sixteenth President of the United States, Abraham Lincoln.
Level: Everyone
Recommendation: Perfect for guests who love the nostalgia of Walt Disney's animatronic storytelling. Personally, we love this attraction for its music, historical detail, and the fun of seeing Abraham Lincoln come to life.
Lightning Lane: None

DISNEYLAND FIREWORKS

Disneyland's stunning classic fireworks display! Watch the magic all around the park as fireworks are set off behind Sleeping Beauty Castle. Our favorite viewing spot is on Main Street between the Emporium shop and the Main Street Cinema. From here, you can see the fireworks, the castle, and the projections that light up the buildings on Main Street. We recommend arriving about 30-40 minutes before showtime (typically 9:30PM on select nights).

There are several different displays of fireworks throughout the year. You may see Wondrous Journeys, Mickey's Mix Magic, Halloween Screams, or Believe in Holiday Magic, depending on the time of year. These nighttime spectaculars may be displayed with projections and other special effects each day of the week. However, fireworks are added on Fridays, Saturdays, and Sundays, and during busier times of the year like the holidays, spring break, and summer. Fireworks may be canceled during high winds and other weather.

MAGIC HAPPENS PARADE

One of Disneyland's best parades ever! See characters from Frozen, Moana, Coco, and more on vibrant floats as they travel through Main Street, U.S.A., and Fantasyland! The parade runs twice a day and switches directions as it travels back through the park. However, the Christmas Fantasy Parade takes this sport during the holiday season.

⋆ Magic Tips ⋆

Watch the parades from Main Street or near the Sleeping Beauty Castle for the best viewing. Find your spot 30-40 minutes before showtime (check map or the Disneyland app for times).

Get reserved seating for the Disneyland parades when you reserve a dining package at Plaza Inn. Meals include a lunch entree, non-alcoholic drink, and parade viewing voucher with up-close seating. Book your reservation by searching Plaza Inn Dining Packages on the Disneyland app.

MAIN STREET SHOPS

Browse several stores in this charming and nostalgic land. There's the large Emporium filled with Disney goods, the Candy Palace where you can see sweets get made, the new Plaza Point holiday store that changes seasonally, and much more! Many guests wait until the end of the night to purchase their goods to take back home. However, you can save time waiting in lines by ordering sweets and doing self checkout with the Disneyland app! Look for the "Order Food" and "Shop in Store" options in the app's menu.

ADVENTURELAND

Discover adventure brought to life with some of Disney's best storylines and attractions set in a dense jungle. Brave a forbidden temple with Indiana Jones or speed down crocodile-infested waters on the Jungle Cruise. Adventureland, one of Disneyland's original themed areas, was redesigned to fit with the Indiana Jones Adventure theming in the 1990s. Guests will find everything here from classic and thrilling rides to delicious treats like Dole Whip floats.

Theme: The jungles of South America, Asia, and Africa

The Dominguez Tree
Adventureland is home to a special landmark known as the Dominguez Family Tree. This exotic palm was planted in the late 1890s and has resided on the property ever since. Disneyland was built in part on the Dominguez family's orange grove and the family specifically requested that the tree stay on property as it had special memories for them. Walt Disney agreed and the tree was replanted in Adventureland where it still stands today! You can easily spot this towering palm between Jungle Cruise and the Indiana Jones Adventure.

RIDES

INDIANA JONES ADVENTURE

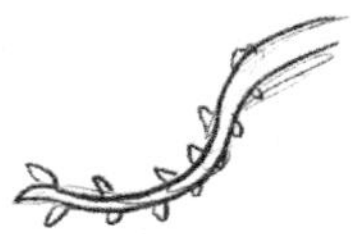

Description: Travel through a hidden jungle temple and hop aboard a classic jeep-like vehicle that holds up to 12 passengers.
Level: Thrill Riders (must be 46"/117cm or taller)
Recommendation: This is a unique ride that is only at Disneyland and it should not be missed by thrill riders.
Lightning Lane: Available with Genie+ / May use Virtual Queue
Ride Secrets: In the spike chamber in the queue, look for a bamboo pole. Shake it until you hear the room rumble and the spikes fall from above. Also, look for a "Do Not Pull Rope!" sign in the queue above the well. Do it and hear the person below yell for help!

Decode It: The temple queue is packed with hidden details including a secret language written on the walls. You can decode these secret messages for free using the Play Disney mobile app.

· Magic Tips ·
The Lightning Lane for Indiana Jones only skips the outside portion of the queue. So only get a Lightning Lane selection for this ride if the wait is longer than 45 minutes. If you're okay not riding with your party, ask the Cast Member at the entrance of the ride (typically they are dressed like Indiana Jones) about the "Single Rider" option. However, at times the Single Rider line doesn't save you much time.

JUNGLE CRUISE
Description: Venture down a massive river on a boat with your comedic tour guide. See animatronic Amazonian and African animals from monkeys and crocodiles to elephants and lions on this 7-minute long ride.
Level: Everyone
Recommendation: A classic, humorous Disneyland ride that most guests will enjoy. Thrill riders may want to skip it.
Lightning Lane: None

ADVENTURELAND TREEHOUSE
Description: A climbable treehouse with inspiration of Swiss Family Robinson. There are different bedrooms and stunning views of Disneyland! It's not an actual tree but a 7-story structure that weighs 150 tons!
Level: Young Kids / Kids / Tweens
Recommendation: Kids ages 10 and under will love this attraction
Lightning Lane: None

SHOWS

ENCHANTED TIKI ROOM
Description: An animatronic show starring birds and Tikis in a tropical island setting.
Level: Family / Everyone
Recommendation: Have a Dole Whip while you watch the 15-minute long show. Thrill-seekers will want to skip this one, as it's a classic attraction that can feel a bit dated.
Lightning Lane: None

FRONTIERLAND

An immersive land inspired by the Wild West! Ride the high-speed Big Thunder Mountain Railroad or catch a classic saloon show at the Golden Horseshoe Stage. The Rivers of America winds around this land with sights of the magnificent Mark Twain Riverboat and Sailing Ship Columbia.

Theme: North America's Wild West

Rustic Charms
Many of the old items found around Frontierland are authentic! When designing attractions like Big Thunder Mountain, Disney Imagineers ventured to old mining locations and foraged for abandoned equipment to place in this land!

RIDES

BIG THUNDER MOUNTAIN RAILROAD
Description: A fast rollercoaster with a few dips called "The Wildest Ride in the Wilderness"!
Level: Thrill Riders (must be 40"/102cm or taller)
Recommendation: Many families and thrill riders will love this fast rollercoaster with short dips and great special effects.
Lightning Lane: Available with Genie+

MORE ATTRACTIONS

THE GOLDEN HORSESHOE STAGE – Laughing Stock Co. is a Western-style stage show with songs and jokes while you dine! During the show, actors may pick a few members of the audience to join them on stage. This is one of the oldest shows at Disneyland and one of Walt Disney's favorites!

MARK TWAIN RIVERBOAT – Explore a beautiful American-style riverboat as you cruise around the Rivers of America on this multi-level boat.

FRONTIERLAND SHOOTIN' EXPOSITION – A paid experience where you can shoot targets with laser-guided rifles.

PIRATE'S LAIR ON TOM SAWYER ISLAND – Board a raft and set sail for an island playground perfect for Kids and Tweens.

SAILING SHIP COLUMBIA – A massive 18th-century ship replica that sails guests around the Rivers of America. Explore below deck for artifacts and hear a unique narration about the original ship's voyage. We prefer Sailing Ship Columbia over the Mark Twain Riverboat for its adventurous feel.

DAVY CROCKETT'S EXPLORER CANOES – Don't come with your arms sore! Guests paddle down the Rivers of America in Frontierland while viewing the stunning waterscape of Disneyland.

NEW ORLEANS SQUARE

Enter The Big Easy in a never-ending celebration of Southern delight. New Orleans Square is filled with shops, unique restaurants, and two very famous rides: Pirates of the Caribbean and the Haunted Mansion! A "square" by name only, this land has tight corners, cobblestone pathways, and plenty of lively New Orleans-style energy to excite guests.

Theme: 19th-Century New Orleans

Members Only
New Orleans Square is home to Disneyland's exclusive Club 33. Originally serving as a local hangout for the 33 investors of Disneyland, the Club provides fine dining and a full bar to its guests. To get access, you'll need a membership or an invitation from a member. The waitlist to join Club 33 is incredibly long, taking some guests years before they are invited. The rumored initiation fee starts at $33,000 plus dues of $12,000 annually.

RIDES

HAUNTED MANSION

Description: A slow-paced ride through a haunted house.
Level: Everyone (though young children may become frightened)
Recommendation: It's a Disneyland classic that many thrill-riders may want to skip for it's slow movement and effects that are only scary enough to terrify young children. The Haunted Mansion will show a 13-minute wait time for anything 10 minutes or less.
Lightning Lane: Available with Genie+
Haunted Mansion Holiday: During Halloween through New Years Day (mid-September through early January), the Haunted Mansion transforms for a spooky surprise! Jack Skellington and his fiendish friends from Tim Burton's *The Nightmare Before Christmas* take over the attraction to celebrate Halloween and Christmas. This temporary

re-theme is popular for its spectacular added special effects and animatronics.

· Magic Tips ·
The Haunted Mansion has a secret "servants' quarters" as part of the queue. In this dimly lit hall, guests walk through a dusty-looking corridor with creepy decor before ending up in the hallway portion of the queue. Though you will skip the normal queue while walking through, this special corridor may be very entertaining to long-time fans. Most of the time you will not have access to the servants' quarters but if you're lucky, a Cast Member may ask your party to enter through it!

PIRATES OF THE CARIBBEAN
Description: Pirate-themed boat ride in the dark. Also a great air-conditioned ride to cool off in on hot days. Over 120 animatronics bring this 15-minute ride to life!
Level: Everyone
Recommendation: A must-see Disney classic ride for all!
Lightning Lane: None

SHOWS

FANTASMIC!
Reopens Spring 2024
Description: An epic nighttime spectacular over the Rivers of America. Displays music and scenes from Disney classic films brought to life with special effects, actors, and floats!
Level: Family / Everyone
Recommendation: A stunning nighttime spectacular for those who enjoy stage shows. This show may run multiple times during the holiday and not at all during the off-season.
Lightning Lane: None

· **Magic Tips** ·
On nights with fireworks, stick around after the first Fantasmic! showing to see the fireworks. Some restaurants including Blue Bayou and River Belle Terrace may offer dining packages with reserved viewing of Fantasmic!

CRITTER COUNTRY

Critter Country feels like a pine forest filled with friendly woodland characters like Winnie the Pooh. The land is sort of a dead end with just one restaurant, The Hungry Bear, a couple of rides, and a store based around Winnie the Pooh. Thus, you likely won't hang out in this area, but there is a pathway along the river that connects to Star Wars: Galaxy's Edge.

Theme: A backwoods and forest-themed land

RIDES

TIANA'S BAYOU ADVENTURE

Opens Late 2024
Description: Water-based log ride with singing animatronic animals. At the end, you plunge down five stories from the mountain!
Level: Thrill Riders (must be 40"/102cm or taller)
Recommendation: If you love water rides with big drops, this attraction is for you!
Lightning Lane: Possibly Individual Lightning Lane with Virtual Queue
Stay Dry: To avoid getting soaked, ask a Cast Member to seat you near the back of the log ride vehicle.

· **Magic Tips** ·
Tiana's Bayou Adventure is a reimagining of the Splash

Mountain ride. It uses the same log flume ride system but with new themes including music, special effects, audio-animatronics, and story. It's expected to open late 2024.

THE MANY ADVENTURES OF WINNIE THE POOH
Description: A slow-paced ride through the brightly-colored world of Winnie the Pooh.
Level: Young Kids / Family
Recommendation: Great for young kids and families.
Lightning Lane: None

FANTASYLAND

Classic Disney animated films come to life in the kid-friendly Fantasyland. Families with young kids especially love Fantasyland for the picturesque scenes designed for them.

Theme: A medieval courtyard and classic Disney wonderland

Look Mom, No Lines!
The most popular lines in Fantasyland are Peter Pan's Flight and Snow White's Enchanted Wish. If you're visiting with a child under 6 years of age, we recommend starting with one of these two rides before the lines exceed 30 minutes.

RIDES

MATTERHORN BOBSLEDS
Description: Swiss mountain-themed rollercoasters and the only thrill ride in Fantasyland.
Level: Thrill Riders (must be 42"/107cm or taller)
Recommendation: Matterhorn is home to two separate tracks. In general, the left track (Tomorrowland side) is more thrilling than the right (Fantasyland side).
Lightning Lane: Available with Genie+

· **Magic Tips** ·
The Matterhorn Bobsleds are technically two separate roller coasters that load on different sides of the mountain. Both tracks move up to the same speed, 27 mph (43.5 km/h), but the Tomorrowland-loading side is about 100 ft (30 m) longer!

PETER PAN'S FLIGHT

Description: Fly along Peter Pan through London and Neverland on a pirate ship!
Level: Young Kids / Everyone
Recommendation: Perfect for all ages and a Disneyland classic that we also recommend to thrill-seekers. Peter Pan's Flight can have one of the longest lines in the park. To avoid this, we recommend riding this first if you are with small children who may have short attention spans.
Lightning Lane: None

ALICE IN WONDERLAND

Description: Hop aboard the Caterpillar and see the whimsical story of Walt Disney's *Alice in Wonderland*.
Level: Kids / Everyone
Recommendation: Perfect for families with kids of all ages. This classic dark ride is also popular amongst Disneyland fans with its charming characters, glow-in-the-dark lighting effects, and newly added magic!
Lightning Lane: None

MAD TEA PARTY

Description: Disneyland's famous tea cups inspired by *Alice in Wonderland*! Spin with your friends (up to 3-4 adults per tea cup).
Level: Kids / Everyone
Recommendation: Perfect for all ages and a Disneyland classic that we also recommend to thrill-seekers (the tea cups can spin fast or slow, depending on how hard you turn them).
Lightning Lane: None

DUMBO THE FLYING ELEPHANT

Description: Soar high while boarding Dumbo! Also, hold a feather to help Dumbo take off.

Level: Young Kids / Everyone
Recommendation: Perfect for families with young children.
Lightning Lane: None

MR. TOAD'S WILD RIDE

Description: Zip in a zany buggy that follows the story of Mr. Toad (from the 1949 animated film, *The Adventures of Ichabod and Mr. Toad*).
Level: Kids / Family
Recommendation: Perfect for all ages. It's a Disneyland-only classic ride (Disney World closed this attraction in 1998 and replaced it with the Many Adventures of Winnie the Pooh).
Lightning Lane: None

CASEY JR. CIRCUS TRAIN

Description: Pretend you're a circus animal on this slow-paced train that takes you up and down the hills from the movie *Dumbo*.
Level: Kids / Family
Recommendation: Perfect for families with young children.
Lightning Lane: None

SNOW WHITE'S ENCHANTED WISH

Description: Travel through the tale of *Snow White and the Seven Dwarfs.*
Level: Kids / Family
Recommendation: Perfect for families with young children. This ride was updated in 2021 with a new, happier storyline and special effects.
Lightning Lane: None

PINOCCHIO'S DARING JOURNEY

Description: A slow-paced but colorful ride that follows the story of Walt Disney's *Pinocchio*.
Level: Kids / Family
Recommendation: Perfect for families with young children.
Lightning Lane: None

KING ARTHUR CARROUSEL

Description: A classic carousel with horses from *The Sword in the Stone*.
Level: Kids / Family
Recommendation: Perfect for families with young children.
Lightning Lane: None

STORYBOOK LAND CANALS

Description: A boat ride through Monstro the whale's mouth with views of miniature models of Disney's best movie settings.
Level: Kids / Family
Recommendation: Perfect for families with young children.
Lightning Lane: None

"IT'S A SMALL WORLD"

Description: A boat floats through several counties with children singing the "It's a Small World" theme song in different languages.
Level: Young Kids / Family
Recommendation: Perfect for families with young children. During the holiday season, this ride dazzles with lights and new costumes. Look for characters like Ariel and Aladdin hidden throughout the ride.
Lightning Lane: Available with Genie+

SHOWS AND ATTRACTIONS

SLEEPING BEAUTY CASTLE WALKTHROUGH

Description: Walk through the Disneyland castle.
Level: Family / Everyone
Recommendation: Walk through, see the art, and take a picture outside of the castle.
Lightning Lane: None

PIXIE HOLLOW

Description: Meet Tinker Bell and her friends between tall blades of grass.
Level: Kids and Young Kids
Recommendation: Great for the pixie fan of any age!
Lightning Lane: None

FANTASY FAIRE

At Royal Hall and Royal Theatre
Description: Meet Princesses in the Royal Hall and watch them perform lives shows (*Beauty and the Beast* and *Tangled*) in the Royal Theatre.
Level: Kids / Family
Recommendation: Perfect for children of all ages who love Disney Princesses. However, the lines can get a bit long midday for these meet and greets.
Lightning Lane: None

BIBBIDI BOBBIDI BOUTIQUE – A shop where kids can dress up in princess clothing and makeup. Perfect for children who are inspired by Disney Princesses. Starting around $100, kids can get their makeup and hair done—and even buy a gown of their favorite Disney Princess. There are more options, including a Knight Package and a *Frozen* Package!
Appointments: Call (714) 781-7895 (up to 60 days in advance)

TOMORROWLAND

One of the original themed lands in the theme park, Tomorrowland has served for decades as a peek into the future. With thrilling rides like Space Mountain and Star Tours, Tomorrowland boasts an assortment of Disney magic.

Theme: The world of tomorrow

More Like the World of Yesterday...
It's no secret that Tomorrowland is ironically outdated. The concrete buildings and neon signage feel like 1990s concepts of the future—because they are. The recent version of Tomorrowland reopened in 1998, but slight changes have occurred since then. Still, it's not enough because the land feels like something from the past. We're not ragging on Tomorrowland, because we love the attractions within this area, but a redo is heavily in order.

RIDES

SPACE MOUNTAIN
Description: Board a rocket ship and blast off into outer space in this classic Disney roller coaster in the dark!
Level: Thrill Riders (must be 40"/ 102cm or taller)
Recommendation: A not-to-be missed attraction for thrill riders and those who love a good roller coaster. Space Mountain has been a Disneyland staple since 1977 and is great fun!

Lightning Lane: Available with Genie+

STAR TOURS—The Adventures Continue
Description: 3D *Star Wars*-themed motion simulation ride.
Level: Thrill Riders
Recommendation: Perfect for those who enjoy motion simulation rides. Each time you ride this attraction it's different. Star Tours has nine different planets and a new scene from recent *Star Wars* films.
Lightning Lane: Available with Genie+

BUZZ LIGHTYEAR ASTRO BLASTERS
Description: Compete against others in this fun *Toy Story*-themed ride. It seems like it's for the kids, but it's fun for everyone to blast the laser guns at targets to rack up points.
Level: Everyone (including most Thrill Riders)
Recommendation: A crowd favorite with a short line
Lightning Lane: Available with Genie+
Scoring Big: These are what the targets are worth in points:
Blue Diamonds = 10,000 each / Purple Triangles = 5,000 each / Green Squares = 1,000 each / Circles = 100 each
Targets are worth more when they light up! You can hit the targets as many times as you'd like (keep hitting the blue diamonds!)

· **Magic Tips** ·
Many of the plants in Tomorrowland are edible! There are fruit trees, lettuce heads, and herbs beautifully planted around the land (though we don't recommend eating anything). This concept comes from Imagineers believing that a perfect world has an abundance of food and healthy, edible vegetation grows in public spaces.

FINDING NEMO SUBMARINE VOYAGE
Description: Nemo and friends join you underwater in this slow-paced ride filled with animation effects.
Level: Family
Recommendation: Great for all ages, but not for those who may be claustrophobic. Thrill riders may also want to skip this one for its slow pace.
Lightning Lane: None

ASTRO ORBITER
Description: Orbit a solar system model on spinning rocket ships.

Level: Kids / Family
Recommendation: Fun for young children
Lightning Lane: None

AUTOPIA
Description: Where kids can drive cars around a track.
Level: Kids / Family (must be 32"/81cm or taller to ride; must be 54"/ 137cm to drive alone)
Recommendation: Designed for Kids to Tweens, but with height restrictions.
Lightning Lane: Available with Genie+

DISNEYLAND MONORAIL
A smooth ride around the Disneyland Resort that drops guests off in Downtown Disney. The monorail runs about every 5 minutes and has limited hours on hot days, usually closing at 11:00am and reopening at 6:00pm. The monorail is recommended for all ages.

SHOWS AND ATTRACTIONS

***STAR WARS* LAUNCH BAY** – Take a photo with Chewbacca, Darth Vader, Rey, or Kylo Ren (these characters may change throughout the year). Also see movie props and more.

TOMORROWLAND THEATER – A large theater often used for seasonal attractions such as movie previews.

MICKEY'S TOONTOWN

A cartoon wonderland with eye-popping colors, play areas, and kid-friendly rides. In Toontown, guests can visit the homes of Mickey Mouse, Minnie Mouse, and their friends—with a chance to meet them at the end! Toontown also is filled imagination and zany cartoon antics perfect for kids ages 5-12 years old. Toontown also implements experiences for kids with varied sensory needs.

Theme: Cartoon town starring Mickey, Minnie, and their friends

> **Toontown is Interactive!**
> Pull the lever near the fireworks and see what happens or take a photo behind the jail cell bars! You can also pry open crates, ring that door bell, and try to open the doors for big surprises!

RIDES

MICKEY & MINNIE'S RUNAWAY RAILWAY

Description: A family-friendly trackless dark ride with projection mapping, animatronics, and cartoonish action! Starring Mickey, Minnie, Goofy, and Donald, this attraction can be enjoyed by most guests as it doesn't have frightening moments or a height restriction. Some segments use motion simulation.
Level: Everyone (no height restriction)
Recommendation: Due to the newness of this attraction for 2023 and the reimagining of Mickey's Toontown, we expect a high demand for this attraction throughout the year. There also may be a virtual queue in place.
Lightning Lane: Likely Individual Lightning Lane and Virtual Queue

> · **Magic Tips** ·
> Mickey's Toontown may also close early due to fireworks displays and other technical reasons, so plan a visit here in the daylight hours.

ROGER RABBIT'S CAR TOON SPIN

Description: A "dark ride" where riders can spin the wheel and make the car turn on the track.
Level: Everyone
Recommendation: Great for kids and possibly some thrill-riders who enjoy spinning rides.
Lightning Lane: Available with Genie+

CHIP & DALE'S GADGET COASTER

Description: A short, kid-friendly rollercoaster.
Level: Kids and Young Kids (must be 35"/ 89cm or taller)

Recommendation: A great first-roller coaster for young kids, though there's often a long wait and the ride is very short. The tiny seats on this junior coaster might be uncomfortable for taller/larger adults.
Lightning Lane: None

ATTRACTIONS

MICKEY & MINNIE'S HOUSES – The best places to snap a photo with Mickey and Minnie Mouse. Walk through their homes and meet them at the end for a picture!
Lightning Lane: None

INTERACTIVE AREAS – Check out several play areas inspired by Goofy, Donald Duck, and more! There are tactical zones as well as water play areas for kids.

STAR WARS: GALAXY'S EDGE

Enter a galaxy far, far away on the planet of Batuu. See famous Star Wars characters and experience epic intergalactic battles! This is a highly immersive, detailed land that brings the elements of the Star Wars universe to life. It's not something straight out of the movies, but instead a place of fun and fantasy displaying Disney's newest creative ventures in themed entertainment. Read more in the next chapter!

CHAPTER SEVEN

STAR WARS: GALAXY'S EDGE GUIDE

INTRODUCTION

For decades Disney theme parks have gone virtually unmatched by competitors. Not only are they the most popular theme parks in the world, but the Disney brand is practically synonymous with themed entertainment. All of that changed when The Wizarding World of Harry Potter opened in Universal's Islands of Adventure in Orlando. Suddenly, there was a theme park experience so stunningly immersive it became a central tourist destination.

To Disney, it was abundantly clear that they needed a realist world of their own. Star Wars felt like the perfect answer to Harry Potter. In its 40-year history, the franchise has earned an estimated $65 billion in merchandise, box office sales, home videos, and more. Its fandom is also wide-reaching and multigenerational, making the storylines familiar to millions of potential park guests.

Disney's impressive plan was to transport visitors to a galaxy far, far away, have them become Jedis, fly the Millennium Falcon, and even meet Chewbacca. With Star Wars: Galaxy's Edge, Disney pulls all of this off and more in its largest, most riveting expansion to date. There are stormtroopers marching down ancient walkways, a secret hideaway where guests can build a lightsaber, and even a danger-filled cantina. Disney even went as far as omitting signage in Galaxy's Edge and uses alien language to make the land feel as authentic as possible.

Galaxy's Edge stretches across 14 acres, which is roughly the same size as 2-3 lands in a typical Disney theme park. The magic is in the details, which took Imagineers about two years just to complete the rock work and paint needed to bring Galaxy's Edge to life. One half of the land is crowded with shops, dining, and the Millennium Falcon! This is where guests can explore and also fly the famous ship on the flight simulator, Millennium Falcon: Smugglers Run.

The other half is the hiding spot of the Resistance. This area isn't as populated, but there are some iconic ships and characters to take photos with. The Resistance side is supposed to look unassuming as it holds a hidden path to the land's signature attraction, Star Wars: Rise of the Resistance. This jaw-dropping dark ride has guests join the Resistance to battle the First Order in an epic intergalactic confrontation!

In this chapter, we review the story, attractions, and tips for exploring Star Wars: Galaxy's Edge. It's like visiting a theme park within another theme park—and is like nothing you've ever seen before!

THE STORY

Star Wars: Galaxy's Edge is an entirely immersive land with a vibrant backstory. Set on the fictional planet of Batuu at the edge of the galaxy, this ancient destination is home to a variety of creatures. Black Spire Outpost is the main area guests explore in Batuu. It's an old trading area once used as a ship refueling station before hyperspace was invented. Black Spire gets its name from an enormous dark, petrified tree at its center. At night, all of the spires around the outpost glow with vibrant hues!

Today, Black Spire Outpost is the home of rogues looking to escape the clutch of the First Order. In this timeline—set shortly after the events of *Star Wars: The Last Jedi (Episode VIII)*—the wicked First Order has indeed arrived. Kylo Ren and his fleet of stormtroopers scour Black Spire Outpost for "rebel scum." Meanwhile, Resistance members like Rey and Chewbacca hide on the outskirts of town.

Now, if Batuu doesn't sound familiar, it's because Disney invented the planet for its theme parks. They wanted a new yet familiar land for Galaxy's Edge. Nearly every major element from across *Star Wars* films and animated TV series can be found on Batuu. The round-top buildings of Black Spire Outpost are reminiscent of Naboo while the lush surroundings look like Alderaan. Oga's Cantina feels a lot like the one found on Tatooine. As you browse the Merchant Row, you'll see creatures and items from the entire Star Wars Universe. This includes species found around Jabba the Hutt's palace like the amphibious Worrt (located in Oga's Cantina) and a Kowakian monkey-lizard (purchasable in the Creature Stall shop). There's even a "live" baby Sarlacc (the sand monster that ate Boba Fett in *Return of the Jedi*) in Dok-Ondar's Den of Antiquities.

Disney made it so that every crevice of Batuu is sprinkled with Star Wars charm. For anyone doubting that a land like this belongs in a Disney theme park, guess again. There's nothing but magic, fantasy, and dazzling storytelling throughout Galaxy's Edge. Even if you've never seen a *Star Wars* film, the spectacular production is mind-blowing. The world appears real, and the fun is abundant. No matter what your expectations are, you're certainly in for a wild ride.

MAP OF GALAXY'S EDGE

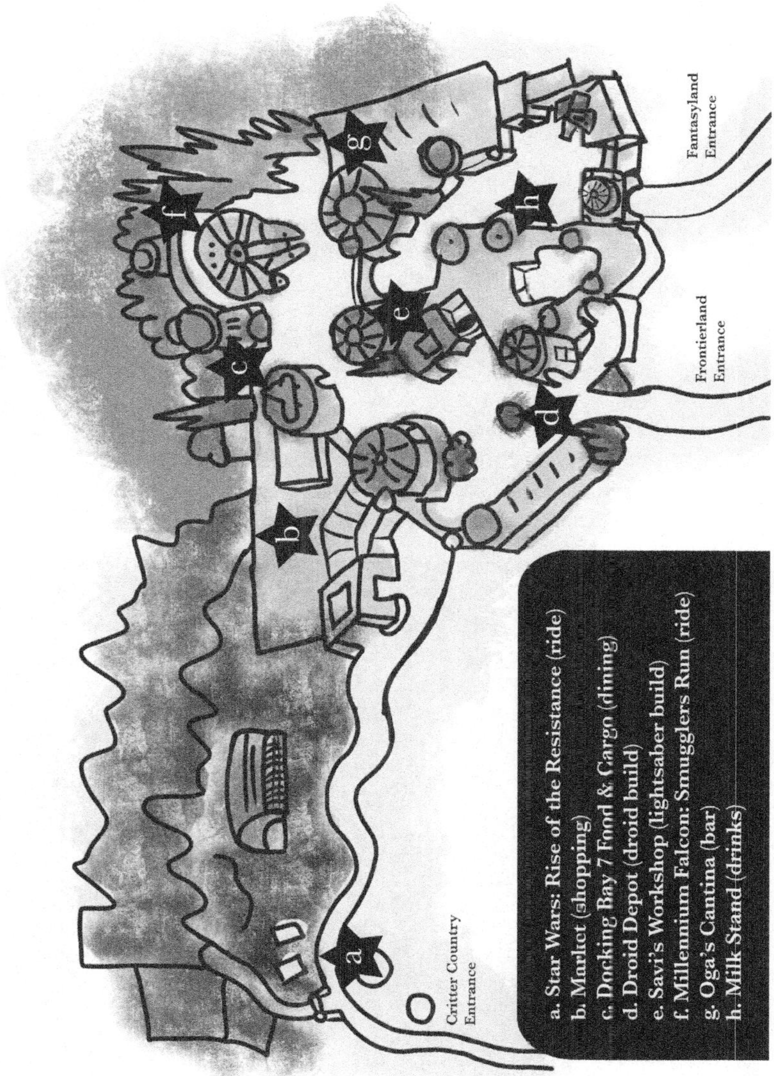

RIDES

There are two featured rides in Star Wars: Galaxy's Edge. The first is Millennium Falcon: Smugglers Run, a flight simulation ride where guests collaborate to fly Han Solo's famous ship. It's incredible to see that Disney built the Falcon from the ground up. We don't mean a *part* of it or a *model* of it. Disney built the entire ship *to scale* —and you get to fly it!

Depending on how poorly you fly the Falcon, you may see damage in the hallway as you exit. However, if you perform well, you'll score points that are recorded on the Disney Play app (make sure you have Bluetooth enabled in the app).

Seeing the Falcon for the first time brings many visitors to tears. It's like meeting a long lost friend in an unexpected place. Disney effectively unveils the ship by making visitors peek around a corner or step down stairs as it comes into view. After the initial shock, you might want to touch the thing, but there's a rusty-looking barrier surrounding the Falcon that keeps us humans at bay. Luckily, Disney photographers happily snap photos in front of her.

*** Magic Tips ***

Flying the pilot position has the best views of the screens, but it also requires the most work. Sadly, you can't choose which job you play. If you want a specific position, you can always ask a Cast Member or switch with someone in your group. Engineers have the easiest job on deck, while pilots have the most work. If someone decides not to press buttons, the ship will automatically take over for them.

The Millennium Falcon ride experience also changes day and night. For example, fly during the day, and you'll see the sun out. At night, it's much darker around Black Spire Outpost!

The main attraction in Galaxy's Edge is Star Wars: Rise of the Resistance. This is a roughly 18-minute role-playing adventure with several ride experiences and plenty of jaw-dropping special effects. During the attraction, guests escape Batuu and find themselves in a dangerous encounter with the evil First Order.

Rise of the Resistance is part walk-through, part motion simulator, and part trackless ride adventure. You'll see real actors, animatronics, mind-blowing special effects, and more in this immersive attraction. We don't want to give away too much but Rise of the Resistance is a must-do experience. Overall, the ride is family-friendly, so most guests will enjoy the ride (it's about as thrilling as Indiana Jones Adventure but has less "dark" parts).

> *** Magic Tips ***
> Keep in mind, if you get motion sickness on rides like Star Tours, you may want to avoid the Millennium Falcon and Rise of the Resistance.

MILLENNIUM FALCON: SMUGGLERS RUN

Best for: Kids, Tweens, Teens, Adults
Restrictions: 38" / 97cm
Lightning Lane: Yes, Disney Genie+

STAR WARS: RISE OF THE RESISTANCE

Best for: Kids, Tweens, Teens, Adults, Thrill Riders
Restrictions: 40" / 102cm
Notes: Due to the overwhelming popularity of Star Wars: Rise of the Resistance, guests may need a boarding pass to ride the attraction. We go over tips for obtaining a boarding group in a later chapter.
Lightning Lane: Yes, Individual

SHOWS

The shows of Galaxy's Edge don't have the same style as the traditional theatrical productions at Disney theme parks. Instead of running on a schedule, they appear to occur at random before unsuspecting guests. The main stage is Kylo Ren's ship where the

First Order dramatically welcomes their leader to Batuu. After the show, guests can take photos with Kylo and his stormtroopers.

> **★ Magic Tips ★**
> Shows in Galaxy's Edge mostly occur during the day, as do most character meetings (though Rey and Chewbacca have been spotted in the evenings).

If you don't know who Vi Moradi is, you're not alone. She's a fairly new character, only having debuted in a *Star Wars* novel back in 2017. Vi Moradi, a rebel spy, is easy to pick out of a crowd. She has black and blue hair and usually wears a bright orange rebel vest. Vi was sent to Batuu by General Leia Organa to spy on Kylo and his troops.

We love the shows in Galaxy's Edge because guests become part of the storyline. Talk to Vi Moradi, and she might tell you about her mission. Kylo Ren also walks through the crowd as he looks for rebels. Additionally, you'll see characters like Rey and Chewbacca roaming Batuu during the day. These moments are ideal times to snap a photo with your favorite Star Wars characters.

DINING

Disney has created out-of-this-world dining experiences for Star Wars: Galaxy's Edge! There's a lively cantina serving alcoholic (and non-alcoholic) beverages, a rustic dining hall, and a stand with the famous blue milk! The food in Galaxy's Edge is somewhat eclectic. Disney purposely made the flavors hard to place so that each bite seems foreign.

OGA'S CANTINA

This high-energy cantina feels incredibly authentic to the Star Wars Universe. The ancient-looking building houses a hodgepodge of equipment, creatures, and a droid DJ! The owner, Oga Garra, is a Blutopian who also runs the cantina. She doesn't take any sass and expects all guests to follow her rules. We never really see Oga, but her staff talks wildly about her as if she's a well-known threat.

For those who recall the captain of the first Star Tours attraction, you're in for a treat. DJ R-3X (voiced by Paul Reubens, a.k.a. “Pee-wee Herman”) spins day and night as bartenders deliver fizzing, bubbling, and steaming drinks to their patrons. Each of the cocktails is named after a Star Wars theme or creature—and comes with a high price tag starting at $15 for an alcoholic beverage. There are drinks for kids, too, like the Blue Bantha with a cookie on top!

Adults craving a drink inside Disneyland will love that there’s finally a bar. Since guests can’t leave Oga’s with their cocktails, this will likely be a favorite hangout for years to come. To get a reservation (up to 60 days in advance), you’ll need to reserve online at disneyland.com or via the mobile app.

Oga’s Cantina also serves separate breakfast and lunch/dinner options. Morning beverages include coffees, juices, and drinks like the Bloody Rancor (Bloody Mary). For lunch/dinner, guests can sample the regular menu with dozens of drinks including cocktails, beers on tap, and hard cider on tap. The cantina serves most styles of alcohol from vodka and rum to beer and wine. If you’re visiting in the morning and don’t like the selection, ask your waiter or bartender for the standard menu.

OGA'S CANTINA RECOMMENDATIONS

- **Fuzzy TaunTaun** (alcoholic beverage) – A sweet drink made with peach vodka, peach schnapps, orange juice, and cane sugar. There’s a fun "Buzz Button Tingling" foam on top that numbs your lips!
- **Yub Nub** (alcoholic beverage) – A sweet drink made with Malibu pineapple rum, Sailor Jerry spiced rum, citrus juices, and passion fruit. Also available eight a souvenir mug.
- **The Outer Rim** (alcoholic beverage) – A bold drink with Patrón Silver Tequila, pomegranate liqueur, lime, and cane sugar, exotic fruit purée, and a black salt rim.

- **Oga's Obsession** (non-alcoholic provision) – A gelatinous mix of lemonade and cotton candy flavors served with dried fruit eaten with a spoon.
- **Cliff Dweller** (non-alcoholic beverage) – A sweet, gingery drink with citrus juices, coconut, hibiscus grenadine, and ginger ale
- **Spiran Caf** (breakfast alcoholic beverage) – A hot coffee with rum, orange marmalade, and vanilla whipped cream. Served during breakfast hours.
- **Not Recommended:** The Jedi Mind Trick is just a bit basic and the make sure that you specify the Yub Nub without the souvenir mug if you don't want to pay the $46 for it.

*** Magic Tips ***
Oga's Cantina may also limit your experience to two drinks per person and a 45-minute max time slot.

DOCKING BAY 7 FOOD & CARGO

This rustic quick-service diner serves a variety of alien eats for guests to enjoy. We think that the food here closely resembles Asian-fusion cuisine with some surprising twists. For example, the sweet and spicy Smoked Kaadu Ribs comes with a blueberry corn muffin. Additionally, there aren't forks and knives in Galaxy's Edge (for now). Instead, guests must use a spork-like utensil to cut, scoop, and eat. Yes, this can be a little tricky at first, but it doesn't take long to get the hang of the spork. It's these unexpected touches that give Black Spire Outpost its alien feel.

DOCKING BAY 7 DINING RECOMMENDATIONS

- **Endorian Roasted Chicken Salad** (lunch/dinner entree) – A hearty salad of mixed greens, roasted veggies, quinoa, and pumpkin seeds topped with delicious marinated chicken, and tossed in green curry ranch.

- **Moof Juice** (non-alcoholic beverage) – A very sweet concoction of fruit juices and chipotle-pineapple.
- **Vintian Mineral Mousse** (dessert) – A complex and creamy dessert with strawberry, vanilla, and chocolate flavors.
- **Not Recommended:** The Endorian Fried Chicken Tip-Yip is fairly bland.

OTHER EATS

RONTO ROASTERS – This snacking spot is popular for its tangy sausage wraps served in a pita. However, we highly recommend the plant-based Ronto-less Garden Wrap with kimchi slaw—it's one of the best snacks in the Disneyland Resort!

MILK STAND – Try blue and/or green milk from the *Star Wars* films. These are plant-based (dairy-free) drinks served like a cold slushy. Blue Milk has a berry flavor and Green Milk is more citrus. We recommend Blue Milk over Green.

KAT SAKA'S KETTLE – Munch on a variety of flavored popcorn. We recommend the sweet and spicy Outpost Mix.

JAT KAA'S COOLERS – Droid-driven carts serving drinks, including very popular round Coke bottles!

SHOPPING

There are seemingly infinite items to purchase in Galaxy's Edge including cute Porg plushies and Jedi robes. You can also purchase a Kowakian monkey-lizard puppet (the small creature found with Jabba the Hutt) that sits on your shoulder and moves with your commands. For more immersion, Disney sells an exclusive metal gift card in Galaxy's Edge called the Batuuan Spira. These gift cards are available at Droid Depot for about $5 and a minimum load of $100.

Sadly, some of the better experiences in Galaxy's Edge come at an extra cost. Savi's Workshop and the Droid Depot are amazingly fun, but you might spend hundreds of dollars entertaining your family. Here we review these experiences to help decide what's best for your visit.

SAVI'S WORKSHOP CUSTOM LIGHTSABERS REVIEW

Savi's Workshop is a secret backdoor area—sort of like a speakeasy—where those seeking the Force can become a Jedi! In other words, you find a secret entrance in a scrap metal yard to build a custom lightsaber for around $220. Because of the hefty price tag, we only recommend this experience for those who are serious Star Wars fans.

These lightsabers are as good as real. They have metal hilts, and the blades make sounds as they draw in and out. You can choose one of four handles: Peace and Justice (Republic-era Jedi), Power and Control (dark side/Sith), Elemental Nature (wild Jedi), or Protection and Defense (ancient Jedi). There are also four different kyber crystals that change the color of the blade: blue, red, green, or violet.

The lightsaber building experience includes a moving pre-show where guests are taught the ways of the Jedi until they are finally sworn in by a mystical guest (give you a hint of who it is, we will...). For true Star Wars fans, Savi's Workshop will be one of the best moments of their trip. Having a "working" lightsaber that both looks and feels real is one thing, but becoming part of the Jedi order is absolutely mind-blowing. John Williams, the original composer of the Star Wars films, scored new music to fit this stunning experience. While we wished for some extra animatronics, Savi's Workshop delivers with great storytelling through script, lighting, and sound. We believe that adults and kids 5 and older will greatly appreciate this experience. Savi's Workshop only allows one guest to accompany each builder, so plan accordingly.

*** Magic Tips ***
Savi's Workshop takes a limited number of guests per day. Thus, time slots can become full very quickly with demand. If you're planning on building a lightsaber, reserve

your experience on **Disneyland.com** up to 60 days in advance.

If you want a different saber hilt, visit Dok-Ondar's Den of Antiquities and see if you can barter or trade for one. Individual lightsaber parts and pieces are sold outside of Savi's, and are limited to two parts per receipt of a purchased lightsaber.

You may be able to ship your lightsaber home rather than taking it on a plane. We recommend inquiring with First Order Cargo store in Galaxy's Edge for shipping prices (they usually start around $17).

If you're not a big Star Wars fan, you might want to skip this one if the price sounds out of your range. Sure, it's a fantastic show, but some of the magic might be missed if you don't appreciate the folklore from this franchise. The lightsabers are also huge—about 45 inches (114 cm)—so small children will have a difficult time wielding these. Also keep in mind that your lightsaber doesn't easily break down, so something this size won't fit in a rental locker. For this reason, you may want to schedule Savi's Workshop around the end of the day or when you can take time to place it somewhere. Otherwise, you'll be riding rollercoasters like Space Mountain with it between your legs!

DOK-ONDAR'S DEN OF ANTIQUITIES

Our favorite shopping spot in Galaxy's Edge is Dok-Ondar's Den of Antiquities. Inside, you'll see an array of Star Wars-themed rarities and exclusive merchandise. Hardcore Star Wars fans will also enjoy the extensive collection of lightsaber hilts, kyber crystals, and holocrons for sale.

Most impressive is the animatronic Dok-Ondar, a finicky Ithorian who might trade with you for one of his prized lightsaber hilts—or you can uncover your own treasure within his collection. Dok-Ondar sells rare white and yellow kyber crystals that change the color of lightsaber blades. Additional blue, red, green, and violet crystals found in Savi's Workshop are sold, too!

⋆ Magic Tips ⋆

If you're looking for a less expensive lightsaber, head over to Dok-Ondar's. He sells kid-sized ones for a fraction of the cost.

Those who buy a red kyber crystal may discover a rare black one instead with a special note! Additionally, some of the red and green kyber crystals react differently inside of a Sith or Jedi holocron.

There are seemingly countless collected goods in Dok-Ondar's Den of Antiquities. Look at the second level of the the shop to spot some classic *Star Wars* and other Lucasfilm items.

DROID DEPOT

See a working factory where guests can make their very own remote-controlled droid! You pick the parts to customize a R2-D2, BB-8, or C-Series unit. The droids start around $100 each and are fun to build for kids and adults (we recommend ages 6 and older, though Disney lists 3 and older). The Droid Depot doesn't have the show elements found in Savi's Workshop, but it likely makes a better take-home toy. Kids might play with lightsabers a bit, but a remote-control toy is fun for just about everyone.

Droid Depot is also home to some luxury finds. Guests can buy and design a fully animatronic R2-D2 for $25,000! If you're dropping the dough on this one, R2 can be customized with personality and a battle-worn appearance. If $25,000 is just a *little* bit out of your price range, R2 also hangs out at the depot for pics and chats with guests!

THE MARKET

Black Spire's prime marketplace is home to a gallery of small shops. Set up like a co-op, guests can browse the shelves and hidden elements within these stores. Most of the items appear handmade so as to add to the authenticity of visiting an alien planet with realistic merchandise.

Black Spire Outfitters – Pick up a Jedi robe and other costumes inspired by characters like Rey and the dark-sided Sith. Clothing pieces come in multiple sizes for kids and adults. Unfortunately, Disney prevents those aged 14 and older from wearing these costumes throughout the park. This ban may be removed in the near future as demand increases for guests to live out their Star Wars story in full garb.

Creature Stall – Set up like a small pet store, this shop is filled with *Stars Wars*-inspired toys from porg puppets to plush tauntauns. There are also several small animatronics here including a sleeping loth-cat found in a crate near the entrance. Loth-cats are furry alien critters made famous from the animated series *Star Wars Rebels*. Outside of the Creature Stall is a small register with Kowakian monkey-lizards (sinister-looking critters that work as puppets that sit on guests' shoulders). These monkey-lizards—like the one found in Jabba the Hutt's palace in *Return of the Jedi*—run about $70 each.

Jewels of Bith – The Bith were an alien race from the planet of Clak'dor VII. They were known for their highly evolved mental and motor skills for playing music and creating fine wares. If you're looking for more day-to-day clothes, this store sells everything from t-shirts and jackets to hats and trinkets. Pick up misting fans, keychains, pins, and several other gifts in this shop. To keep with authenticity, nothing in this store will say "Star Wars: Galaxy's Edge" but instead read "Black Spire Outpost" or "Batuu." If you're looking for merchandise with "Star Wars: Galaxy's Edge" on it, shop at The Star Trader store in Tomorrowland or the Emporium on Main Street, U.S.A.

Toydarian Toymaker – Discover wooden and hand-sewn toys perfect for collectors of all ages. There are also instruments and games for sale here. The store gets its name from the flying alien species, Toydarians, like Watto who appeared as a junk dealer in *The Phantom Menace*. You can see the Toydarian shop owner, Zabaka, flying around her shop through a foggy window.

OTHER STORES

The Resistance Supply – Kiosks found near the Rise of the Resistance attraction selling various gifts, clothes, and toys.

First Order Cargo — A store near Kylo Ren's ship that sells goods fitted for the light or the dark side. Buy everything from clothing to trinkets made famous by Star Wars characters. Look above First Order Cargo and spot stormtroopers on the roofs!

STAR WARS: BATUU BOUNTY HUNTERS

Disney brings Star Wars adventure to life with an interactive game within Galaxy's Edge! Batuu Bounty Hunters sends guests on missions around Black Spire Outpost to find bounties hidden. To play, you'll need a MagicBand+ and the free Play Disney app on your smartphone. The game uses augmented reality to help guests uncover bounties before turning them in for virtual credits (unfortunately, the credits aren't redeemable for physical prizes).

Batuu Bounty Hunters is a lot of fun for Star Wars fans. The interactive features pull players into the story, and it feels rewarding to collect credits. To play, guests should head to the Guild Master's Hideout, located just outside the market (near the vehicles on display). Players will see a large digital board where they can opt in to play, and follow instructions on the Play Disney app. Guests will also meet a gruff alien named Raga Bua who comes to life in a very animated way!

While playing, your MagicBand+ works like a tracking device, changing different colors to help decide if you're "hot" or "cold" from your target. When you're close, the MagicBand+ will light purple, and then you can use the Play Disney app to uncover the hidden target. When finished, head back to the Guildmaster's Hideout and speak with Raga Bua for your credits. The entire game takes around 2-3 hours to complete.

MORE TO EXPLORE

Data Pad Interactions

The Play Disney mobile application has a special data pad designed just for Galaxy's Edge. Open the app, click on the icon in Galaxy's Edge, and follow the instructions to hack, decode, and interact with the world around you. You'll earn points as you crack simple codes, and even make things like droids move around the land!

The Language

Learn the language of Batuu from the locals! They say many words and phrases that aren't used on Earth. Some are a bit self-explanatory while others can be somewhat confusing to hear for the first time. For example, there are several ways to say "hello" or "goodbye" when visiting Batuu. To keep you up to speed, here are several of the phrases we've gathered:

BATUUAN SPEAK	ENGLISH MEANING
Datapad	mobile device / phone / credit card machine
Credits	dollars (money)
Credentials	Disney discount card (VISA, DVC Card, etc.)
Hydrator	water fountain
Scans	photos
Image Scanner	camera / phone camera
Cargo Manifest	receipt
Holograms	Magic Shots (added effects to Disney PhotoPass images)
"Good Run!"	"Good Luck!"
"Bright Suns!"	"Good Day!" or "Hello!" said in the daytime
"Rising Moons!"	"Good Evening!" or "Hello!" said at night
"May the Spires Keep You!"	"Goodbye!"
"Till the Spire!"	"Goodbye!" or "Until We Meet Again!"

"For the Order!"	a First Order salute
"May the Force Be With You"	a Resistance salute

LIFE DAY

During the holiday season, Disneyland transforms into a winter wonderland. Though Earth holidays aren't celebrated in the Star Wars galaxy, Life Day is! Usually running from mid-November through early January, this small, seasonal celebration is available for all guests.

Technically Life Day is celebrated on November 17th each year. The Wookiee holiday is all about finding harmony with friends and family members. Wookiees have celebrated Life Day for thousands of years and have since spread the traditions across the galaxy—including the planet of Batuu.

⋆ Magic Tips ⋆
Life Day originated in the Star Wars Holiday Special on CBS in 1978. The cult classic television special was poorly received by audiences for its strange themes, characters, and cheesy storylines. In the special, Chewbacca's family awaits his arrival to celebrate Life Day on his home planet of Kashyyyk. The special has only aired once.

In Black Spire Outpost, you can celebrate Life Day with special food and merchandise available around the land. The most famous beacon of the holiday is a glowing orb. If you've purchased Disney PhotoPass, you may be able to take advantage of a Magic Shot that places a glowing orb in your hand.

CHAPTER EIGHT

DISNEY CALIFORNIA ADVENTURE PARK

INTRODUCTION

While Disneyland is the iconic theme park, Disney California Adventure is the newer cool kid in town! The park opened in 2001 and is now home to seven themed lands. With even more Disney-style rides that aren't found in any other park, like the Incredicoaster rollercoaster, Guardians of the Galaxy—Mission: Breakout!, and the Pixar Pal-A-Round Wheel, California Adventure brings sunny-themed surprises for everyone. Some say that Disney California Adventure is the "adult park" because of its edgier rides and delicious restaurants that serve beer, wine, and specialty cocktails.

Thrill riders will love this side of the Disneyland Resort because of its rollercoaster with a loop, dangerous Guardians of the Galaxy—Mission: Breakout!, and the *Cars*-themed Radiator Springs Racers. However, there's something for everyone in Disney California Adventure from The Little Mermaid "dark ride" to high-flying Soarin'.

BUENA VISTA STREET

Step back to the Los Angeles of the 1920s, just as Walt Disney gazed upon it when he first arrived in Southern California. Buena Vista Street acts like Main Street, U.S.A. at Disneyland with rows of shops, dining, and a Starbucks to help start your day. The Red Car Trolley and several street performers also make their way down this area throughout the day.

Theme: 1920s Los Angeles

The Storyteller's Statue
Near the hub at the end of the street is The Storyteller's Statue, a sculpture of Walt and Mickey smiling at passing guests. This bronze statue has been replicated in several Disney theme parks around the world including Tokyo and Shanghai. The Storyteller Statue keeps the energy of the Disneyland Resort alive with the printed phrase "We are just getting started." It's a message to guests about Walt's vision for an ever-expending, ever-changing theme park. Take a photo with Walt and Mickey to commemorate your visit to a theme park beyond its founder's wildest dreams.

RIDES

RED CAR TROLLEY
Description: Slow moving cable car ride.
Thrill Level: Everyone
Recommendation: Kids might be fond of this trolley ride to Hollywood Land.
Lightning Lane: None

SHOWS

PAINT THE NIGHT (May return in 2023)
Description: Neon nighttime parade.
Recommendation: Disney fans of all ages will enjoy this vibrant nighttime parade starring favorite characters from Mickey to Tinker

Bell! The spinning lights will catch the eye of everyone around in this dazzling attraction. We recommend lining up at least 30 minutes before the parade to get the best viewing in Hollywood Land (Paradise Gardens Park doesn't have great sound for the parade).
Get Preferred Viewing: Book a reservation at select dining locations and receive an "on-the-go" meal as well as preferred seating to Paint the Night. To book, visit Disneyland.com or call (714) 781-4565 up to 60 days in advance.

HOLLYWOOD LAND

Dive into classic Hollywood as Walt Disney saw it! Experience a back lot area, stellar theatre, and a Disney animation studio. Hollywood Land serves as an unexpected kid-friendly area. With entertainment like Turtle Talk with Crush in the Animation Building, Mickey's PhilharMagic 3-D show, and Disney Junior Live on Stage, preschool-aged kids will love this land!

Theme: 1920s downtown Hollywood

Amazing Shopping
The Backlot Premiere Shop is located at the back of Hollywood Land and to the left of the Monsters Inc. ride. Here you'll find all sorts of merchandise and even photo ops here. This shop often changes seasonally, so it could have Halloween, holiday, and/or Avengers-themed merchandise throughout the store, depending on the time of year. We highly recommend checking it out during your visit.

RIDES

MONSTERS, INC. MIKE & SULLEY TO THE RESCUE!
Description: Slow moving dark ride.
Thrill Level: Kids / Family
Recommendation: Fun for kids and fans of the movie.
Lightning Lane: Available with Genie+

· **Magic Tips** ·
You can get a "buddy pass" to help skip the Monsters, Inc. line. This pass gets two riders into the attraction through the exit. Just ask a Cast Member at the front of the queue for the buddy pass, but they don't issue them at all hours of the day.

SHOWS AND ATTRACTIONS

DISNEY ANIMATION
Description: A collection of animation-themed attractions to view and experience.
Thrill Level: Everyone
Recommendation: For fans of classic Disney animated films.
Lightning Lane: None
Animation Academy – We highly recommend this unique attraction. A Disney animator shows you how to draw a character in a simple way. The best part is that you can keep your free animation paper! Check outside the building for character drawing times.
Sorcerer's Workshop – See how classic Disney animated movies were brought to film and even make a short animation of your own!
Turtle Talk with Crush – Interact with Crush the turtle from *Finding Nemo* in this unique and hilarious theatre-like event designed for Young Kids. Ask the Cast Member for a free "I Totally Talked Turtle" sticker at the end of the experience (these may not always be available).

DISNEY JR. DANCE PARTY!
Description: A stage show designed for preschoolers. See their favorite Disney Jr. characters from The Lion Guard, Doc McStuffins, Sofia the First, and Mickey and the Roadster Racers!

Thrill Level: Young Kids
Recommendation: For families with very young children only.
Lightning Lane: None

MICKEY'S PHILHARMAGIC
Description: A 4-D film show starring Mickey, Donald Duck, and their friends. Sing along to popular Disney theme songs that have debuted over the decades.
Thrill Level: Everyone
Recommendation: A great way to beat the summer heat in this large theatre. We especially recommend this attraction for parents with young kids.
Lightning Lane: None

CARS LAND

Cars Land is one of the most spectacular places in any Disney theme park. From the gorgeous backdrop of the Cadillac Mountains to fun roaming characters, this area has heaps of appeal. Cars Land is totally immersive and makes you feel as though you've stepped right into the popular Pixar franchise!

Theme: Route 66 comes to life with Pixar's *Cars*!

Cars Land Neon Lighting Ceremony
This unlisted ceremony occurs nightly around 5 minutes after sunset. See the neon lights come to life on Flo's V9 Café and other surrounding buildings!

Ready for the Holidays
Cars Land is one of the few themed areas that fully decorates for the holidays. During Halloween (early September through October 31) you'll see plenty of spooky car-themed decor. Afterward, the land transforms into a festive automobile-inspired Christmas with lights, music, and special attractions through the first week of January.

RIDES

RADIATOR SPRINGS RACERS

Description: High-speed simulated race car ride.
Level: Family / Thrill Riders (must be 40"/ 102cm or taller)
Recommendation: A high-speed car ride suitable for all ages. Enter the world of *Cars* in this imaginative, fan-favorite attraction. If the line gets too long, you can also choose the "Single Rider Line." You likely won't sit next to your friends or family but the line is often much shorter than the regular line. Loading for Single Riders is at the start of the queue.

Lightning Lane: Available as an individual (no Genie+)

LUIGI'S ROLLICKIN' ROADSTERS

Description: Spin and move to the music in colorful cars. Each time is different!
Level: Kids / Family (must be 32"/ 81cm or taller)
Recommendation: Perfect for kids.
Lightning Lane: None
Swinging Holiday: This attraction changes its decorations and song for the holiday season ("Luigi's Honkin' Haul-O-Ween" for Halloween and "Luigi's Joy to the Whirl" for Christmas).

MATER'S JUNKYARD JAMBOREE

Description: Get flicked and whirled around while riding the back of Mater's truck.
Level: Kids / Family (must be 32"/ 81cm or taller)
Recommendation: Great for kids, and thrill riders might also enjoy this unpredictable ride.
Lightning Lane: None
Holiday Overlay: During Halloween and Christmas time, this attraction gets a new song and decoration for the holidays. Disney will also temporarily rename it ("Mater's Graveyard JamBOOree" for Halloween and "Mater's Jingle Jamboree" for Christmas).

PIXAR PIER

A pier and boardwalk-style land themed after Pixar animated films. Pixar Pier has something for everyone, from kid-friendly rides like Inside Out Emotional Whirlwind to the looping Incredicoaster for thrill seekers. We also enjoy the dining spots on the pier, like the Adorable Snowman serving lemon-flavored ice cream and the popular Lamplight Lounge with a full bar and delicious menu options. Guests entering the end are treated to an animatronic Luxo Jr. lamp perched on top of the Pixar Pier sign. If you're looking for a Pixar character to snap a photo with, chances are they hang out in this land. New Pixar films will also debut popular characters within this area of Disney California Adventure.

Theme: Californian ocean pier with Pixar characters

Howdy, Neighbor!
Pixar Pier is divided into four neighborhoods based on popular Pixar films. These include Incredibles Park, Toy Story Boardwalk, Inside Out Headquarters, and Pixar Promenade, which celebrates all Pixar films.

RIDES

TOY STORY MIDWAY MANIA!
Description: A 4-D game where riders attempt to score the most points by shooting at animated targets with a plunger canon.
Level: Everyone
Recommendation: All ages will enjoy this ride, including preschoolers, families, and thrill riders. Not recommended if you have trouble seeing with 3-D glasses.
Lightning Lane: Available with Genie+
Scoring Big:

1. Many "pro" riders hold the plunger between two fingers with their palm facing them.
2. Higher-point targets are at the bottom of the screens.

3. Scene #1 (Hamm and Eggs) – Hitting the pigs on the fence will make a cat appear that can be hit multiple times for big points.
4. Scene #2 (Rex and Trixie) – Pop the lava balloons on the volcano to make it erupt with 500-point balloons.
5. Scene #3 (Green Army Men) – Look for the yellow-tinted plates that are worth 2,000 points.
6. Scene #4 (Alien Ring Game) – On the far sides are rocket ships and aliens worth big points.
7. Scene #5 (Woody's Western Theme) – Aim for the doors of the saloon to reveal higher point targets. At the end of this scene there are mine carts that roll toward you. Look for the bats above the mine carts that are worth some major points.

· Magic Tips ·
If you have a party of 1-2 (or 3 with a small child), ask a Cast Member at the ride entrance for a "buddy pass" that may help skip the line. This pass may not always be available.

INCREDICOASTER

Description: A fast steel rollercoaster with big drops and a loop themed after Pixar's *Incredibles*.

Level: Thrill Riders (must be 48"/ 122cm or taller)

Recommendation: The Disneyland Resort's only looped rollercoaster—a thrill rider's dream! Needless to say, it's not for those who don't enjoy intense rollercoasters.

Lightning Lane: Available with Genie+

Go It Alone: The "Single Rider Line" could save you time on a busy day. Look for the blue sign that says, "Single Rider Line," on the left side of the queue (where the ride unloads passengers).

JESSIE'S CRITTER CAROUSEL

Description: A classic carousel with western-style critters. This attraction is a redesigned version of the previous King Triton's Carousel of the Sea.

Level: Young Kids

Recommendation: A perfect ride for families with Young Kids.

Lightning Lane: None

· **Magic Tips** ·

Disney will sometimes give out a "Deed to the Toy Box," which is an exclusive item to the Toy Story Boardwalk portion of Pixar Pier. This "deed" allows front-of-the-line entry to Jessie's Critter Carousel, Toy Story Midway Mania, and Toy Story character meets! Usually we see Cast Members give this privilege to young kids dressed up as Toy Story characters during their visit. Really, it's up to certain Cast Members to decide who will receive this prestigious experience. If your child gets it, we'd love to know! Send us a message on our website: www.magicguidebooks.com!

PIXAR PAL-A-ROUND

Description: A massive multi-colored Ferris wheel that has both swinging and stationary gondolas themed after Pixar characters.

Level: Everyone

Recommendation: Thrill riders will love the swinging gondolas and slow-paced riders will enjoy the stationary ones. The line for this ride can be very long and slow moving on busy days. The top has some amazing sights of Disneyland and downtown Los Angeles! The swinging gondolas may cause motion sickness. If someone in your party becomes unexpectedly ill, look for the motion sickness bags tucked near the seats in your gondola.

Lightning Lane: None

INSIDE OUT EMOTIONAL WHIRLWIND

Description: A colorful, spinning ride.

Level: Young Kids

Recommendation: This slow-paced ride is great for families with Young Kids. Each colorful seat has a different emotion with sounds unique to characters from Pixar's *Inside Out*. The ride was once the Flik's Flyers attraction in the former A Bug's Land, but has since been

repurposed into a colorful spinning attraction for the *Inside Out* film. At night, this attraction glows with wonderful colors!
Lightning Lane: None

PARADISE GARDENS PARK

The central land of Disney California Adventure that showcases both classic and new seaside attractions. Many of the rides here appeal to kids ages 5-12 years old while the restaurants serve adult-friendly items. Fans of classic carnival attractions will enjoy Disney's spin on rides like the Crazy Mouse rollercoaster (Goofy's Sky School) and the swings (Silly Symphony Swings). Paradise Gardens Park seems a little out of place with some of the cheaper-looking rides versus the other unique experiences found around the theme park.

Theme: Seaside park

Feeling Festive
Paradise Gardens Park serves as a dining row during festivals at Disney California Adventure. Several dining kiosks line its main pathway during the Food & Wine Festival in the spring and the Holiday Foods Marketplace from November through early January. The paths can become crowded during these times as guests dine on light bites and sip delicious drinks. We recommend trying some of these foods as they are quite unique and tasty!

RIDES

THE LITTLE MERMAID – ARIEL'S UNDERSEA ADVENTURE

Description: A family-friendly "dark ride" telling the story of the animated *The Little Mermaid* with bright colors and music.
Level: Young Kids / Kids / Family
Recommendation: Great for families and fans of Disney's *The Little Mermaid*.
Lightning Lane: None

GOOFY'S SKY SCHOOL

Description: A twisting family-friendly rollercoaster based on the 1940s animated short, "Goofy's Glider." The ride plays on the sensation that the car might fly off the track at any moment.
Level: Kids / Thrill Riders (must be 42"/ 1027m or taller)
Recommendation: Great for Thrill Riders of all ages. The seats can be a bit uncomfortable for larger riders.
Lightning Lane: Available with Genie+

GOLDEN ZEPHYR

Description: Whirl in a giant, slow-paced circle on a metallic aircraft.
Level: Young Kids / Family
Recommendation: Truthfully, we've never understood this ride. It seems oddly out of place, the experience isn't exciting for anyone, and it lacks any sort of Disney theming. Still, young kids might enjoy its spinning motion.
Lightning Lane: None
Note: Disney will close this ride at the sign of wind or rain that could disrupt the cables and spinning method used in this attraction.

SILLY SYMPHONY SWINGS

Description: Classic spinning carnival swings that fly around to orchestral music.
Level: Everyone (must be 40"/ 102cm or taller)
Recommendation: Kids, Tweens, Teens, and Thrill Riders will love this one. Tandem swings are available and very limited.
Lightning Lane: None

JUMPIN' JELLYFISH

Description: Bob up and down on these jellyfish-shaped parachute seats.
Level: Young Kids / Kids
Recommendation: Perfect for kids of all ages.
Lightning Lane: None

SHOWS

WORLD OF COLOR

Description: A stunning nighttime water show with dazzling technical effects that takes guests through several Disney films. A newer version of this show called World of Color–One debuts on

January 27, 2023. It'll feature an all-new story as part of the Disney100 celebration.
Thrill Level: Everyone / Family
Recommendation: Must see for all! Snag a spot early, at least 30 minutes before showtime. However, don't stand too close or you could get wet! World of Color may only run on select nights and have multiple showings during summer hours.
Lightning Lane: None, but may use a Virtual Queue
Holiday Overlay: World of Color runs a holiday version called World of Color: Seasons of Light from November through early January.

· **Magic Tips** ·
Some restaurants including Wine Country Trattoria and Storytellers Cafe may offer dining packages with reserved viewing of World of Color. This is for standing room only.

For seats, there's also a World of Color Dessert Party offered with pricing starting at $89 per guest. Seats for this experience are often elevated and to the back of the standing area. Guests receive a tray of sweets with two smaller alcoholic beverages of choice for adults 21+. Book 60 days in advance on the Disneyland app by searching for "World of Color Dessert Party."

GRIZZLY PEAK

Inspired by California National Parks like Yosemite, Grizzly Peak is centered around a bear-shaped mountain. This lush, foliage-rich land is home to two of Disney California Adventure's main attractions: Soarin' and Grizzly River Run.

Theme: Californian national park

Map It Out
There's a faux park map of Grizzly Peak located near an old station wagon with a canoe on it. Look for this cool detail across the path from Smokejumpers Grill.

RIDES

GRIZZLY RIVER RUN

Description: Board a massive raft and travel up and down a gushing river.
Level: Everyone / Thrill Riders (must be 42"/ 107cm or taller)
Recommendation: Perfect for those who love water rides.
Lightning Lane: Available with Genie+

· Magic Tips ·
Grizzly River Run has complimentary lockers located to the left side of the ride (as you face it). Store your belongings here at no charge for up to 2-hours ($7 per hour after).

SOARIN'

Description: A hang glider simulation that takes you over stunning views, and landmarks, with scents that fill the air.
Level: Everyone / Thrill Riders (must be 40"/ 102cm or taller)
Recommendation: A unique, must-see experience for all ages. Guests who don't like thrill rides usually love Soarin. Though the flight can take you high into the air, it's an overall gentle experience.
Lightning Lane: Available with Genie+

REDWOOD CREEK CHALLENGE TRAIL

Description: Inspired by the Pixar movie *Up* and Disney's *Brother Bear*, kids can earn Wilderness Explorer badges by completing challenges. Several activities and character encounters occur throughout the day in this attraction. Kids might race ducks down a river or explore other challenges with Disney and Pixar characters.
Level: Kids / Family
Recommendation: A playground for kids of all ages.
Lightning Lane: None

SAN FRANSOKYO SQUARE

San Fransokyo Square is a small dining area with several restaurants and shops for hungry park guests. Based on Disney's *Big Hero 6*, the area combines San Fransisco with Tokyo as well as a blend of other cultures. There aren't traditional rides within this land, but instead food-based attractions and a character greeting spot.

Theme: A *Big Hero 6*-themed multicultural food court on the water

· **Magic Tips** ·
If you're having a trouble finding a spot to dine in Disney California Adventure, head over to San Fransokyo Square. There are plenty of tables here for anyone to enjoy!

ATTRACTIONS

MEET BAYMAX

Description: An outdoor character meet and greet with healthcare Robot Baymax and Hiro Hamada from Disney's *Big Hero 6!*
Thrill Level: Everyone
Recommendation: Great for fans of Baymax—he gives great hugs!
Lightning Lane: None

THE BAKERY TOUR

Description: Take a tour of the Boudin Bakery and sample bread.
Thrill Level: Everyone
Recommendation: Fun for bread-lovers and fans of Boudin.
Lightning Lane: None

AVENGERS CAMPUS

Disney's Marvel-themed land, Avengers Campus, stars superheroes from blockbuster films including Spider-Man, Captain America, Ant-Man, Black Panther, Doctor Strange, Black Widow, and more. The area replaced the former A Bug's Land which closed in 2018. Avengers Campus has two rides, tasty dining spots, and several shows throughout the land. We detail all that Avengers Campus has to offer in the next chapter.

· **Magic Tips** ·
There's also a smaller "land" called Performance Corridor. Here you'll find places to eat, a parade route, and pathways leading to other lands. Performance Corridor is in the middle or the park between Grizzly Peak and Cars Land. However, it's usually not marked on the map and doesn't contain any major attractions.

CHAPTER NINE

AVENGERS CAMPUS

INTRODUCTION

When Guardians of the Galaxy—Mission: BREAKOUT! opened at Disney California Adventure in 2017, guests were not prepared for this next-level experience. Taking the ride system and structure of the popular Twilight Zone Tower of Terror attraction, Guardians literally drops guests into a whole new thrilling storyline around a favorite Marvel franchise. When the attraction opened, fans also noticed the Avengers logo between the tower and A Bug's Land. This marker was Disney's promise of things to come.

So in 2017, two years before Disney Parks would launch its highly anticipated Star Wars: Galaxy's Edge, the company announced plans for another ambitious land. Avengers Campus would open in just a few years at Disney California Adventure. Disney's first-ever Marvel-themed land would bring entertainment based on popular superheroes like Spider-Man, Doctor Strange, Black Widow, and more to the Disneyland Resort.

The new land would take over the spot previously occupied by the kid-friendly A Bug's Land. Work had quietly already begun in the former "It's Tough to Be a Bug" Theatre as Disney Imagineers worked to transform the space into an exciting new Spider-Man-themed ride. Though Avengers Campus promised to feel immersive like Star Wars: Galaxy's Edge, this new land would use bolder, brighter colors. It would feel more like a futuristic "Tomorrowland" than an ancient alien planet.

Avengers Campus was set to debut in July of 2020 but was put on an indefinite hold as park closures stopped construction. However, only eleven months later, the land opened to great fanfare on June 4, 2021.

Avengers Campus brings both heroes and villains from the Marvel Cinematic Universe to life. There are two rides, epic stunt shows, heavily themed dining, and plenty of comic book-inspired easter eggs to spot in this area. Though much of Avengers Campus is modeled after the Marvel Cinematic Universe films, the stories aren't exactly the same. For example, characters like Iron Man, who have since passed in the film series, are still alive and well in Avengers Campus.

Nonetheless, the Avengers Campus is still completely immersive and committed to telling exciting stories. As guests enter the land, they'll see their favorite heroes leaping from buildings, battling on rooftops, mystically appearing in ancient ruins, and even dancing to their favorite tunes. Whether you're a huge Marvel fan or just a casual viewer of the franchises, there's something for everyone to enjoy in Avengers Campus.

THE STORY

Each piece of Avengers Campus has its own individual story that is under the umbrella of a much larger one. The arching storyline covers a gentrified Californian industrial area. In the past, it was owned and operated by Stark Industries, where Tony Stark's (Iron Man's) father once worked closely with other brilliant minds. Today, guests can still explore the old brick buildings of Stark Motors,,,, which has now been converted into the Worldwide Engineering Brigade—or WEB—where Peter Parker and other talented young scientists showcase their inventions.

On the opposite side of the campus, guests can sample food that grows and shrinks in the Ant-Man-themed Pym Test Kitchen. Further from that is the Collector's Fortress where the Guardians of the Galaxy are on display for guests to see. Taneleer Tivan, also known as The Collector, picked a spot next to Avengers Campus to showcase his collection. In addition to the Guardians of the Galaxy, Doctor Strange, Thor, Loki, Black Panther, and many other fan-favorites also appear throughout the land to greet guests.

· ***Magic Tips*** ·

Look down around the Collector's Fortress that houses the Guardians of the Galaxy ride and you'll see a strange, iridescent spatter. In the Avengers Campus story, this is cosmic radiation set off by the tower when it teleported to Earth. Disney Imagineers were inspired by Marvel artist Jack Kirby who drew the cosmos in this style (commonly referred to as the "Kirby Crackle").

Though all of this feels very light-hearted, the idea behind Avengers Campus is based on a potential threat to Earth. Tony Stark worries that more alien assailants could end up on our planet, so he decided to train more humans to defend themselves. With the help of the other Avengers, guests can learn several techniques that could make them mighty superheroes!

Marvel Theme Park Universe

There are three Avengers-themed locations throughout the world: Disney California Adventure, Walt Disney Studios Park in Disneyland Paris, and the Stark Expo in Hong Kong Disneyland.

RIDES

Avengers Campus is home to two adventure-filled rides. WEB Slingers: A Spider-Man Adventure uses augmented reality for guests to shoot webs like Spider-Man! The ride feels much more like a giant video game with slow-moving ride vehicles (similar to Toy Story Mania). Guests also wear 3-D glasses that allow them to shoot webbing from their wrists to destroy targets.

The second attraction is the thrilling Guardians of the Galaxy: Mission—BREAKOUT! This extreme drop ride takes guests up and down 13 terrifying stories! During Halloween, the attraction transforms into the even scarier Monsters After Dark.

WEB SLINGERS: A SPIDER-MAN ADVENTURE

Help Spider-Man wrangle up runaway spider-bots by shooting webbing from your wrists! Guests can explode targets, pull apart sets, and even fling robots in this family-friendly adventure. Destroying certain targets allows guests to gain more points. In the end, each vehicle gives group and individual scores. The day's best scores are displayed around the land including the WEB Suppliers store.

Best for: All Ages

Restrictions: No minimum height

Power Ups: Guests also have more power options than just webs for this ride. A WEB Power Band allows guests to shoot a triple shot during the attraction. An Iron Man repulsor attachment also fits onto the Power Band for the wearer to fire beams like Iron Man on the ride! There's also an Electro-Dynamic Web-Shooter that blasts targets with explosive energy. These attachments are sold at WEB Suppliers in Avengers Campus ($29.99 for the Power Band and $24.99 for each additional attachment).

Scoring Tips: Each color spider-bot is worth a different amount of points. Gold is the highest, followed by green, blue, and red in that order. Typically gold bots hang out in the background or quickly run onto the screen before they leave again. Hit the green spider-bots to send off a chain reaction of explosions! We also recommend that you move your hands quickly to shoot the most web. Short, back and forth movements are all you need to rapid fire!

GUARDIAN OF THE GALAXY: MISSION—BREAKOUT!

Get ready to plummet 13 stories in this Marvel-themed thrill ride! There are 6 different classic songs that play during the attraction, each with their own drop sequences and scenes. Guests can ride Guardians more than once in a day and have completely different experiences each ride.

· Magic Tips ·

During the Halloween season, Guardians of the Galaxy transforms into Monsters After Dark in the evenings. Serving as a sort of sequel to the ride, guests must find Baby Groot as he escapes a series of terrifying monsters. The attraction is set to a heavy metal song also called "Monsters After Dark." This Halloween version typically runs from early September through Halloween Day. Guests can experience the regular Guardians of the Galaxy attraction until around 2pm before it reopens as Monsters After Dark at 3pm. The ride also stays open for Oogie Boogie Bash.

SHOWS

The superheroes in Avengers Campus help make the land come to life. There are five stages around the campus that host the Avengers as they interact with audiences and even battle villains.

THE AMAZING SPIDER-MAN

Spider-Man greets guests near the WEB building in an amazing way. You'll be able to see him literally jump 65 feet into the air before climbing down a wall to snap selfies with his fans. Disney created its own realistic "stuntronic" that makes it appear that Spidey just jumped over the building!

DOCTOR STRANGE: MYSTERIES OF THE MYSTIC ARTS

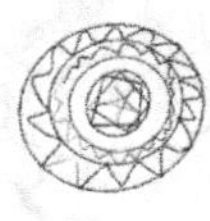

Something strange is going on at the edge of Avengers Campus. Just behind the WEB Suppliers building, you'll find odd artifacts and ancient ruins. During certain times, you also may hear rumblings before Doctor Strange appears. In this short show, the Sorcerer Supreme performs magic and even opens up dangerous portals to the Dark Dimension!

· *Magic Tips* ·
Time and space work differently around the Ancient Sanctum. Look for cool photo ops, including a warped black and white tile that appears to bend into the ground when guests snap a photo on it! At night, the Sanctum comes to life with brilliant colors.

WARRIORS OF WAKANDA
Wakanda's own Dora Milaje display their prowess and amazing skills as they encourage guests to find their inner hero.

AVENGERS ASSEMBLE! & AVENGERS HEADQUARTERS
The Avengers' Quinjet aircraft sits atop the headquarters near the middle of the land. Here guests will see epic stunt shows that take place on the rooftop. Between the shows, heroes like Thor and Captain Marvel often stand near the Quinjet and wave to guests below.

AVENGERS HEADQUARTERS
Greet your favorite superheroes at the base of the Quinjet. Disney gets really immersive with these characters so expect them to frequently change out as new MCU content is released. For example, as *Loki* aired on Disney+, the character would change costumes weekly. Guests could see Time Variant Loki and President Loki over the weeks.

GUARDIANS OF THE GALAXY: AWESOME DANCE OFF!
See characters from Marvel's Guardians of the Galaxy perform hilarious dance moves in front of the Collector's Fortress.

· *Magic Tips* ·
The Disneyland app lists show times for most of the stages around Avengers Campus. To view these times, either search for the specific attraction or find them on the interactive map. When using the map, make sure to toggle to "entertainment" and zoom in on Avengers Campus in Disney California Adventure. Tap the attraction to see show times.

DINING

The food in Avengers Campus is mostly based on American favorites like chicken sandwiches and peanut butter and jelly. There's also a microbrewery where adults 21 and older and try a variety of beers and mixed drinks. However, these are revamped versions of the classics that bring new flavors that are impressive enough to please an Avenger! Oh, and there's Shawarma, too!

PYM TEST KITCHEN

The Ant-Man-themed Pym Test Kitchen uses "Pym Particles" to grow food and shrink waste. The concept behind this restaurant is to feed the world and reduce the amount of pollutants when done. The end results are both fun and delicious!

PYM TEST KITCHEN RECOMMENDATIONS

- **Pym-ini Sandwich** (lunch and dinner entree) – A scrumptious sandwich served with salami, ham, sun-dried tomato spread, and provolone between toasted focaccia. Each sandwich comes with tangy marinara dipping sauce and a light arugula salad. There's also a giant Family-sized Pym-ini that serves 6-8 guests (and costs about $100)!
- **PB3 Superb Sandwich** (lunch and dinner entree) – A classic peanut butter and jelly sandwich with a twist! Pym Test Kitchen warms the peanut butter, adds in a slice of banana, crispy candied bacon, and serves it with a tiny banana smoothie. Comes with a side of crispy potato bites (similar to tater tots).
- **Not So Little Chicken Sandwich** (lunch and dinner entree) – It's more like a giant piece of fried chicken breast than a sandwich because the shrunken bun is so tiny! Though we wished for more of a bun, the chicken tastes great as its covered with teriyaki and red chili sauces. Comes with crispy potato bites.
- **Celestial-sized Candy Bar: Choco-Smash CANDY Bar** (dessert) – A massive, shareable candy bar with layers of chocolate brownie, nougat, caramel, peanuts, and dark chocolate.

PYM TASTING LAB

Next to Pym Test Kitchen you'll find a microbrewery with a similar theme. All of the drinks here are alcoholic beverages for adults 21 and older. We're bigger fans of the drinks at Oga's Cantina because there's more variety and the flavors pack a better punch. However, there are some real gems at Pym Tasting Lab, especially if you're a fan of beer.

PYM TASTING LAB DINING RECOMMENDATIONS

- **Molecular Meltdown** (beer cocktail) – A dark stout beer served with a scoop of vanilla ice cream and dried mini marshmallows. We recommend mixing the ice cream into the beer!
- **X-Periment** (cocktail) – A tequila mixed drink with mango and habanero flavors and boba. It's more sweet than spicy and the boba are more like "popping pearls."
- **Honey Buzz** (cocktail) – A sweet gin cocktail with lemon juice and honey syrup. This delicious drink is also served with a crunch stick of honey that's kind of like a tall Jolly Rancher.
- **Snack Molecules** (to-go snack) – A mixed bag of flavorful tiny pretzels, honey-roasted peanuts, and sweet and spicy popped sorghum. It all comes in an easy-to-carry bag for snacking on throughout the day.

MORE EATS

SHAWARMA PALACE

Try the Avengers' favorite food! We recommend the New York's Tastiest chicken wrap or the Impossible Victory Falafel wrap. Both are well seasoned, served in delicious flakey wraps, and come with a side of coconut yogurt-tahini sauce for dipping.

TERRAN TREATS

Snack on treats that are out of this world! Try new takes on churros like the Sweet Spiral Rations. Or try our favorite, the Cosmic Cream Orb—a dessert puff filled with raspberry cheesecake mousse.

SHOPPING

There are three shops in Avengers Campus: WEB Suppliers (near WEB Slingers), Avengers Vault (below the Quinjet), and The Collector's Warehouse (inside the Guardians of the Galaxy tower). These stores are fairly small but still offer a wide variety of souvenirs and apparel. WEB Suppliers is mostly for toys based on Spider-Man (and where guests can purchase attachments for WEB Slingers). The Collector's Warehouse has more apparel with shirts, costumes, and bags based on Guardians of the Galaxy and other MCU properties. The Avengers Vault is a mix of the two with its own unique supplies.

SECRETS & EASTER EGGS

The Marvel Cinematic Universe movies are filled with easter eggs from the comics and more. Avengers Campus is no acceptation! Here are some of the fun surprises you can find throughout the land:

- ☐ **Miles Morales Was Here** - The Spider-Man of Harlem, Miles Morales, left his mark on Avengers Campus—literally. The street art on the WEB building was created by the other Spidey himself!

- ☐ **The Incredible... Tree?** - There's a hulked-up tree near the WEB building. Look for a bulbous tree with a green trunk! Next to it are sewage drains that read, "CAUTION: GAMMA RADIATION."

- ☐ **This Spot Is Taken** - Just behind the Hulk Tree, look for old parking signs on the brick walls. You'll see reserved spots for H. Stark (Tony's father) and E. Jarvis, two prominent figures of S.H.I.E.L.D. who first developed the area where Avengers Campus stands.

- ☐ **Formative Days** - Look for the Stark Industries Complex map near WEB Suppliers (it's on a post just outside the front door). Here you'll see an "old map" of Avengers Campus before its gentrification. Where Cars Land now stands, it's labeled "Quarantine Zone."

- ☐ **Locked Up** - In the queue for WEB Slingers, look for rows of lockers just before you get your 3D glasses. These lockers have the insignias of several Marvel characters including Mary Jane Watson (Spider-Man's girlfriend), Harley Keener (who first appeared in *Iron Man 3*), and Miles Morales. There are 20 lockets in total—who else can you spot?

- ☐ **The Claw!** - In the pre-show for WEB Slingers, look for a claw machine. There are dozens of easter eggs hidden as prizes within the pile of prizes—including an alien from Toy Story!

- ☐ **Cleanup Crew** - Around Avengers Campus you'll see several strange-looking boxed labeled "Damage Control." These are crews in the Marvel universe sent out to clean up alien wreckage.

- ☐ **Old Farming Town** - After grabbing your food in Pym Test Kitchen, you'll likely spot two large condiment containers near the ceiling. The ketchup and mustard bottles have "Bountiful Valley Farm" labels—a nod to Disney California Adventure's fictional farming community that later became A Bug's Land (before Avengers Campus).

- ☐ **"Get Me Outta Here!"** - In the story of Guardians of the Galaxy—Mission: BREAKOUT, Rocket the raccoon escapes his enclosure before setting free the rest of his team. You can see Rocket's red footprints on the sign outside of the ride and even coming from a hole in the left side of the building.

MORE TO COME!

As more Marvel Cinematic Universe films and shows debut, we expect more characters and easter eggs throughout the land. So keep your eyes peeled as these changes will likely debut in 2023.

CHAPTER TEN

SKIPPING THE LINES

NO MORE WAITING

On average, our readers worry the most about waiting in long lines during their Disneyland visit. Over the decades, guests have complained about spending hours in a queue for a ride that only lasts two minutes. Disney is very conscious of this common guest complaint. As millions flock to the Disneyland Resort each year, the company wants to give the best impression for its visitors—after all, a positive word-of-mouth review is the best marketing!

To combat the long lines, Disney has implemented features like Virtual Queues to keep guests out of the lines. For Disney, having guests roaming the parks is a big win because they'll often spend money instead of waiting in line. With so much fun food and immersive shopping experiences, it only makes sense that guests would rather spend money than wait in a one-hour line for Space Mountain.

In the past, Disney used FastPass to help guests skip the line. However, this product was replaced by the updated Disney Genie, an in-app tool for avoiding long wait times. When Star Wars: Rise of the Resistance first opened, Disney implemented a new Virtual Queue option. Also using their mobile device, guests can snag a virtual place in line and return to the attraction when called.

Disney says that it plans to keep Virtual Queues well into the future. However, both Genie and Virtual Queues have a number of flaws that can make them not-so-user-friendly. In this chapter, we give you the best tactics for using these products avoid lines.

VIRTUAL QUEUES

INTRODUCTION

When Disney first introduced the epic Star Wars: Rise of the Resistance, they ran into a giant issue: more guests want to ride the attraction than there are available seats for the day. To keep up with the demand, Disney implemented a virtual "boarding pass" for this attraction. When WEB Slingers: A Spider-Man Adventure opened at Disney California Adventure, guests could also obtain a virtual queue spot for this attraction as well.

HOW THE VIRTUAL QUEUE WORKS

To obtain a boarding pass, guests need the Disneyland mobile app on their phone and park tickets linked to their account. Boarding passes "drop" at certain times throughout the day, typically before park opens and again later in the afternoon. During these drops, guests should move quickly to reserve spots for their party. Boarding groups are often gone in *seconds* (we're not exaggerating here)!

Once a guest joins a boarding group, they will see an estimated wait time on the app, and will be notified via a pop-up message when it is their time to return to the attraction. Typically, the guests have an hour to return to the ride (the pop-up message will tell you when you must arrive). The app will issue each person in your party a code that is scanned by the Cast Member near the attraction entrance.

However, rules often change for how Virtual Queues work at Disneyland. For example, when Rise of the Resistance first opened, guests could only join the Virtual Queue from inside Disneyland. When the parks reopened, guests could join the Virtual Queue beginning at 7am each day from their home or hotel room. A second time slot was added at 12pm for guests once they scanned into Disneyland or Disney California Adventure.

To see which attraction will use Virtual Queue on the day of your visit, open the Disneyland app, select menu, followed by "Virtual Queues." We recommend checking this the day before your visit or even the same morning before 7am.

VIRTUAL QUEUE TIPS

When guests secure boarding passes for their group while in the parks, they often cheer. The excitement comes from very real uncertainty as boarding passes are not guaranteed. With that said, here are some important tips to improve your chances:

Link Your Party – Before you head to the parks, you'll need to link all of your party's theme park tickets to the Disneyland app. This can be done by scanning the barcodes or entering them manually under "Tickets and Passes" in the app's menu. Each person may also need a theme park reservation for that day.

Designate Someone – Though multiple people in your party can try for a boarding pass, we don't recommend it. Disneyland Cast Members have warned us that having multiple people try using the same tickets could confuse the system. We've tried both methods and have found that having one person on one device is the most reliable.

So Refreshing – Before you try for the Virtual Queue, look for the tab under the Disneyland app's menu (it's also often on the main screen). When you enter the Join Boarding Group screen, it will refresh. The page will not show a "Join" button until the time has dropped. You may also be able to drag down the screen and let go to refresh the page right when the time comes.

· **Magic Tips** ·

You may only be allowed one boarding group at a time. You'll need to have scanned your first boarding pass to try for the second one.

Other rides may use the Virtual Queue differently. For example, World of Color may sometime use a virtual queue to manage heavy crowds.

Full Bars – We highly recommend that you have a great signal on your phone before you try for a boarding pass. So give yourself a few minutes before the time drops to find a nice spot. We also recommend against using Disneyland's Wi-Fi as it is often much slower than cellphone carriers.

Right on Time – Since boarding groups book up in seconds, time is of the essence. Disneyland apparently syncs its clock with the official one on www.time.gov. We recommend having one person in your party holding their phone to show the Pacific Daylight Time on this website. As soon as the time strikes, the boarding group portion of the app should be refreshed. If successful, a "Join" button will appear.

Keep Moving – There may be a few screens to move through before securing boarding passes. Keep moving through the screens until you've seen that you are successful!

DISNEY GENIE

INTRODUCTION

As you may have realized by now, planning a trip to the Disneyland Resort can feel overwhelming. With virtual queues, restaurant reservations, and organizing your desired activities, it's easy to feel worn out even before your vacation begins. We've noticed in recent years that organizing a trip to Disneyland has required more and more pre-planning. Almost to the point where it could feel like a chore.

So to overcome all of these planning issues, Disney introduced a new product to help guests easily manage their visit. Disney Genie is supposed to work like "magic" by giving suggestions, forecasts, and recommendations to plan your day. Using the Disneyland app, guests tell Genie which attractions, dining, and other experiences they would like to enjoy that day. Genie goes to work by building itineraries and other suggestions during the visit.

While all of that sounds amazing on paper, of course there are some flaws. For example, everything Genie tells guests is through Disney's filter. Meaning, you won't hear that a suggested restaurant actually has lackluster food. Nevertheless, Disney Genie does a good job of helping alert guests to the shortest wait times. This is mostly done through Genie's suggestions and works very well for those unpredictable times when rides like Radiator Springs Racers unexpectedly has a super-short wait.

⋆ **Magic Tips** ⋆
Disney Genie+ can sell out but usually only on very busy days like the holiday season and spring break. We recommend purchasing Disney Genie+ before 10am to avoid sell outs.

HOW TO USE DISNEY GENIE

1. Sign in to the Disneyland app and make sure that your park tickets are linked to your account.
2. Before heading to the park, select the attractions and dining you'd like to experience.
3. If you have dining reservations, these will show up here and Genie will automatically plug them into your itinerary.
4. When you're ready to visit the parks, Genie will give you suggested times to experience your choice of attractions. These suggestions may also update throughout the day to improve your experience.

DISNEY GENIE+

Though Disney Genie is free, it does have paid options for guests wishing to skip the lines on their own. Disney Genie+ costs $25+ or more per person, per day, and allows guests to use a "Lightning Lane" to skip the lines at both theme parks. You may have already guessed but the Lightning Lanes are just the former FastPass lines renamed. These dedicated lines form separately from the standard queues to skip the bulk of the wait. Lightning Lanes can save you hours of waiting in long lines in one day.

Pricing for Disney Genie+ varies depending on the day you visit. Unfortunately, Disney does not reveal how much pricing will be in advance. To save on cost, you can bundle Genie+ with your park ticket for a flat $25 per person per day. However, if you've already purchased your tickets, you will need to wait until you enter the park to purchase Disney Genie+ on the Disneyland app.

ABOUT LIGHTNING LANES

Dozens of attractions at the Disneyland Resort have access to the Lightning Lanes. Most of these are accessible with the Disney Genie+ paid feature. You will not be able to use a Lightning Lane without paying for it.

Guests are able to book one attraction at a time. Lightning Lanes are restricted to once per ride per day. Meaning, you cannot use Lightning Lane twice for the same attraction in one day. Once you've used a Lightning Lane, you'll be able to book another with Genie+. The $25+ per day fee works at both theme parks in a single day. Just keep in mind that park hopping restrictions may prevent you from using Genie+ at the other park.

However, some attractions have Lightning Lanes that do not work with Genie+. Popular rides including Star Wars: Rise of the Resistance and Radiator Springs Racers require guests to pay an *à la carte* fee for these Individual Lightning Lanes. Prices start around $15 and can vary depending on how busy the parks are that day. Guests are also limited to two Individual Lightning Lane reservations per day.

· **Magic Tips** ·

You can mix and match paying for Disney Genie+ and Individual Lightning Lanes. However, you do not have to pay for Genie+ to pay for an Individual Lightning Lane and vice versa. Furthermore, no attraction requires that you pay for the Lightning Lane to experience it. The special lane is just created to help save you time waiting in a standby line.

WHO SHOULD GET DISNEY GENIE+

1. **Love to Ride** – Guests who want to experience as many rides as they can in one day should certainly consider Disney Genie+. You may be able to experience twice as many rides in a single day with Lightning Lane.
2. **Sleeping In** – If you like to sleep in, Genie+ is a great feature. You won't need to get to the parks at opening to have shorter wait times. However, we still recommend getting to the parks by late morning to maximize your Disney Genie+ benefits.

3. **Park Hopping** – Since Genie+ works at both of the parks, you'll be able to book your next attraction before you leave. Since either park can become busy midday as guests hop, we think Disney Genie+ can be well worth your money to skip the lines.
4. **Breakfast with Characters** – Some of the best times to meet characters is at one of the breakfast spots. If you've booked a character breakfast and want to enjoy the parks after, you may see that lines increase once you arrive. You'll be able to book your Lightning Lane reservations while dining and then head to the attraction once you've finished.

What did Simba say while in line for the Matterhorn?

"I wish this line would Mufasa!"

WHEN NOT TO GET DISNEY GENIE+

1. **Slow Days** – We don't recommend getting Disney Genie+ on very slow days. If you're seeing Space Mountain at a 20-minute wait and Jungle Cruise at 10 minutes, it may be a waste of money to upgrade.
2. **Very Busy Days** – Though Disney Genie+ is limited in quantity per day, guests may find using it on very busy dates difficult. For example, you may only get to use the Lightning Lane a few times on a very busy day. Even worse, you'll still have to wait in very long lines for rides not covered by Disney Genie+. In this instance, it may be better to pay *à la carte* to skip the lines for rides like Radiator Springs Racers.
3. **Long Vacation** – If you're planning for a long vacation, you may not need the Genie+ upgrade for each day of your trip. Instead, you may wish to put the money toward extra days on your park tickets to visit more often.

4. **For Moral Reasons** – It's clear that we live in a world of "haves and have-nots," but are products like Disney Genie+ digging that line even deeper? After all, Lightning Lanes used to be free when they were part of FastPass. So arguably, Genie+ is just a product that only gives FastPass to families with money.

DISNEY GENIE+ TIPS

1. **Be Dedicated** – Dedicate one person in your party to be in control of booking the Lightning Lanes. This will make it much easier to get the same time slot as the rest of your guests.
2. **Don't Be Drained** – Carry a portable battery to charge the phone in case your battery drains.
3. **Get Ready** – Genie+ reservations may be redeemed by scanning the barcode on your phone or the individual physical tickets.
4. **Time for Seconds** – If your Lightning Lane reservation is later in the day, you can book a second reservation two hours after booking the first. For example, if your Lightning Lane reservation is for 5pm but you reserved it at 12pm, you'll be allowed to book a second reservation two hours later at 2pm. This tip only works for Lightning Lane reservations more than two hours out.

GENIE+ RECOMMENDATIONS

We've listed the Genie+ reservations by their demand and wait time length. High and Very High attractions book the quickest while Low and Very Low attractions may not need Lightning Lane purchases:

∑ = Individual Lightning Lane attractions that do not work with Disney Genie+

DISNEYLAND

Autopia	Low
Big Thunder Mountain Railroad	Medium
Buzz Lightyear Astro Blasters	Low
Haunted Mansion	Medium
Haunted Mansion Holiday (seasonal)	High
Indiana Jones Adventure	High
"it's a small world"	Low
"it's a small world" Holiday	Medium
Matterhorn Bobsleds	Medium-High

Mickey & Minnie's Runaway Railway ∑	High
Millennium Falcon: Smugglers Run	Medium
Roger Rabbit's Car Toon Spin	Medium
Space Mountain	High
Tiana's Bayou Adventure	High
Star Tours – The Adventures Continue	Low
Star Wars: Rise of the Resistance ∑	Very High

DISNEY CALIFORNIA ADVENTURE

Goofy's Sky School	Low
Grizzly River Run	Medium
Guardians of the Galaxy – Mission: BREAKOUT!	High
Guardians of the Galaxy – Monsters After Dark (seasonal)	High
Incredicoaster	Medium
Monsters, Inc. Mike & Sulley to the Rescue!	Low
Radiator Springs Racers ∑	Very High
Soarin' Around the World	Medium
Toy Story Midway Mania	High
WEB Slingers: A Spider-Man Adventure	High

· **Magic Tips** ·

It's possible that the Disney Genie+ list will update in the future to include more attractions in 2024. For more tips, see our Genie+ booking recommendations by interest and age group in our Pre-Planned Attraction Lists chapter.

MODIFYING A RESERVATION

Once you've booked a Lightning Lane with Disney Genie+, you can modify it within the Disneyland app. To do this, find your Lightning Lane reservation, tap the 3 dots (•••) in its box and then tap "Modify Plan." You'll then be able to see new available times for your current and different attractions.

OTHER DISNEY GENIE+ FEATURES

Your purchase of Disney Genie+ also comes with augmented reality lenses to capture very cool snaps around the park. These filters can usually be used even after you're home from vacation! You'll also get a tour with Audio Tales that gives you secrets about the theme parks as you travel through them.

NOT USING THE DISNEY GENIE

Though the Disney Genie is a very cool piece of technology, you may not be interested in using it. Perhaps you're not that tech savvy or you just don't want to bother using your phone all day. That's totally fine! In fact, we've designed our tips so that you don't have to rely on the Genie at all to have fun in the parks.

With that said, it's still pretty difficult to get away from technology at the Disneyland Resort. As Disney sees more and more guests staring at their phone screens in line, it makes sense to use these devices within the parks. For consumers, using a device they are familiar with often makes things easy. However, there could be instances when the technology fails. For example, if you're unable to install an application or connect to the internet. Even worse, something might happen to your device, rendering it useless during your vacation. If this were to happen, we recommend talking with a Cast Member during your visit. There are often several around the parks at various information desks waiting to assist guests. If plans aren't working out, don't give up before talking to one of them. From our experience, Disney can work wonders to make good when things go wrong!

DISNEY PHOTOPASS

Even if you're planning not to get Disney Genie+ for your entire party, you still may want to purchase it. The PhotoPass feature of Genie+ is certainly worth the $25+ daily price. Disney Photographers will take memorable photos that you can freely post around the internet. These are great ways to remember your visit. Only one person in your party will need to purchase Genie+ and all photos will need to be synced to their account (usually by having the photographer scan their park ticket).

SINGLE RIDER

The single ride line is designed for those willing to ride alone in a row of strangers. Disney is all about efficiency, and sometimes rides have an off-number of seats per row (like the Radiator Springs Racers), so filling in that extra space loads more people at a time. The benefit to the single rider is a quicker way onto the attraction as Disney uses a specialized line for single riders. Only a handful of rides in each park have this feature. While the line often saves time, in many instances it doesn't (the Indiana Jones Adventure is often known for this). If you're lucky and in a single rider line with your party, you might get seated together! Either way, we highly recommend this for teens and adults, but not so much for families with younger kids who wouldn't be seated with a guardian.

SINGLE RIDER LOCATIONS

This option may not be available every day. Some attractions only run Single Rider lines during busy seasons.

DISNEYLAND

- **Matterhorn Bobsleds** – It's the same line as the Lightning Lane return, but the Cast Members will split you up before heading onto the ride.
- **Millennium Falcon: Smugglers Run** – Ask the Cast Member at the queue start for a Single Rider pass. You will skip most of the elements in the queue including some of the amazing animatronic pre-show scenes. The biggest downside is that many Single Riders don't get to pilot the Falcon.
- **Space Mountain** – Usually guests enter the single rider line for Space Mountain through the attraction exit. Go past the ride photo displays and look for the Single Rider sign.

CALIFORNIA ADVENTURE

- **Goofy's Sky School** – Look for the yellow sign near the start of the queue and by the Lightning Lane.
- **Grizzly River Run** – Move up the exit stairs and meet the Cast Members at the rotating platform to ask about the Single Rider Line.
- **Incredicoaster** – Another hidden line (though it's marked with a blue sign) located by walking through the left side of the queue where you will see a gate (it takes you to the opposite side of the rollercoaster boarding).
- **Radiator Springs Racers** – A clearly marked queue at the start of the queues.
- **Soarin' Around the World** – Ask a Cast Member at the entrance for a Single Rider ticket to access the queue. You may be given a pass for single rider.
- **WEB Slingers: A Spider-Man Adventure** – Find a clearly marked sign near the ride's entrance.

CHAPTER ELEVEN

DOWNTOWN DISNEY

INTRODUCTION

Downtown Disney is the premier hangout location at the Disneyland Resort. It's surrounded by the Resort hotels, bursting with shops, including World of Disney, and filled with treats like an enormous Starbucks and a tasty Jamba smoothie bar. You can also go for a round of bowling at Splitsville or enter the immersive Star Wars Trading Post store. Best of all, theme park admission isn't required to experience the fun of Downtown Disney.

MONORAIL

Save your feet from walking and take Walt Disney's monorail system into Disneyland's Tomorrowland station. The ride comes with some great narration and tips about the park. You must have a park ticket to board.

PARKING

If you're just visiting Downtown Disney, you may park in one of the lots nearby. Road signs will direct you to the parking areas with quick and easy access to the dining, shops, and entertainment. The first 3 hours of parking are free with validation from a purchase of $20 at the shops or restaurants. If you dine at a table service restaurant like Splitsville, you can receive up to 5 hours of complimentary parking validation. Otherwise, parking is $14 an hour with a maximum parking charge of $66. Disney rounds up to the hour, so if you validate for 3 hours, but stay for 3 1/2, you'll be charged for the full extra hour. Guests visiting the theme parks may not use the Downtown Disney parking areas.

SHOPS

DISNEY BRANDED STORES

World of Disney - This ultimate Disney store is massive and located close to the parks.

Disney Home - High-end housewares for the Disney lover.

Disney's Pin Traders - A place to buy Disney pins and other collectables.

The Disney Dress Shop - Get a dapper look at this dress and accessory shop by Disney.

Marceline's Confectionary - Order a variety of sweets and shop for houseware in this shop inspired by Walt Disney's hometown of Marceline, Missouri.

Star Wars Trading Post - Discover collectibles and apparel from a galaxy far, far away! The Star Wars Trading Post is an immersive and eclectic store that's perfect for any Star Wars fan. Find items here that you would typically only find in Star Wars: Galaxy's Edge including exclusive lightsaber hilts, kyber crystals, and Jedi robes.

· **Magic Tips** ·
The Star Wars Trading Post used to be the Rain Forest Cafe but has since transformed into this amazing new store. Look near the ceiling for all sorts of Star Wars easter eggs. Also look for Rey's speeder bike just outside of the entrance! You can snap a photo next to it.

WonderGround Gallery - Specialized Disney artwork by famous Disney artists! At times, WonderGround will host signings and other events with the artists present.

· Magic Tips ·
Many stores including World of Disney, Elias & Co. (Disney California Adventure), and the Emporium (Disneyland) use mobile checkout for a speedier purchase. Find the "Shop in Store" button on the Disneyland app to use it.

MORE STORES

California Sole – Trendy shoes and sandals.

Curl Surf – Beach-inspired clothing and accessories for men and women.

The LEGO Store – Purchase and play with building blocks. Also check out the enormous Disney characters made entirely of Legos!

PANDORA Jewelry – Elegant jewelry and some Disney-inspired collections.

Sephora – Makeup and beauty supplies.

Sunglass Hut – High-end sunglasses and accessories.

MORE FUN

Splitsville – Bowl, drink, and dine at this family-friendly alley and restaurant.

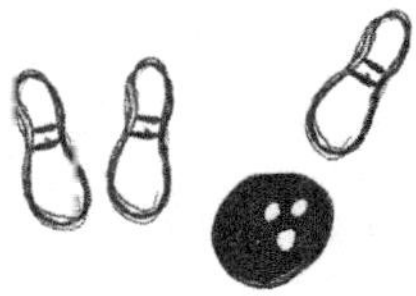

Stages – Both day and night, Downtown Disney comes alive with live music.

Hotel Restaurants – Visit one of the three Resort Hotels and dine at one of their restaurants, stop at a bar, or recline in a lounge.

DISCOUNTS

Like any other mall, Downtown Disney will often run seasonal discounts at its stores. While many of these sales go unlisted from Disneyland's website, you can usually see signs posted on storefront windows. Additionally, Disney Vacation Club Members, and those with a Disney Visa Card can score merchandise discounts at Disney-owned stores like the World of Disney, Disney Home, Disney's Pin Traders, and the WonderGround Gallery. Some other retail locations, including dining spots, may offer 10-20% discounts for these types of memberships.

Note: We cover Downtown Disney's many delicious restaurants in the next chapter!

CHAPTER TWELVE

DINING GUIDE

INTRODUCTION

Many visitors of the Disneyland Resort tell us that they primarily come for the world-class rides and meeting their favorite Disney characters. Sometimes they'll mention a particular show like the nighttime fireworks or Fantasmic, but rarely do they mention one of our favorite attractions: the food! If you haven't already thought about the dining options at Disney, we recommend that you start now. The Resort holds a wide variety of famous mouthwatering treats and even better little-known delights! Sometimes we visit the Resort just to try our favorite snacks and sneak in a ride or two in between munchies—we're not kidding!

RESERVATIONS

Most restaurants take reservations up to 60 days in advance via the Disneyland app, disneyland.com, or by calling (714) 781-DINE. We highly recommend this for popular locations like the Blue Bayou at Disneyland and the Lamplight Lounge at Disney California Adventure. If you can't get a reservation, you can still get a spot at your dining place, you just may have to wait. On busier days, we recommend planning to dine earlier (around 11:30am for lunch and 4pm for dinner) to avoid the rush. Make sure to book reservations and count every member of your party, including kids under 3 years old.

Note: We place "*Top Choice!*" next to our favorites or a "❤" by other highly recommended spots and items.

MOBILE ORDERING

The Disneyland App is your ticket to fast and easy ordering to some of the best dining locations in the parks! Not every restaurant has this option, but some with infamously long lines—like the Bengal Barbecue at Disneyland—now have a way for you to cut ahead! We highly recommend mobile ordering instead of waiting. Disneyland has streamlined this system to make it quick and easy for your food availability. Additionally, mobile food orders are freshly prepared for each guest. Those with Disney discounts can access a discount when ordering at participating locations.

Using Mobile Ordering:

1. Download the Disneyland App
2. Create a login (or use with your existing Disney account)
3. Select "Order Food"
4. Choose your destination and arrival time
5. Select your items
6. Review the order and purchase with credit card
7. When your order is ready, head to the restaurant and alert a Cast Member that you have arrived for pickup!

We've marked all restaurants with mobile ordering using this icon: ‡ — Keep in mind, Disney will add more restaurants and possibly change options, so use the Disneyland App for a more up-to-date list.

· **Magic Tips** ·

Disney's commitment to the environment has taken its theme parks away from using many plastics. This means that Quick-Service dining spots distribute soft drinks without a lid or straw. If you'd like a paper straw, ask a Cast Member at your dining location.

WALK-UP RESERVATIONS

Popular Disneyland Resort restaurants book up quickly! If you didn't get a spot at your choice of restaurant, you can always try for the walk-up list. Not all dining spots have this option but its easy to find.

To join the walk-up list, you'll need to be near the restaurant and open the Disneyland app. Usually there's a QR code you can scan near the restaurant or find the spot on the app. If available, you'll see "Join Walk-Up List" under the restaurant's name. Tap it and you'll be able to join virtually. Just wait until you're called to dine.

Restaurants with Virtual Walk-Up Lists*

1. Blue Bayou (DL)
2. Cafe Orleans (DL)
3. River Belle Terrace (DL)
4. Carthay Circle Restaurant (DCA)
5. Carthay Circle Lounge – Alfresco Dining (DCA)
6. Lamplight Lounge – Boardwalk Dining (DCA)
7. Wine Country Trattoria (DCA)
8. GCH Craftsman Bar (Grand Californian Hotel)
9. Storytellers Cafe (Grand Californian Hotel)

*This list is subject to change. Other popular dining spots—including Blue Bayou and Oga's Cantina—will often take walk-ups in person. To do this, speak with the Cast Member near the entrance when you're ready to dine. It's not guaranteed but worth a shot!

RESTAURANT TYPES

- **Table Service** - Restaurants with a waiter. It is suggested that you tip based on the service you receive.
- **Quick-Service** - Restaurants that you can order at and get seated right away.
- **Character Dining** - A buffet meal with Disney characters greeting guests at their tables.

OUR RESTAURANT PRICING

- **$** – Under $15 (typically snack carts)
- **$$** – $15 - $25 (typically Quick-Service Restaurants)
- **$$$** – $25 - $35 (more expensive Quick-Service Restaurants)
- **$$$$** – $35 or more (premium dining and character dining)

DISNEYLAND DINING

MAIN STREET, U.S.A.

CARNATION CAFE – *Top Choice!*
Description: Early 20th-century American café
Type: Table Service
Pricing: $$ / **Reservations:** Yes
Menu:
Breakfast: breakfast skillet, pancakes, omelets, Mickey waffles, juice, coffee, adult beverages
Kids Breakfast: waffles, pancakes, eggs
Lunch & Dinner: Walt's chili, burgers, sandwiches, short rib, pie, soda, coffee, juice, tea, adult beverages
Kids Dinner: fried chicken, burger, mac & cheese
Recommendation:
Breakfast: Mickey-shaped waffles
Lunch and Dinner: Walt's Chili, Parmesan Toasted Patty Melt

❤ ‡ JOLLY HOLIDAY BAKERY CAFE
Description: Early 20th-century American café
Type: Table Service
Pricing: $$ / **Reservations:** No
Menu:
Breakfast: steak and eggs, pancakes, omelet, parfait, Mickey waffles, bacon, sausage, toast, oatmeal, eggs benedict, coffee
Kids Breakfast: eggs, potatoes, bacon, fruit, waffles, pancakes
Lunch & Dinner: chili, salad, sandwiches, burgers, melts, meatloaf, fried chicken, ice cream, shakes, malts, cheesecake, soda
Kids Dinner: fried chicken, burger, mac & cheese
Recommendation:
Breakfast: Gourmet Donuts ❤
Lunch and Dinner: Sourdough Bacon-Cheese Melt, Classic Malt

MARKET HOUSE (STARBUCKS COFFEE)
Description: Starbucks Coffee
Type: Quick-Service
Pricing: $ / **Reservations:** No
Recommendation: The lines can be somewhat long in the morning, but they are quick to serve everyone. It might be a little hard to find the Market House sign, but it is right across from the Carnation Cafe, on your right as you walk toward the castle.

‡ PLAZA INN
Description: A classic, wonderfully detailed restaurant on the corner of Main Street and Tomorrowland.
Type: Character Breakfast Buffet / Quick-Service Lunch-Dinner
Pricing: $$-$$$ / **Reservations:** Yes (only for breakfast)
Menu:
Breakfast: breakfast buffet with eggs, bacon, sausage, made-to-order omelets, Mickey waffles, fruit, muffins, french toast, coffee, tea, soda
Lunch & Dinner: fried chicken, pot roast, salmon, pasta, salad, soda, coffee, tea, desserts
Kids Dinner: baked chicken, pasta
Recommendation: Fried chicken (lunch and dinner)

MORE EATS

‡ GIBSON GIRL ICE CREAM PARLOR ($) – Serving up Disneyland's scrumptious ice cream. Get it in a waffle cone.

❤ ‡ LITTLE RED WAGON ($) – A small, red wagon with a mighty following! Here you can get one of Disneyland's famous corn dogs with special dipping sauces.

‡ REFRESHMENT CORNER ($) – Get a Coke soft drink, or, better yet, a famous chili dog here.

ADVENTURELAND

❤ ‡ BENGAL BARBECUE – *Top Choice!*
Description: South Asian-style barbecue

Type: Quick-Service
Price: $-$$ / **Reservations:** No
Menu: meat skewers, vegetable skewers, breadsticks, rice plates, hummus, spring rolls, pork sandwich, coffee, tea, soda
Recommendation: Safari Skewer (bacon-wrapped asparagus), Jungle Julep (pineapple slush with orange, grape, and citrus flavors)

❤ ‡ TIKI JUICE BAR
Description: Soft-serve ice cream stand
Type: Snack Cart
Price: $ / **Reservations:** No
Menu: Pineapple Dole Whip, pineapple spears, pineapple juice
Recommendation: Dole Whip float (pineapple ice cream in pineapple juice)

· **Magic Tips** ·
Disneyland will often have seasonal snacks that you can find at various quick-service locations. These seasonal snacks are only available for a limited time. For example, you may find pumpkin-spiced churros in the fall or ginger bread cookies during the holiday season. Find these snacks listed on dining spot menus in the Disneyland app.

❤ ‡ THE TROPICAL HIDEAWAY – *Top Choice!*
Description: Sneak away to the tropics and greet skippers from the Jungle Cruise in this unique and fun location!

Type:
Price: $ / **Reservations:** No
Menu: Bao buns, Dole Whip flavors (orange, raspberry, and pineapple), chilled ramen, dessert lumpia, fruit, chips, soda
Recommendation: Loaded Whip (pineapple- and orange-flavored Dole Whip with fruit and crystalized hibiscus topping), Bulgogi Beef Bao, and Sweet Lumpia (crispy dessert filled with fruit and served with sweet dipping sauce)
Secret Menu Item: You can ask for candied bacon to add to the top of you Dole Whip here!

FRONTIERLAND

‡ THE GOLDEN HORSESHOE

Description: A western dining experience with American fare. Hear live music while dining on some of Walt Disney's favorite food (the chili he loved is now served at Carnation Cafe) in this classic venue with piano players.
Type: Quick-Service
Price: $$ / **Reservations:** No
Menu: fish and chips, chicken tenders salad, desserts
Kids: chicken tenders, power pack
Recommendation: Fish and Chips

RIVER BELLE TERRACE

Description: Western dining experience with American BBQ
Type: Table Service
Price: $$ / **Reservations:** Yes
Menu:
Brunch and Lunch: biscuits & gravy, pancakes, eggs, sandwiches, adult beverages, coffee, tea, juice
Dinner: pork chop, pot pie, fish, pasta, adult beverages, soda
Kids: BBQ ribs, mac and cheese
Recommendation: Smoke Burnt Ends Grilled Cheese, Biscuits & Gravy, Monkey Bread (pull apart cinnamon bread with whipped topping and candied pecans)

‡ STAGE DOOR CAFE

Description: Western dining experience with American favorites
Type: Quick-Service
Price: $ / **Reservations:** No
Menu: chicken tenders, corn dog, spinach wrap, fried steak sandwich
Kids: chicken slider, power pack
Recommendation: Hand-dipped Corn Dog, Funnel Cake

RANCHO DEL ZOCALO RESTAURANTE

Description: Mexican food
Type: Quick-Service
Price: $$ / **Reservations:** No
Menu: grilled chicken, tacos, burrito, carne asada, southwestern salads, soda, coffee, tea, flan

Kids: bean and cheese burrito, chicken taco, chicken and rice, beans and rice
Recommendation: Fire-grilled Chicken or a Burrito

MORE EATS

❤ **SHIP TO SHORE MARKETPLACE** ($) - Turkey legs, chimichangas, coffee, hot cocoa, and frozen lemonade. Before 10:30am, this cart offers delicious breakfast chimichangas with eggs, bacon, and cheese.

NEW ORLEANS SQUARE

❤ **CAFE ORLEANS** – *Top Choice!*
Description: French-style soups and outdoor dining
Type: Table service
Price: $$$ / **Reservations:** Yes
Menu: Monte Cristo sandwich, short rib, pasta jambalaya, chicken, salad, garlic parmesan fries, soda, coffee, tea, adult beverages
Kids: chicken, fish, mac and cheese, beef, shrimp and grits
Recommendation: Monte Cristo Sandwich, Pommes Frites

· **Magic Tips** ·
Disneyland limits its restaurant reservations so they may be difficult to book in advance. If you can't find a reservation, we highly recommend joining the walk-up. You can easily do this for most table service restaurants in the parks by opening the Disneyland app when you're near the dining location. Search for the restaurant name or find it on the map. if there's walk up list availability, you'll be able to secure a spot for your party,

❤ **BLUE BAYOU** – *Top Choice!*
Description: Disneyland's premier dining experience with some of the best entrees the Disneyland Resort has to offer. Located inside of the Pirates of the Caribbean ride, this is exceptional Louisiana-style dining with Creole food and more!

Type: Table Service
Reservations: Yes (highly recommended)
Price: $$$-$$$$
Menu:
Lunch: Monte Cristo sandwich, steak, pork loin, jambalaya, pasta, chicken maison, lamb, salad, gumbo, soda, coffee, tea, mixed soft drinks, crème brûlée, beer, wine, some mixed drinks
Dinner: lobster and steak, pork loin, pasta, salmon, chicken maison, lamb, salad, crab hush puppies, gumbo, soda, coffee, tea, mixed soft drinks, crème brûlée, eight-layer chocolate cake, beer, wine, some mixed drinks
Kids Lunch & Dinner: chicken, fish, mac and cheese, beef and vegetables
Recommendation: Monte Cristo Sandwich (lunch), Surf & Turf (dinner), Louisiana Lemonade (lemonade, Sprite, mango, and raspberry with a glow cube decoration—served at lunch and dinner)

> · **Magic Tips** ·
> Only table service restaurants in Disneyland Park serve alcohol. It's mostly beer, wine, and a special hurricane cocktail designed for the restaurant. However, unlike at Disney California Adventure, guests must drink their beverage inside of the restaurant.

❤ ‡ TIANA'S PALACE – *Top Choice!*
Description: Creole specialties inspired by *The Princess and the Frog*
Type: Quick-Service
Price: $$ / **Reservations:** No
Menu: gumbo, sandwiches, chicken, cornbread, mac and cheese, filled beignet, cold brew, coffee, juice, tea, soda
Kids: mac and cheese, pasta
Recommendation: House Gumbo, Gulf Shrimp and Grits

‡ ROYAL STREET VERANDA
Description: French-style soups
Type: Quick-Service
Price: $$ / **Reservations:** No
Menu: clam chowder, fritters, soda, coffee, tea
Recommendation: Creamy Clam Chowder (served in a sourdough bread bowl), New Orleans Fritters

MORE EATS

❤ ‡ **MINT JULEP BAR** ($) – Mickey-shaped beignets, lattes, mochas, and, of course, mint juleps

---

CRITTER COUNTRY

❤ ‡ HUNGRY BEAR RESTAURANT
Description: Picnic-style sandwiches, burgers, and fries
Type: Quick-Service
Price: $ / **Reservations**: No
Menu: burgers, chicken sandwiches, fish sandwiches, turkey wrap, salad, fries, onion rings, soda, coffee, tea, funnel cake
Kids: hamburger, chicken nuggets, mac and cheese, power pack
Recommendation: Turkey Caesar Wrap, Onion Rings, House-made Funnel Cake
Secret Menu Items: Loaded Fries or Loaded Onion rings with cheese, bacon, green onions, and cilantro sour cream on top

❤ ‡ HARBOUR GALLEY
Description: Waterfront-style food with lobster entrées
Type: Quick-Service
Price: $ / **Reservations**: No
Menu: lobster roll, lobster mac and cheese hot dog, clam chowder, tuna sandwich, salad, fruit, soda, coffee, tea, mixed lemonade
Kids: power pack
Recommendation: Mac 'n' Cheese in a Sourdough Bread Bowl

FANTASYLAND

❤ ‡ RED ROSE TAVERNE
Description: French- and American-fusion restaurant styled after the live-action *Beauty and the Beast* movie.
Type: Quick-Service
Price: $$ / **Reservations**: No
Menu:

Breakfast: breakfast burger, breakfast platter (eggs, potatoes, bacon, croissant), french toast, hash browns, pancakes, juice, soda, coffee, tea
Lunch/Dinner: burger, chicken sandwich, poutine, flatbread, salad, soda, coffee, tea, the grey stuff, mixed soft drinks
Kids: turkey sandwich, cheese pizza, burger, mac and cheese (toddler)
Recommendation: Chicken Sandwich a la Lumiere (lunch or dinner), Grey Stuff Gateau, and Gaston's Famous Brew (a drink flavored with apple, mango, and passion fruit whipped topping)

‡ TROUBADOUR TAVERN
Description: Italian-, German-, and American-fusion restaurant
Type: Snack
Age Group: Everyone
Price: $ / **Reservations**: No
Menu: turkey leg, sausage, stuffed baked potato, pretzel bites, popcorn, soda, coffee, tea, mixed soft drink
Recommendation: Stuffed Baked Potato

MORE EATS

‡ EDELWEISS SNACKS ($) – A snack cart serving Disneyland's famous giant turkey legs, chimichangas, and other treats.

MAURICE'S TREATS ($) – European-style pastries served from a cart inspired by *Beauty and the Beast*. Try the savory Garlic Cheesy Pretzel Bread!

MICKEY'S TOONTOWN

❤ ‡ CAFE DAISY – *Top Choice!*
Description: Find American food favorites that are ideal for the entire family.
Type: Quick-Service
Age Group: Everyone
Price: $$ / **Reservations**: No

Menu: pizza, hot dogs, garden wrap, mac and cheese, cold brew, lemonade, coffee, milk, juice, soda
Recommendation: Pepperoni Pizza Flop-Over

GOOD BOY GROCER ($) – Grab and go snacks and picnic baskets!

TOMORROWLAND

‡ ALIEN PIZZA PLANET
Description: Pizza and other Italian-American favorites themed after *Toy Story*.
Type: Quick-Service
Price: $$ / **Reservations**: No
Menu: pizza, pasta, breadsticks, salad, soda, coffee, tea
Kids: pasta, pizza
Recommendation: Mega Pepperoni

‡ GALACTIC GRILL
Description: American-style breakfast, lunch, and dinner
Type: Quick-Service
Price: $$ / **Reservations**: No
Menu:
Breakfast: breakfast burrito, French toast sticks, breakfast sandwich, juice, soda, coffee, tea, mixed soft drinks
Kids Breakfast: breakfast slider (egg and turkey bacon in a bun), power pack
Lunch/Dinner: burger, fried chicken sandwich, veggie wrap, fries, salad, soda, coffee, tea, mixed soft drink
Kids: burger, chicken nuggets, mac and cheese (toddler)
Recommendation: Galactic Grill serves pretty tasty breakfast options! Try the American Breakfast Burrito with eggs, cheese, bacon, sausage, hash browns, and salsa.

DINING EXPERIENCES

TOMORROWLAND SKYLINE LOUNGE EXPERIENCE
Description: Snack, sip, and savor a delicious view of the Disneyland nighttime fireworks from a high-up lounge in Tomorrowland!
Type: Special Event Dining — $60/person
Recommendation: If you're craving a great view of the fireworks, but also want to relax at night in a posh setting, this experience is for you! Of course, it does come at an extra premium cost ($50/person), but you'll have a wonderful, full view of the castle and the show while snacking on a tray of fruit, cheese, and sweets. There is also a selection of hot or cold beverages (usually sodas and coffee, but no alcohol). The lounge is pretty cool, too, with futuristic light-up tables and swanky seating positioned at the top of the Tomorrowland Expo Center (once the Innoventions building, but now houses Star Wars Launch Bay).
Reserve Your Table: https://disneyland.disney.go.com/dining/disneyland/tomorrowland-skyline-lounge

---

STAR WARS: GALAXY'S EDGE

❤ ‡ DOCKING BAY 7 FOOD AND CARGO – *Top Choice!*
Description: An intergalactic canteen in a rustic, Star Wars-inspired building. The food here is a mix of flavors that will tickle the tastebuds of adventurous eaters.
Type: Quick-Service
Price: $$ / **Reservations**: No
Menu: breakfast items, ribs, salads, air-fried chicken, noodles, juice soda, coffee, tea, desserts
Kids: air-fried chicken
Recommendation: Smoked Kaadu Ribs, Oi-oi Puff (dessert), Cold Brew Black Caf (creamy coffee cold brew topped with crunchy chocolate cereal)

❤ **OGA'S CANTINA** ($-$$) – This is a lively bar filled with Star Wars surprises and cocktails. This is one of the few locations in Disneyland that serves alcohol to its guests (ages 21+), but there are treats for kids as well. We recommend the T-17 Skyhopper (vodka, melon, and kiwi blend) and the non-alcoholic Hyperdrive (Punch It!), a blend of berry flavors and Sprite.

· **Magic Tips** ·
We recommend getting a reservation for Oga's Cantina or you may not gain entry. However, walk-up seating may be available, especially early in the morning.

KAT SAKA'S KETTLE ($) – Flavored kettle corn! We recommend the sweet and spicy Outpost Popcorn Mix and eating the many flavors together for the best taste!

‡ **MILK STAND** ($) – Blue and green "milk" made famous by Star Wars films. These are non-dairy (plant-based) slushy drinks with lightly sweet flavors. Blue Milk is a fan favorite for its creamy berry flavor. Green Milk is a bit earthier with a hint of melon.

❤ ‡ **RONTO ROASTERS** ($) – Tangy sausage wraps served for breakfast, lunch, and dinner. These are filling enough for one and great to split if you're just snacking. We recommend the incredibly tasty Ronto-less Garden Wrap made with a plant-based sausage and Korean-fusion flavors, wrapped in a pita.

· **Magic Tips** ·
Outside of Ronto Roster, cranking the spit of meat, is a lesser known droid named 8D-J8. In the folklore of Galaxy's Edge, this bot was once a smelter droid who has been reprogrammed for his meat-cooking post. The simulated roaster he's cranking under is a podracer engine reworked into a grill!

CALIFORNIA ADVENTURE DINING

BUENA VISTA STREET

❤ **CARTHAY CIRCLE RESTAURANT** – *Top Choice!*

Description: A signature dining location with some of the best entrees the Disneyland Resort has to offer.
Type: Table Service with adult beverages available
Price: $$$-$$$$ / **Reservations**: Yes
Menu: Carthay Circle has a seasonal menu but the dining is always unforgettable. There's also a full bar with signature cocktails.
Recommendations: Carthay Signature Fried Biscuits

MORE EATS

❤ **CARTHAY CIRCLE ALFRESCO DINING & LOUNGE** ($$-$$$) – A snacks and bites lounge for adults 21 and older only. Serves sushi and alcoholic drinks. A reservation may be required for the Alfresco Dining experience (when available). Recommendations: Vietnamese Twice-cooked Beef Tacos, Duck Confit Emparadas, and Rose Petal Soda (non-alcoholic).

‡ **CLARABELLE'S HAND SCOOPED ICE CREAM** ($) – We recommend the Oswald Sundae (also available in a souvenir holder shaped like a kitchen sink).

FIDDLER, FIFER, AND PRACTICAL CAFE ($) – Starbucks Coffee and treats.

MORTIMER'S FISH MARKET ($) – Snacks and bottled water.

AVENGERS CAMPUS

❤ ‡ **PYM TEST KITCHEN**
Description: Growing and shrinking American favorite food items in a restaurant inspired by Ant-Man.

Type: Quick-Service
Price: $$ / **Reservations**: No
Menu: sandwiches, salad, giant pretzel, plant-based, desserts, soda, beer, coffee, smoothies, juice
Kids: sandwiches, pasta
Recommendation: Pym-ini Sandwich, Quantum Pretzel, Proton PB&J Punch, Celestial-sized Candy Bar: Choco-Smash (dessert)

· **Magic Tips** ·
Seating in Avengers Campus is very limited. You might find more spots near the Hyperion Theatre.

MORE EATS

‡ **PYM TASTING LAB** ($$) — A mixology bar with fresh new drink concoctions that come in a beaker cup! We recommend the X-Periment and Molecular Meltdown.

❤ **TERRAN TREATS** ($) – Sweets and sodas. We recommend the Cosmic Cream Orb, a pastry filled with raspberry cream cheese mousse.

❤ ‡ **SHAWARMA PALACE** ($) – A snack cart serving delicious wraps. Get the chicken or falafel shawarma. There also may be a second cart, Shawarma Palace Too, near the Hyperion Theatre.

HOLLYWOOD LAND

❤ ‡ AWARD WIENERS
Description: Gourmet hot dogs and sausages.
Type: Quick-Service
Price: $ / **Reservations**: No
Menu: hot dogs, fries, funnel cake fries, soda, coffee, tea, beer
Kids: hot dog, power pack
Recommendation: Bacon Street Dog, Beer Cheese Fries, Funnel Cake Fries (dessert)

‡ STUDIO CATERING CO.
Description: Food truck with bites inspired by *Guardians of the Galaxy*
Type: Quick-Service
Price: $ / **Reservations**: No
Menu: nachos, tacos, soda
Recommendation: Obviously Nachos (slightly spicy with chicken)

MORE EATS

‡ HOLLYWOOD LOUNGE ($$) – An outdoor bar with mixed drinks and beer.

FAIRFAX MARKET ($) – A stop for healthy snacks and vegetarian options like hummus and coconut water.

❤ ‡ SCHMOOZIES ($) – Blended fruit smoothies and sweet snacks.

CARS LAND

❤‡ FLO'S V8 CAFE
Description: Classic American Diner
Type: Quick-Service
Price: $$ / **Reservations**: No
Menu:
Breakfast: eggs, breakfast potatoes, bacon, sausage, fruit, juice, coffee, tea, soda
Kids' Breakfast: waffles, American breakfast plate, fruit plate
Lunch/Dinner: pork ribs, burger, turkey avocado bacon club, tuna sandwich, fried chicken, pot pie, salad, fries, soda, coffee, tea, shakes, seasonal pies, beer, wine, sangria
Kids' Lunch/Dinner: burgers, chicken strips, mac and cheese, sliders
Recommendation:
Breakfast: Brioche French Toast (with caramel sauce and bananas)
Lunch/Dinner: Blue Plate Special (breaded chicken with garlic mashed potatoes)

‡ COZY CONE MOTEL
Description: Snack huts that serve several types of delicious treats in cones. Each cone "hut" serves different types of treats.
Type: Quick-Service Snacks
Price: $ / **Reservations**: No
Menu: chili, bacon mac and cheese, churros, soft-serve ice cream, pretzels, popcorn, soda, coffee, tea, specialty mixed sodas, mixed alcoholic drinks, beer
Recommendation: Bacon Mac 'n' cheese Cone

· **Magic Tips** ·
Most breakfast meals at Disneyland are served until only 11am. Since the morning hours are the best times to experience short waits, breakfast can get in the way. To minimize time spent on dining, use options like mobile ordering in between rides.

MORE EATS

FILLMORE'S TASTE-IN ($): Quick-Service snacks, juice, and water.

PIXAR PIER

❤ LAMPLIGHT LOUNGE – *Top Choice!*
Description: Disney California Adventure's popular bar with a view of the Pier.
Type: Casual Table Service and Bar
Price: $$ / **Reservations**: Yes (recommended)
Menu:

Brunch: potato flautas, chilaquiles, brunch burger, avocado toast, brunch quesadilla, omelet, soda, juice, cocktails
Lunch/Dinner: sushi, lobster nachos, chicken sandwich, ratatouille, burgers, donuts, salad, mixed drinks, cocktails (full bar), wine, beer
Kids: PB and J Roll (peanut butter and jelly rolled to look like sushi), burger slider, pasta, chicken

Recommendation: Spotlight Nachos: Barbacoa (zesty nachos supreme with tortilla chips, pinto beans, chipotle cheese, and many flavorful bits of beef)—only available upstairs in the lounge.

· Magic Tips ·
If you can't grab a reservation to Lamplight Lounge, try joining walk-up list in the Disneyland app. Lamplight Lounge offers "Boardwalk Dining" with outdoor spots for those needing a last-minute table. The only downside is that these spots may not have any shade.

MORE EATS

‡ ADORABLE SNOWMAN FROSTED TREATS ($) – Soft-serve ice cream and other treats. Try the Lemon Soft-serve—it tastes like a lemon Dole Whip!

ANGRY DOGS ($) – Spicy and mild hot dogs.

JACK-JACK COOKIE NUM NUMS ($) – Large melt-in-your-mouth chocolate chip cookies served warm. At around $6 each, the cookies served here are drastically overpriced. Still, they are incredibly delicious and something you'll likely crave again and again.

POULTRY PALACE ($) – *The* place to get Disney's famous giant turkey legs and chicken entrees. We recommend the Chicken Drumstick Box. The meal comes with breaded and baked chicken legs, dipping sauces, and a side of coleslaw.

SEÑIOR BUZZ CHURROS ($) – Get a red hot churro here.

SAN FRANSOKYO SQUARE

‡ AUNT CASS CAFE
Description: Find sandwiches and soups in bread bowls here! The restaurant is based on *Big Hero 6*.
Type: Quick Service

Price: $$ / **Reservations:** No
Menu: soups in bread bowls, sandwiches, clam chowder, soda, beer, wine, cocktails
Recommendation: San Fransokyo Clam Chowder, Turkey Pesto Club, Honey Lemon-Ade

❤ ‡ COCINA CUCAMONGA
Description: Tasty Mexican-American quick-service food
Type: Quick Service
Price: $$ / **Reservations:** No
Menu: tacos, beer, wine, margaritas, cocktails, soda
Recommendation: QuesaBirria street-style tacos

‡ LUCKY FORTUNE COOKERY
Description: Asian-fusion quick-service food
Type: Quick Service
Price: $$ / **Reservations:** No
Menu: chicken sandwich, ramen, pot stickers, macaron, cocktails, beer, wine, tea, soda
Recommendation: Karaage-inspired Crispy Chicken Sandwich, Pork Wonton Nachos, Lychee Tea

MORE EATS

‡ CAPPUCCINO CART ($$) – Fan-favorite drinks and snacks presented by Joffrey's Coffee.

‡ PORT OF SAN FRANSOKYO CERVECERIA ($) – Order a variety of Karl Strauss beer at this window.

‡ RITA'S TURBINE BLENDERS ($) – Find a variety of blended margaritas and non-alcoholic slushees. We recommend combining Rita's Grand Strawberry Margarita with Rita's Grand Lemon-Lime Margarita!

❤ ‡ GHIRARDELLI SODA FOUNTAIN AND CHOCOLATE SHOP – Shop chocolates and gifts or order a sundae. We recommend the Magical Sundae with hot fudge. There's also a dairy-free one!

PERFORMANCE COORIDOR

❤ MAGIC KEY TERRACE

Description: Exclusively for Magic Key holders, this lounge serves elevated snacks with fantastic views of Disney California Adventure.
Type: Bar and Lounge
Price: $$ - $$$$ / **Reservations:** Yes
Menu: meatballs, flatbread, bruschetta, charcuterie and cheese board, soda, coffee, tea, wines, cocktails
Recommendation: This dining spot is typically only for those with a Magic Key holders and their guests. The cocktails and small bites are fantastic here! Try the Charcuterie Cheese Board!

MORE EATS

WINE COUNTRY TRATTORIA ($$) – Try the Red Sangria (21 and older) and the Bolognese.

‡ SONOMA TERRACE ($) – Try local Californian craft beer.

MENDOCINO TERRACE ($$) – Wines and soft drinks. We recommend pairing wine with the Italian Meat and Cheese Box.

GRIZZLY PEAK

❤ ‡ SMOKEJUMPERS GRILL

Description: A hanger-shaped American grill for burgers and fries
Type: Quick-Service
Price: $$
Reservations: No
Menu: burgers, sandwiches, chicken tenders, chili, chili cheese fries, onion rings, salad, beer, wine, margarita, soda, coffee, desserts
Kids: chicken skewer, burger, grilled cheese sandwich, chicken tenders, mac and cheese (toddler)
Recommendation: Brisket Mac 'n Cheese

PARADISE GARDENS PARK

‡ BOARDWALK PIZZA & PASTA
Description: Pizza joint with Italian-American favorites
Type: Quick-Service
Price: $$ **Reservations:** No
Menu: spaghetti, chicken pesto, ravioli, pizzas, salads, tiramisu, soda, tea, beer
Kids: cheese pizza, turkey meatball sandwich
Recommendation: Try one of their pizzas

‡ PARADISE GARDEN GRILL
Description: Grill with Mexican-inspired eats
Type: Quick-Service
Price: $$ **Reservations:** No
Menu: tamales, queso, chicken and rice, tacos, parfait, soda, coffee, tea, beer
Kids: quesadilla, taco
Recommendation: Yucatan-inspired Vaporcitos (chicken tamales)

ADULT POURS

‡ **BAYSIDE BREWS** ($) – American beer on tap. Try their sweet and salty Cream Cheese-filled Pretzel!

MORE EATS

❤ ‡ **CORN DOG CASTLE** - Get a delicious battered hot dog with Disney's famous recipe. Try the semi-spicy Hot Link Corn Dog!

RESORT HOTEL DINING

DISNEYLAND HOTEL

❤ GOOFY'S KITCHEN

Description: American breakfast and dinner with buffet options.
Type: Table Service (Breakfast and Dinner)
Price: $$$$ / **Reservations:** Yes
Menu:
Breakfast/Brunch Buffet: omelet station, Mickey waffles, Mickey pancakes, French toast, bacon, sausage, eggs, fruit, eggs benedict, peanut butter pizza, soft-serve yogurt, coffee, tea, soda, juice
Adult Breakfast Beverages (additional cost): mimosa, bellini, screwdriver, bloody mary
Dinner Buffet: carving station, vegetables, fish, salad, fruit, hot dogs, pizzas, mac and cheese, dessert station
Recommendation: Brunch buffet

❤ ‡ TANGAROA TERRACE TROPICAL BAR & GRILL

Description: American and Polynesian Cuisine
Type: Quick-Service (Breakfast, Lunch, and Dinner)
Price: $$ / **Reservations:** No
Menu:
Breakfast: breakfast burritos, eggs, bacon, pancakes, French toast, avocado toast, breakfast bowl, pastries, soda, tea, coffee, Dole Whip
Kids Breakfast: pancakes, French toast, and egg scrambles
Lunch/Dinner: poke bowl, ramen, salad, fried shrimp, burgers, poutine, wings, gyoza, sodas, milk, tea, juices, coffee, and Dole Whip
Kids Lunch/Dinner: cheeseburger and rice bowls
Recommendation:
Breakfast: Pineapple Upside-Down Pancakes
Lunch/Dinner: Tempura Shrimp

· Magic Tips ·
Tangaroa Terrace is one of the few places outside of Disneyland Park to get a Dole Whip—without a theme park ticket. The restaurant also sells Dole Whip Floats with rum for those 21 and older!

BARS AND LOUNGES

❤ **TRADER SAM'S ENCHANTED TIKI BAR** – *Top Choice!*
Description: A tropical Disney "dive bar" with themed magic! Certain drinks cause the room to swirl into a storm or the volcano artwork to erupt! Trader Sam's is fun for everyone (though it becomes 21 and over after 8pm). The menu is virtually the same as Tangaroa Terrace.
Type: "Dive Bar" and Lounge
Price: $$ / **Reservations:** No
Menu: burgers, shrimp, asian-fusion food, gyoza, sodas, milk, tea, juices, coffee
Kids: cheeseburger and rice bowls / Full bar
Recommendation:
Cocktails: The Uh Oa! (rum blends with passion fruit), Krakatoa Punch (rum punch), and Ka-blue-ie! (tropical rum with blue curacao)
Food: Hawaiian Cheeseburger or Tempura Shrimp

MORE EATS

THE COFFEE HOUSE ($$) – This small coffee joint sells cold and hot beverages and treats.

DISNEY'S GRAND CALIFORNIAN

❤ **STORYTELLERS CAFE** – *Top Choice!*
Description: American breakfast, lunch, and dinner with buffet options. You can meet several Disney characters here including Mickey Mouse!
Type: Table Service (and Character Breakfast)
Price: $$$- $$$$ / **Reservations:** Yes
Menu:
Breakfast/Brunch Buffet: omelet station, potatoes, French toast, bacon, sausage, eggs, fruit, eggs benedict, spanish rice, oatmeal, roasted chicken, coffee, cappuccino, chai latte, tea, soda, juice

Adult Breakfast Beverages (additional cost): mimosa, bellini, bloody mary, raspberry champagne
Lunch/Dinner (not a buffet): pizza, steak frites, short rib grilled cheese, croque monsieur, spaghetti, turkey club, Wagyu burger, salads, soda, coffee, tea, cocktails, beer, chocolate cake, cheesecake, crème brûlée
Dinner Buffet: carved turkey, salmon, pasta, chicken nuggets, mac and cheese, vegetables, salad, desserts
Recommendation:
Breakfast: Brunch Buffet
Lunch/Dinner: Slow-roasted Turkey Clubhouse

❤ **NAPA ROSE** – *Top Choice!*
Description: California-themed upscale dining with entrées designed by gourmet Napa chef Andrew Sutton.
Type: Dinner
Price: $$$$ / **Reservations:** Yes
Menu: fish, veal chop, chicken, lamb, mac and cheese, rabbit bratwurst, soda, coffee, tea, wines, cocktails
Kids: pasta, fish, steak, pizza, salad
Recommendation:
Starter: Roasted Breast of Pheasant with Duck Liver Mousseline
Lunch: Any of the main courses as they were all designed by gourmet chef Andrew Sutton.
Dinner: Dinner Buffet

BARS AND LOUNGES

NAPA ROSE LOUNGE ($$) – The bar lounge inside of the Napa Rose (more casual than Napa Rose) with wine, cocktails (full bar), and wood-fired pizza.

HEARTHSTONE LOUNGE ($$) – A lounge in Disney's Grand Californian with bites and cocktails (full bar).

‡ **GCH CRAFTSMAN BAR & GRILL** ($$) – A casual eatery with breakfast, lunch, and dinner items. The bar services hotel guests at the pool and the grill is open to the general public. On weekends, you may hear live music and other entertainment. We recommend the Double Baked Beef Nachos served in the Grill portion outside near the pool. Mobile ordering is available for the GCH Craftsman Bar and reservations may be available for the Grill.

PIXAR PLACE HOTEL

❤ GREAT MAPLE

Description: A Southern California favorite dining spot that's known for its "elevated comfort food." A great place to visit for brunch and dinner with large portions and delicious entrees. They're famously known for the maple bacon donuts.
Type: Table Service
Price: $$$
Brunch Menu: pancakes, French toast, scrambles, bacon, eggs
Lunch & Dinner Menu: pasta, tacos, burgers, ribs, desserts
Recommendation: Get the Maple Bacon Donuts with your meal!

DOWNTOWN DISNEY DINING

BALLAST POINT

Description: A 7,000 square foot brewery and restaurant located on the second story of Downtown Disney. Ballast Point is a great hangout spot for adults, as it's home to an extensive beer list. The entire family will enjoy the delicious bites to eat here as well as the top-story views of Downtown Disney.

Type: Table Service

Price: $$$

Menu: burgers, salads, wings, burritos, tacos, pizzas, steaks, beer

Recommendation: Duck Nachos, Ballast Point Wagyu Burger

⋆ **Magic Tips** ⋆

Downtown Disney is transforming! Some restaurants may become unavailable as new ones open. While Disneyland has not updated the list for 2023, upcoming dining experiences include the popular Din Tai Fung!

BLACK TAP CRAFT BURGERS & SHAKES

Description: Award-winning burgers, beers, and designer milkshakes

Type: Table Service / Counter Service

Price: $$-$$$ / **Reservations:** No

Menu: burgers, salad, shakes, beer on tap, sodas

Recommendation: The burgers are good, but the Crazy Shakes are even better! Get one of these delicious concoctions inside at the table service restaurant or at the shake window outside.

NAPLES RISORANTE E PIZZERIA

Description: Italian

Type: Table Service

Price: $$$ / **Reservations:** Yes

Menu: pizzas, calamari, soup, pasta, soda, wine, beer, tiramisu, gelato, cheesecake

Kids: pizza, pasta, mac and cheese, chicken, risotto

Recommendation: Any of their pizzas!

NAPOLINI
Description: Build-your-own pizza
Type: Table Service
Price: $$ / **Reservations:** No
Menu: build-your-own pizza, salad, sandwiches, Italian desserts, soda, beer, wine
Recommendation: Build-your-own pizza

❤ JAZZ KITCHEN COASTAL GRILL
Description: Cajun food with a lounge bar
Type: Table Service / Lounge
Price: $$ / **Reservations:** No
Menu: Po'boys, sandwiches, poutine, gumbo, jambalaya, salad, mac and cheese, steak, beignets, cocktails, beer, wine, soda
Recommendation: Fried Chicken Po-Boy, Beignets
Xpressed: You can order beignets to go next to the Jazz Kitchen. There's a small part of the restaurant where they hand make beignets. Order a box to-go!

❤ SPLITSVILLE LUXURY LANES – *Top Choice!*
Description: Bowling and dining known for its sushi and pizza
Type: Upscale Bowling Alley Lounge
Price: $$ / **Reservations:** Yes
Menu: sushi, burgers, pizza, salads, fish n' chips, ribs, taco bowl, chicken alfredo, fries, nachos, soda, coffee, tea, wines, cocktails on tap
Kids: burger, pizza, chicken tenders, hot dog, pasta, grilled cheese
Recommendation: Crouching Dragon sushi roll with tempura fried shrimp, asparagus, and avocado with spicy krab and eel sauce

TORTILLA JO'S
Description: Mexican food with a lounge bar
Type: Table Service / Lounge
Price: $$ / **Reservations:** Yes
Menu:
Brunch: French toast, breakfast burrito, chilaquilas, breakfast enchiladas, juice, soda, coffee, tea, wines, cocktails
Kids' Breakfast: pancakes, egg scramble
Lunch/Dinner: tacos, burritos, nachos, quesadilla, fajitas, combination plates with rice and beans, salads, chips and guacamole, empanadas, soda, coffee, tea, beer, margaritas, tequila, wines, horchata, fruit smoothie

Recommendation: Fajita de Tres (sizzling chicken, steak, and shrimp served with corns tortillas, rice, and beans), Shredded Beef Burrito (served with rice and refried beans), or the TJ's Grilled Chicken Caesar Salad
Quicker Option: For a fast order, visit the Taqueria next door.

MORE DINING OPTIONS

MORE DINING

EARL OF SANDWICH ($) – Delicious hot & cold sandwiches.

JAMBA ($) – Blended fruit smoothies and breakfast bowls.

SALT & STRAW ($) – Handmade artisan ice cream.

STARBUCKS ($) – Coffee, pastries, and breakfast sandwiches.

WETZEL'S PRETZELS ($) – Savory and sweet pretzels.

BREAKFAST AT THE DISNEYLAND RESORT

Finding breakfast at Disneyland is a little tricky. Since not all venues serve morning meals, it's a bit difficult to find. However, Disneyland's breakfast items are usually much cheaper than the lunch counterparts and can be very tasty! We've created a list of our favorite dining spots and what to get to satisfy your hunger.

Character Breakfasts – If you're in the mood for a big buffet breakfast with a Disney feel, we highly recommend booking a character breakfast. These buffets typically come with waffles, pancakes, bacon, pastries, fruit, coffee, and juice. Storytellers Cafe (Grand Californian Hotel) and Plaza Inn (Disneyland) are our top choices for these experiences.

Disneyland Breakfast Snacks – Disneyland's best breakfast snacks include the Breakfast Chimichanga (Ship to Shore Marketplace in Frontierland), Mickey-Shaped Beignets (Mint Julep Bar), and the Ronto Morning Wrap (Star Wars: Galaxy's Edge). The gourmet donuts at Jolly Holiday (Main Street, U.S.A.) are also a fantastic choice!

Disney California Adventure Breakfast – Flo's V8 Cafe in Cars Land and Pym Test Kitchen in Avengers Campus often serve up some tasty breakfast options. In addition, the Lamplight Lounge may serve brunch (reservation recommended).

Starbucks – Each theme park has a Starbucks near the entrance and there are two locations within Downtown Disney. While these lines become very long in the early morning, there are plenty of coffee flavors and snacks to choose from.

PLANT-BASED DINING

Disney's commitment to the environment also meant a shift toward planet-based options. While many guests identify as vegan or vegetarian, Disney instead opts for the phrase "plant-based" as it more accurately describes the food ingredients. In the coming years, Disneyland will add several more plant-based options, but we've listed our favorite snacks and entrees (keep in mind that menu options and ingredients can always change, so be sure to ask a Cast Member before ordering):

· Magic Tips ·
Disney partnered with Impossible Foods to bring many more plant-based dining options in the future. Star Wars: Galaxy's Edge has the most extensive plant-based menu options. We highly recommend dining at Docking Bay 7 for the most choices.

BEST PLANT-BASED ENTREES

- **Ronto-less Garden Wrap** (Ronto Roasters in Disneyland) – A plant-based sausage with Korean-fusion flavors. Find it in Star Wars: Galaxy's Edge.

- **Felucian Kefta and Hummus Garden Spread** (Docking Bay 7 Food & Cargo in Disneyland) – Plant-based meatballs served with herb hummus and pita. Find it in Star Wars: Galaxy's Edge.
- **Impossible Spoonful** (Pym Test Kitchen in Disney California Adventure) – A giant plant-based meatball over a pile of pasta and served with tomato sauce and dairy-free cheese. Find it in Avengers Campus).
- **Impossible Victory Falafel Shawarma** (Shawarma Palace in Disney California Adventure) – Plant-based falafel with tasty garlic spread in a cauliflower wrap.

BEST PLANT-BASED SNACKS & SWEETS

- **Dole Whip** – Tropcial Hideaway, Adventureland (Disneyland)
- **Churro** – Various churro carts (Disneyland & California Adventure)
- **Mint Julep** – Mint Julep Bar, New Orleans Square (Disneyland)
- **Seasonal Vegan Ice Cream** – Salt & Straw (Downtown Disney)
- **Blue & Green Milk** – Milk Stand, Galaxy's Edge (Disneyland)
- **Popcorn** – Various carts (Disneyland & California Adventure)

OUTSIDE OF THE RESORT

There are dozens of restaurants near the Disneyland Resort that provide alternatives to what you might find on site. Many of these businesses are restaurant chains that appeal to American tourists. There are also some great choices for low cost and/or fantastic flavor. We outline these nearby spots here.

RESTAURANTS WITHIN WALKING DISTANCE

❤ PUESTO

1040 W Katella Ave, Anaheim, CA 92802

Description: A delicious Mexican-inspired dining experience with gourmet tacos, cocktails, and more. Puesto is located inside the Westin Anaheim but all guests are welcome to dine there.

Type: Steakhouse

Price: $$-$$$ / **Reservations:** Yes (https://www.eatpuesto.com/location/anaheim/)

Menu: tacos, chips, salads, guacamole, enchiladas, desserts, cocktails, soda, coffee, tea, juices, beer, wine

Recommendations: Any three tacos—we love the Short-Rib Quesabirria Tacos

DENNY'S

1610 S Harbor Blvd, Anaheim, CA 92802

Description: An inexpensive American diner famous for its breakfast items. Depending on who you ask, this restaurant chain may have a great or poor reputation. This location is across the street from Disneyland's main gate and serves quick breakfasts to tourists. Denny's is also open 24 hours and offers a late-night dining menu.

Type: American Diner

Price: $$ / **Reservations:** No

Menu: American breakfast items, burgers, fries, salads, sandwiches, steaks, pasta, chicken, soda, coffee, tea, juices

Notes: You may order your food to-go via their website: www.dennys.com.

TONY ROMA'S

1640 S Harbor Blvd, Anaheim, CA 92802

Description: A steakhouse made famous by its barbecue ribs recipe, Tony Roma's offers family-friendly dining. This location is right across from Disneyland's main gate and will satisfy those looking for an inexpensive but tasty steak.
Type: Steakhouse
Price: $$-$$$ / **Reservations:** Yes
Menu: steaks, ribs, salads, fries, soups, seafood, chicken, burgers, sandwiches, desserts, soda, coffee, tea, juices, alcoholic beverages
Recommendations: Try the baby back ribs

BUBBA GUMP SHRIMP CO.
321 W Katella Ave, Anaheim, CA 92802
Description: A seafood diner inspired by the film *Forrest Gump*. This is a lively dining experience that the entire family can enjoy. Waiters are very friendly and the food is delicious—especially if you like fried shrimp! Play trivia while you wait and use a unique "run Forrest run" or "stop Forrest stop!" call method to signal your waiter. There are plenty of items here for the entire family to enjoy. This location is about a 10-15 minute walk from the Disneyland Resort.
Type: Southern seafood diner with American favorites
Price: $$-$$$ / **Reservations:** Yes
Menu: seafood, burgers, fries, salads, ribs, chicken, steak, desserts, soda, coffee, tea, juices, alcoholic beverages
Recommendations: Shrimper's Heaven (coconut shrimp, bacon wrapped shrimp, crispy shrimp, and tempura shrimp with dipping sauces), Lava Flow (alcoholic beverage with piña colada, rum, and strawberry sauce)

THE CHEESECAKE FACTORY
321 W Katella Ave, Anaheim, CA 92802
Description: Located about 10-15 minutes walking distance from the Disneyland main gate, The Cheesecake Factory has an extensive menu. This restaurant doesn't take reservations and the line can be quite long during dinner hours, especially on the weekends. The restaurant lives up to its name with delicious cheesecake.
Type: Wide variety of American favorites
Price: $$$ / **Reservations:** No
Menu: burgers, fries, salads, ribs, chicken, steak, Asian, American, pasta, desserts, soda, coffee, tea, juices, alcoholic beverages
Recommendations: Chicken Madeira, Orange Chicken, any one of their famous slices of cheesecake

MORE DINING TIPS

QUICK DINING WITHIN WALKING DISTANCE

MCDONALD'S ($-$$)
1500 S Harbor Blvd, Anaheim, CA 92802
Distance from Disneyland: 5-10 minute walk
Description: Quick burgers, fries, and more from this classic fast food chain.

PANERA BREAD ($-$$)
1480 Harbor Blvd, Anaheim, CA 92802
Distance from Disneyland: 5-10 minute walk
Description: A cafe with sandwiches, soups, and salads.

SUBWAY ($-$$)
1770 S Harbor Blvd, Anaheim, CA 92802
Distance from Disneyland: 10-15 minute walk
Description: Custom sandwiches and sides made to order. Open 24 hours!

7-11 ($)
611 W Katella Ave, Anaheim, CA 92802
Distance from Disneyland: 10-minute walk
Description: Inexpensive snacks, drinks, and quick bites at this convenience store.

· **Magic Tips** ·
In-N-Out Burger is a local favorite, but unfortunately not within walking distance to Disneyland. The closest is located about 10-minutes away at 1168 State College Blvd, Anaheim, CA 92802. We recommend getting the Double-Double Cheeseburger and animal-style fries! Keep in mind that waiting 20 minutes for your order is typical.

SPECIAL DIETS

Disneyland recognizes that its guests have a wide variety of special dietary needs and desires. Though theme park food has a reputation for being unhealthy, this isn't always the case. Vegan and vegetarian options are available around the Disneyland Resort as well as gluten-free and dairy-free options.

If you have a food allergy or other dietary need, please inform your waiter. Often, they will ask if anyone at the table has a food allergy before taking orders. Your waiter will then ensure that your food is prepared as needed. Not all dietary requests can be met. For example, the corn dog batter may not be changed, same as with the churro mix—though you can ask for a churro without the sprinkles, if desired.

Quick-Service dining spots offer a wide selection of allergy-free options. For example, the Galactic Grill in Tomorrowland has an extensive selection of menu options for those with gluten, egg, fish/shellfish, milk, peanut, and/or soy allergies. These menu items are found on disneyland.com.

If you'd like to see an overview of options, we recommend stopping by City Hall in Disneyland at the start of your visit. Here, you can request an allergy guide with a list of substitutions offered around the park.

Vegetarians and vegans will be happy to know that many of the park's best snacks are plant-based. Dole Whip, Mickey Pretzels, cotton candy, and the milks served in Star Wars: Galaxy's Edge are all vegan-friendly options!

PACKING YOUR OWN FOOD

Disneyland allows guests to pack their own food and drink with certain guidelines. Coolers filled with ice aren't permitted within Disneyland Resort. This is a safety measure as banned items could be hidden inside of these coolers and making security dig through heaps of ice slows down the scanning process. Of course, if you need ice for medical purposes, this may be allowed. If you're planning on packing your own soda (which we recommend as bottles cost around $4 each at the parks), you can ask any Quick-Service dining location for a cup of ice to enjoy with your drink.

Disneyland also won't provide plates, utensils, or heating for your food (though those traveling with babies may use microwaves in the Disneyland Baby Center for infant food). We recommend bringing food you can keep cool with ice packs—which are allowed—and meals that don't require heating. Additionally, any of the condiments found outside of Quick-Service dining spots (like ketchup and mustard packets near the Little Red Wagon in Disneyland Park) are pretty much fair game for anyone inside the theme parks. Meaning, you can grab some of these to use with your food from home if needed.

Guests can use any of the Quick-Service seating areas to dine. Our favorites are the ones located at the Jolly Holiday Bakery Cafe on Main Street in Disneyland and the tables at Pacific Wharf in Disney California Adventure. There is also a designated picnic area in the Esplanade near the locker rentals by Disneyland's main gate.

· **Magic Tips** ·

A trip to Disneyland can require 10-15 miles of walking per day! This means that you should stay hydrated at all times to avoid fatigue. Bring your own water bottle into the Resort and replenish it at one of the many filtered refill stations in the parks. Water refill stations are located in Galaxy's Edge (near the Milk Stand and in the Marketplace), Tomorrowland (near Autopia), and by the Rancho del Zocalo Restaurant in Frontierland. If you forget your water bottle, you can ask for a free cup of water at a Quick-Service restaurant and refill it at these bottle fill stations.

CHAPTER THIRTEEN

MEETING CHARACTERS

INTRODUCTION

Character meets have been a long-running staple of Disney theme parks since Disneyland first opened in 1955. Decades later, the characters have stretched to Disney, Marvel, Pixar, and Star Wars franchises. Some of these characters roam the land, greeting guests casually throughout the day. The most popular characters will have special posts with queues that could last more than an hour on busy days!

Meeting characters is a surreal and sometimes awkward experience, but it's fun nonetheless. After all, it is a person dressed in a giant suit acting like an animated figure. We recommend just playing along, answering their questions if they are speaking characters, and snapping the photo you desire. Many will also take a selfie with you!

Even if you're not crazy about meeting characters, we recommend doing it. There's nothing more Instagram-able than a snapshot with a Disney icon. These types of photos make great free souvenirs and memories to last a lifetime.

Also keep in mind that if you've purchased the Disney Genie+, you will get digital professional photos by photographers who station themselves by characters. However, the roaming characters, like the ones found in Star Wars: Galaxy's Edge, may not have a special photographer.

· **Magic Tips** ·
We highly recommend using the Disneyland App for spotting characters. These will update daily as not every character appears each day.

MEETING CHARACTERS WITH KIDS

Kids are the most excited about meeting their favorite characters during their visit. Make time to introduce them to their top choices throughout your day. The characters are each trained to specially sign their name, so bring something to write on! Disneyland also sells autograph books in the shops on Main Street, U.S.A. (Buena Vista Street in DCA and the World of Disney in Downtown Disney also sell these). See how many character autographs you can collect in a day and keep the book for your next visit!

Character dining experiences are the easiest way to greet most of your favorites in a single sitting. Anywhere from 6-10 characters might greet your traveling party while you eat a scrumptious buffet. Most of these dining experiences happen during breakfast and reservations are recommended before visiting.

· **Magic Tips** ·
Social distancing guidelines could affect how and where characters appear. This could mean canceled parades, and character dining experiences, as well as changes in location throughout the parks.

CHARACTER DINING EXPERIENCES:

- **Goofy's Kitchen (Disneyland Hotel)** – Join Goofy and several Disney classic characters wearing chef costumes. This delicious dining event occurs during breakfast and dinner, so come hungry! Keep in mind that the breakfast buffet is about half the cost of the dinner version, so you may want to book early to save some cash.

- **Mickey's Tales of Adventure Breakfast Buffet** (Storytellers Cafe in Disney's Grand Californian Hotel) – Mickey and other classic characters join this scrumptious breakfast event. The characters will wear adventurous outfits.

- **Minnie & Friends Breakfast in the Park** (Plaza Inn at the Disneyland Park) – This event scores well for greets as many Disney characters appear in their traditional costumes. The food and service quality isn't as great as the Resort hotels and the cost is about the same. You can also meet most of these characters around Fantasyland with little wait times.

- **Disney Princess Breakfast Adventures** (Disney's Grand Californian Hotel) – Meet Disney Princesses, have story time, and take photos during this extra-paid morning event. Some of the characters will be dressed in ball gowns while others might wear their classic Disney costumes. Kids are encouraged to dress up, too! Keep in mind that this magical experience is a steep $125 per guest. We detail the Disney Princess Breakfast Adventures in our Visiting with Kids chapter.

Note: Reservations can be made for character dining experiences by using disneyland.com, the Disneyland mobile app, or by calling (714) 781-3463.

· **Magic Tips** ·
If you're staying near the Disneyland Resort, we recommend planning a character dining experience on a day you're not in the parks. This way you're also not wasting precious morning hours eating when you could experience shorter attraction waits instead. The hotel character breakfasts don't require a theme park ticket and many will validate parking for nearby lots. So maybe plan it for your arrival date or the a day you leave.

CHARACTER LOCATIONS

KEY
DL – Disneyland Park
DCA – Disney California Adventure Park
Δ – Rare Character
Characters are listed in alphabetical order

Δ **Aladdin** – Fantasyland (DL)
Alice – Fantasyland (DL)
Anna – Animation Academy in Hollywood Land (DCA)
Ant-Man – Avengers Campus (DCA)
Ariel – Royal Hall in Fantasyland (DL)
Aurora – Fantasyland (DL)
Δ **Baloo** – Adventureland (DL)
Baymax – San Fransokyo Square (DCA)
Belle – Princess Fantasy Faire (DL)
Bert (*Mary Poppins*) – Main Street & Fantasyland (DL)
Black Panther – Avengers Campus (DCA)
Black Widow – Avengers Campus (DCA)
Bo Peep – Pixar Pier (DCA)
Boba Fett – Tomorrowland (DL)
Buzz Lightyear – Pixar Pier (DCA)
Captain America (Steve Rogers) – Avengers Campus (DCA)
Captain America (Sam Wilson) – Avengers Campus (DCA)
Captain Hook – Fantasyland (DL)
Captain Marvel – Avengers Campus (DCA)
Chewbacca – Star Wars: Galaxy's Edge (DL)
Chip 'n Dale – Main Street (DL), Grizzly Peak (DCA)
Cinderella – Royal Hall in Fantasyland (DL)
Clarabelle Cow – Main Street, U.S.A. (DL), Mickey's Toontown (DL)
Cruella De Vil – Main Street, U.S.A. (DL)
Crush – *Turtle Talk with Crush* at Disney Animation (DCA)
Daisy Duck – Main Street, U.S.A. (DL), Buena Vista Street (DCA), Mickey's Toontown (DL)
Darth Vader – Star Wars Launch Bay in Tomorrowland (DL)
Doctor Strange – Avengers Campus (DCA)
Donald Duck – Main Street, U.S.A. (DL), Buena Vista Street (DCA), Mickey's Toontown (DL)

Eeyore – Critter Country (DL)
Edna Mode – Pixar Pier (DCA)
Elena – Fantasy Faire in Fantasyland (DL)
Elsa – Animation Academy in Hollywood Land (DCA)
Fairy Godmother – Fantasyland (DL)
Fancy Nancy – Hollywood Land (DCA)
Δ **Flynn** – Fantasy Faire in Fantasyland (DL)
Frozone – Pixar Pier (DCA)
Gamora – Avengers Campus near Guardians of the Galaxy (DCA)
Goofy – Goofy's Playhouse in Toontown (DL), Main Street, U.S.A. (DL), Buena Vista Street (DCA), Goofy's Kitchen (DL Hotel)
Groot (Adult) – Avengers Campus near Guardians of the Galaxy (DCA)
Hiro Hamada – San Fransokyo Square (DCA)
Δ **Horace** – Buena Vista Street (DCA)
Iron Man – Avengers Campus (DCA)
Jack Sparrow – New Orleans Square and Frontierland (DL)
Jack Skellington – New Orleans Square (DL, during Halloween and Holiday)
Δ **Jasmine** – Fantasyland (DL)
Jessie – Pixar Pier (DCA)
Joy – Pixar Pier (DCA)
Judy Hopps – San Francisco Street in Pacific Wharf (DCA)
Kylo Ren – Star Wars: Galaxy's Edge (DL)
Loki – Avengers Campus (DCA)
Lightning McQueen – Cars Land (DCA)
Mad Hatter – Fantasyland (DL)
Mandalorian & Grogu – Star Wars: Galaxy's Edge (DL)
Mary Poppins – Fantasyland (DL)
Mater – Cars Land (DCA)
Mickey Mouse – Main Street (DL), Mickey's Home in Toontown (DL), Buena Vista Street (DCA), Storytellers Café (Disney's Grand Californian Hotel)
Miguel – Frontierland (DL)
Mike Wazowski – Pixar Pier (DCA)
Minnie Mouse – Main Street (DL), Minnie's House in Toontown (DL), Buena Vista Street (DCA)
Δ **Moana** – Adventureland (DL)
Mr. Incredible – Pixar Pier (DCA)
Mrs. Incredible – Pixar Pier (DCA)
Mr. Potato Head (Audio-Animatronic) – Pixar Pier (DCA)
Δ **Naveen** – Frontierland (DL)
Nick Wilde – San Francisco Street in Pacific Wharf (DCA)

Olaf – Animation Academy in Hollywood Land (DCA)
Δ **Oswald** – Buena Vista Street (DCA)
Pete – Toontown (DL)
Peter Pan – Fantasyland (DL)
Δ **Phillip** – Fantasyland (DL)
Piglet – Critter Country (DL)
Pluto – Main Street (DL), Toontown (DL), Grizzly Peak (DCA)
The Queen (*Snow White*) – Fantasyland (DL)
Δ **Queen of Hearts** – Fantasyland (DL)
Rapunzel – Fantasy Faire in Fantasyland (DL)
Rey – Star Wars: Galaxy's Edge (DL)
Sandess – Pixar Pier (DCA)
Sally (*The Nightmare Before Christmas*) – New Orleans Square (DL, during Halloween and Holiday)
Snow White – Royal Hall in Fantasyland (DL)
Spider-Man – Avengers Campus (DCA)
Star Lord – Avengers Campus near Guardians of the Galaxy (DCA)
Stormtroopers – Star Wars: Galaxy's Edge (DL)
Δ **Sulley** – Hollywood Land or Pixar Pier (DCA)
Thor – Avengers Campus (DCA)
Tiana – Frontierland (DL)
Tigger – Critter Country (DL)
Tinker Bell – Pixie Hallow in Fantasyland (DL)
Vampirina – Hollywood Land (DCA)
Vi Moradi – Star Wars: Galaxy's Edge (DL)
Wasp – Avengers Campus (DCA)
Winnie the Pooh – Critter Country (DL)
Woody – Frontierland (DL), Pixar Pier (DCA)

MORE TIPS

1. During the holidays, Mickey & friends are often dressed in seasonal outfits (Halloween, Christmas, and other special days). Find them in the Town Square on Main Street, U.S.A.!
2. The Princess Fantasy Faire is the best way to take a photo with a Disney Princess.
3. Fantasyland characters typically appear in the early morning but may conclude their visits by 330pm.
4. New Marvel characters will debut in Avengers Campus as movies and shows are released.
5. Sadly, not every character comes out each day, though one of your favorites is sure to be there!

CHAPTER FOURTEEN

VISITING WITH KIDS

INTRODUCTION

The Disneyland Resort is known for being "The Happiest Place on Earth" and we truly believe that it is! Part of Walt Disney's vision was to provide a place for families to enjoy themselves with fun for everyone. Many of the rides at Disneyland are designed for the kid in us all, but this section is all about babies and kids.

We hear a lot of horror stories about parents visiting Disneyland with young kids and not having a great time. While the parks are designed with families in mind, it can still feel like a lot of chaos. This is why pre-planning your visit is more important when traveling with kids. The key is not to overdo it! Your trip should be all about fun, but packing too much into your schedule (or trying to "wing it") will likely end in misery. We recommend combing through this chapter and making a short to-do list (we offer a planning list in the back of this book, too). It's easiest to select the attractions, characters, and dining spots you'd like to try before the start of your visit. This will help make the trip feel like a win when you know what to expect.

BABIES AND TODDLERS

We hear a lot of parents asking if they should bring their baby to Disneyland. The answer is *yes*! Many parents love bringing their babies to the parks because Disneyland provides a stimulating and kid-friendly environment (people don't get mad if your baby cries because they are too busy having fun of their own). As we said earlier, we wouldn't recommend bringing a child of any age unless you know what to expect. To help better prepare you, we've compiled a helpful list of items to bring for your baby or toddler.

WHAT TO BRING

Protection from the Sun – We recommend sunscreen, hats, blankets, and a covered stroller to keep your little one safe.

Blankets and Warm Clothes – These items are essential for cooler days (or at night when the temperatures drop).

Diapers, Wipes, and a Change of Clothes – Just in case of a mess, a change of clothes can be a lifesaver.

Bottles and Formula – Don't forget the liners!

Baby Food – The Disneyland Resort will allow small glass jars as long as they contain baby food.

Backpack – This is for you to carry your baby's items. Sometimes you can hide these in a stroller, but just in case you leave your stroller for a ride, we recommend carrying your items with you.

Stroller – Disneyland prohibits double-wide strollers and stroller wagons of any kind. However, guests with special needs for their child may be able to bring a wagon into the parks. Strollers must be within 31" (79 cm) and 52" (123 cm) which is within the range of most store-bought strollers and tandem jogging strollers. Disneyland stroller rentals start at $18 a day ($36 for a double) at Guest Services. To save money, we recommend bringing your own stroller.

The Disneyland Baby Care Center
Just in case you forget something, Disneyland is equipped with nannies that are there to help. Get baby food, diapers, wipes, and medicine in these spots. They offer nursing rooms, changing tables, highchairs for feeding, a microwave, water, and more.

BABY CARE CENTER LOCATIONS

Disneyland – Main Street, U.S.A., next to First Aid.

Disney California Adventure – In Pacific Wharf, next to the Ghirardelli Store.

Changing Rooms – These are found in most restrooms (men and women).

Breast Feeding – Feeding your baby is a top priority and you shouldn't be nervous to do so at Disneyland. If you want privacy (or quiet), head to the Baby Care Centers in the parks.

First Aid – Located next to the Baby Care Center in Disneyland on Main Street, U.S.A.

Emergencies – If you experience an emergency, call 911.

NAVIGATING WITH BABIES AND TODDLERS

The Disneyland Resort is very large and spread out which can make traveling with kids a bit challenging. Strollers are essential to a successful trip as kids even as old as age 9 may feel tired and need a walking break. Strollers aren't allowed in lines for rides and some dining locations. Most lands in the theme parks have designated stroller parking spots while you wait in line or dine in restaurants. Cast Members regularly patrol these areas for safety.

Strollers are the most hassle when traveling from the parking structures and onto busses. You'll need to remove your child and then physically lift the stroller onto the bus. If this is too difficult, ask a nearby Cast Member for assistance. The monorails are similar and many parents complain that the tight walkways make mobility more challenging than the bus.

Within Disneyland, we recommend riding the Disneyland Railroad to move from distant lands (ie: Mickey's Toontown to Main Street, U.S.A.). This is a fun and easy way to get young kids to see a lot of the theme park without navigating through large crowds. Your child will need to sit on the train bench and your stroller must be folded to ride the Disneyland Railroad.

Keep in mind that if you rent a stroller from Disneyland, you won't be able to use it outside of the theme parks and the esplanade between them.

RIDES FOR BABIES AND TODDLERS

"it's a small world" (Fantasyland) – A gentle boat ride with colors and singing children.

The Many Adventures of Winnie the Pooh (Critter Country) – A slow ride through the story of Winnie the Pooh. See his friends from Tigger to Piglet in this cute and florescent ride.

Dumbo the Flying Elephant (Fantasyland) – Circle round while flying on Dumbo. This ride was designed for kids, but the line can be long.

Mickey's Toontown – Meet Mickey, Minnie, Donald, and Goofy in this toddler-friendly zone. Also a great place for kid-friendly meals.

Carousels: Jessie's Critter Carousel (California Adventure) and King Arthur's Carrousel (Disneyland) are two classic carousels, one in each park.

Jungle Cruise (Adventureland) – A slow moving boat through the African and Amazonian wilds.

Pirates of the Caribbean – A long, dark ride on a boat with two drops at the beginning. If you think these will startle your baby, it's best to avoid it.

Disneyland Railroad – An easy ride around the perimeter of Disneyland.

MORE TIPS

See a Show or Parade – With wonderful music and dancing characters, your baby or toddler will be delighted. Disney Junior: Live on Stage (California Adventure) is a live stage show designed for toddlers. Check the map for a schedule of shows and parades.

Don't Try to Do It All – Young kids can love Disneyland, but that doesn't mean they'll have the energy for a continuous, all-day outing. Space out rides and times waiting in line simple joys like looking at the baby ducks in the moat around Sleeping Beauty Castle or eat a snack under some shade.

Take a Break – As a parent you know that babies and toddlers can wear out fast. At the Disneyland Resort, this is no exception. Plan to go back to the hotel, hang under the shade of trees or umbrellas, or find the Baby Care Center for some peace and quiet. When your baby is ready to go again, head back to the park until he or she is spent.

RIDER SWITCH

Do you have a young child with you, but all of the older kids and adults in your party want to ride? Many Disneyland Resort rides give you the option to wait and switch places when finished. Keep in mind that Rider Switch can be used with Genie+ and Lightning Lane for attractions with both options!

DISNEYLAND RIDER SWITCH LOCATIONS

Autopia, Big Thunder Mountain Railroad, Gadget's Go Coaster, Indiana Jones Adventure, Matterhorn Bobsleds, Millennium Falcon: Smugglers Run, Space Mountain, Star Tours – The Adventures Continue

CALIFORNIA ADVENTURE RIDER SWITCH LOCATIONS

Incredicoaster, Goofy's Sky School, Grizzly River Run, Luigi's Rollickin' Roadsters, Radiator Springs Racers, Soarin', Mater's Junkyard Jamboree, Silly Symphony Swings, Jumpin' Jellyfish

· Magic Tips ·
Kids can usually ride again if it means that one parent would otherwise ride solo. For example, if you have a family of four with two adults and two kids, but "Kid Two" is too short/ scared to ride, use Rider Switch. "Kid One" will take turns riding with the adults during the exchange with "Kid Two" waiting nearby!

KIDS (AGES 3-9)

Since every kid is different, their interests with Disneyland may vary greatly. Many children love fast rides while others look forward to meeting their favorite characters. With so much to do at the Disneyland Resort, we've detailed how each attraction area fairs depending on your child's interest.

DISNEYLAND WITH KIDS

MAIN STREET, U.S.A.

This land is filled with souvenir shops and places to eat. We recommend checking out The Magic Shop to see all of the fun trinkets and old school magic tricks that you can purchase. The Emporium store is crammed with Disney souvenirs, but it can feel a bit claustrophobic with all of the people for a young kid. If you desire a slow-paced ride, hop on a horse-drawn street car and take a ride down Main Street. This option is especially popular for preschool-aged kids. To sweeten your Main Street experience, finish your tour at the Gibson Girl Ice Cream Parlor for a scoop!

Disneyland's character dining experience is at the end of Main Street. The Plaza Inn is home to heroes and villains alike with Peter Pan and Captain Hook ready to take photos with dining guests. We especially like this experience for families with young kids. The restless little ones might want to run around and the Plaza Inn is a spacious, family-friendly place for them to interact with half a dozen characters. Book a breakfast here to start your day off right or come for lunch and try the delicious fried chicken (also served at Carnation Cafe on Main Street).

We recognize that Main Street is often skipped over because of the beckoning Sleeping Beauty Castle. If you don't get to Main Street at the start of your Disneyland journey, it also looks fantastic at night when the lights are twinkling.

FANTASYLAND

This land has rides for all ages, but is especially geared towards kids. The Sleeping Beauty Castle is a must-see experience and if you purchased the PhotoPass (or Disney Genie+), look for a Disney photographer standing in front of the castle.

Disney Princess fans love the Fantasy Faire which is to the left of the castle as you face it. Kids can meet several of their favorites and watch a live show in a small theatre starring Disney Princesses.

In the center of Fantasyland are classic attractions like Peter Pan's Flight, Pinocchio's Daring Journey, Snow White's Enchanted Wish, Alice in Wonderland, and Mr. Toad's Wild Ride. These are all family-friendly "dark rides" with generally short lines. Peter Pan's Flight is the exception, as lines are rarely under 30 minutes.

More Fantasyland Attractions for Kids:

1. Storybook Land Canal Boats – A slow-moving guided boat ride around miniature sets from Disney movies.
2. Casey Jr. Circus Train – A slow-moving train ride through a green hillside and back.
3. Dumbo the Flying Elephant – Fly around and around while holding Dumbo's flying feather on this classic attraction.
4. Pixie Hollow – Meet Tinker Bell and her pixie friends.
5. Mad Tea Party – The classic Disneyland tea cups. You can control how fast you spin the tea cup by turning the wheel in the center.
6. The Matterhorn Bobsleds – If your child enjoys slower rollercoasters, the right side of the Matterhorn is less intense than the left. However, this ride does feature a scary Abominable Snowman. (Must be 42" / 107cm or taller)
7. Dining – If you're looking for dining away from the crowds, try the Red Rose Taverne. There are plenty of options for kids as well as indoor and outdoor seating.

CRITTER COUNTRY

We love this small, mostly kid-friendly land! Critter Country is home to Tiana's Bayou Adventure, but Winnie the Pooh and his friends also take residence here. Meet Tigger or go on the dark ride, The Many Adventures of Winnie the Pooh. We love this attraction because the line is generally very short even on crowded days. Plus, everyone digs the trippy Heffalumps and Woozles scene!

If your child isn't tall or brave enough to plunge down Tiana's Bayou Adventure, invite her or him to watch other guests drop from nearby. It's a lot of fun to see people's faces as they scream down the mountain.

The Hungry Bear Restaurant makes for a great dining spot, especially for large families. Grab a burger, wrap, or fries, and chow down at one of the many picnic tables (there are several kid meal choices as well). Most of the dining area is well shaded and has great views of the Rivers of America and Tom Sawyer Island.

ADVENTURELAND

This land is a jungle-themed area with a couple of great attractions with kids and families in mind. The Jungle Cruse is another popular attraction for all ages. Kids love the cheesy jokes and animatronics.

For kids looking for a thrill, take them on the Indiana Jones Adventure. It's a rough and scary ride, but the bravest kids will certainly boast that they chanced this one (must be 46"/117cm or taller to ride).

If you're looking for a healthier dining option, try the Bengal Barbecue. There are both meat and veggie skewers to try as well as juice drinks. For an added treat, wait in line for a soft serve pineapple Dole Whip. Kids usually like the floats with the pineapple juice at the bottom.

Many people believe that Adventureland is Disneyland's smallest area, but if you count the space taken by the Jungle Cruise, it's nearly the size of Tomorrowland. Adventureland's single walkway becomes crowded in the morning (especially if the park opens at 10am) and in the mid-afternoon as guests bustle to its popular rides. When the Indian Jones Adventure line is over an hour, the queue sometimes stretches into the walkways. To avoid this, ride Indiana Jones in the late morning, early afternoon, or after sunset.

MICKEY'S TOONTOWN

Toontown is a fun, wacky land with plenty for kids to do. There are rides, play houses, character meets, and colorful scenery. Take a picture with Mickey and Minnie Mouse in their interactive areas or visit play areas for kids including based on Donald Duck, Goofy, and more!

Rides include Roger Rabbit's Car Toon Spin, a family-friendly "dark ride" with a wheel to spin the car, and Chip & Dale Gadget Go Coaster, a short, family-friendly rollercoaster with a typically long line. There's also the zany Mickey and Minnie's Runaway Railway! This attraction is great for all ages as they travel around a cartoon world brought to life! Toontown is also filled with kid-friendly eateries with plenty of seating. You can purchase hot dogs, pizza, and kids meals that are specially designed for most hungry kids.

NEW ORLEANS SQUARE

This land is filled with great places to eat for those who enjoy Creole and French dining. Though these treats tend to please adults, kids might like to try a warm Mickey-shaped beignet at the Mint Julep Bar. Cafe Orleans also makes a great dining reservation for kids to people watch from its patio. This table service restaurant serves dishes like macaroni and cheese and chicken breasts for kids. The Blue Bayou restaurant is only a great choice if your child can sit still in a restaurant seat for an hour. The tables are fairly close together, so that often becomes distracting for little ones.

Rides like Pirates of the Caribbean and the Haunted Mansion can be hit or miss for kids ages 3-9. These rides can be a bit spooky and the drops on Pirates can often scare children. Since there isn't a height requirement, we've even taken babies on this boat ride. Some notice the drops (Haunted Mansion does not have drops), but most don't notice.

FRONTIERLAND

Jump into the Wild West in this land filled with runaway trains, cowboys, and plenty of space for families to eat. The classic kids attraction, Tom Sawyer Island, is now home to Jack Sparrow's Pirate's Lair. This island playground has bridges and hiding spots designed for kids of all ages. Most fun of all is taking a raft across the Rivers of America to the island and back.

Kids who like thrill rides or want to try a roller coaster should look to Big Thunder Mountain. Dubbed "the wildest ride in the wilderness," this quick-moving family-friendly rollercoaster only has a few small drops. Riders must be 40"/102cm or taller to experience this attraction. For dining, the Stage Coach Cafe is popular for its chicken nuggets and french fries—kids love them!

TOMORROWLAND

While this futuristic land is known for its thrilling rides like Space Mountain and Star Tours, Tomorrowland offers a variety of attractions for the entire family. Autopia has kids driving their own car and Buzz Lightyear Astro Blasters is a dark ride where you take on the evil Zurg with your laser blaster!

The Finding Nemo Submarine Voyage is a bit hit-or-miss for parents. If you have children that can sit still while waiting in line and on the ride, then this is a great match. You'll want to skip it if your child is feeling restless and unable to sit in a confined area for the nearly 14-minute duration of this ride. Personally, we'd choose a Fantasyland attraction like "it's a small world" over this one.

Space Mountain is a fine choice for kids who love roller coasters and are a height of 40"/102cm or more. However, we don't recommend this fast ride as a first roller coaster experience as its darkness can be too scary. Instead, try the Matterhorn or Big Thunder Mountain Railroad.

Alien Pizza Planet is a popular dining location for families. This cafeteria-style restaurant has everything from pizza, salads, pasta, sweets, and drinks with plenty of indoor and outdoor seating set to a *Toy Story* theme.

· Magic Tips ·
If you'd like to experience the Finding Nemo Submarine Voyage but worry that your child won't enjoy the tight space, ask a Cast Member near at attraction about the accessible room. It simulates taking guests through the ride!

STAR WARS: GALAXY'S EDGE

Even with all of its special details and massively immersive feel, Galaxy's Edge isn't Disney's best place for kids. Instead, we believe that this land was created for a growing population of young adults who frequent the parks each year.

Still, this doesn't mean that many kids won't enjoy themselves. If your child enjoys the rides, make sure to space out long wait times with sips of blue milk at the Milk Stand and maybe a trip to Oga's Cantina where they can try a sweet non-alcoholic beverage. Docking Bay 7 Food & Cargo is better for adventurous eaters as the mix of flavors don't alway appeal to picky eaters—even on the kids menu.

CALIFORNIA ADVENTURE WITH KIDS

BUENA VISTA STEET

This entry portal is filled with souvenir shops and places to eat. While there's not much to do for kids on Buena Vista Street, they might catch a glimpse of Mickey Mouse riding down on the Red Car Trolley! If you're looking for dining in the morning, head to the Fiddler, Fifer & Practical Cafe for a baked good from Starbucks Coffee.

AVENGERS CAMPUS

Marvel fans of all ages love Avengers Campus. Kids can meet their favorite superheroes including Spider-Man, Black Panther, Iron Man, and Captain Marvel. WEB Slingers: A Spider-Man Adventure is an interactive video game-like ride where kids can shoot webbing from their wrists just like Spidey! Pym Test Kitchen also has some great bites that both kids and adults will enjoy.

PIXAR PIER

A Pixar-themed land based on a California pier setting. Young kids will like Jessie's Critter Carousel and everyone will want to try the 3-D shooting game, Toy Story Midway Mania! Adventurous kids might want a crack at the swinging gondolas of the enormous Pixar Pal-A-Round Ferris wheel. If the swinging looks like too much for you, stand in line for a stationary gondola.

Brave kids enjoy the Incredicoaster, a classic boardwalk wooden coaster without the rickety feeling. Race along with the characters from Pixar's The Incredibles as you launch through this unique looping coaster (must be 48"/122cm to ride). Pixar Pier is home to several dining stands. Our favorite is the Adorable Snowman Frosted Treats that serves lemony soft serve in a cone.

PARADISE GARDENS PARK

A California-themed oceanside land with hit (and a miss) waterfront attractions. The Little Mermaid: Ariel's Undersea Adventure is a family-friendly slow-moving "dark ride" through the story and music of Disney's *The Little Mermaid*. Kids ages 3-9 will especially love this one! Older kids might want to try the Goofy's Sky School coaster, the bouncing Jumpin' Jellyfish, or the spinning Silly Symphony Swings. Each of these rides has a 42"/107cm height requirement (except for The Little Mermaid, which does not). At night, experience the World of Color, a stunning water show filled with Disney characters and color that makes a great ending to a day at Disney.

The Golden Zephyr is an odd, slow-moving ship that spins in circles on a cable. While toddlers might enjoy this one, it could be boring for older kids. For dining in Paradise Gardens Park, we recommend the Corn Dog Castle. Disney, after all, has the best corn dogs in the world!

CARS LAND

Set to the beautiful, mountainous landscape of Route 66, Cars Land is as breathtaking as it is fun for the entire family. Every ride in Cars Land is great for kids (though all have height restrictions). Mater's Junkyard Jamboree flicks and turns guests on a swinging track (must be 32"/81cm or taller to ride). Luigi's Rollickin' Roadsters has cars dancing and turning to the music. This ride is "trackless" so you never know where your car will move next (must be 32"/81cm or taller to ride).

The Radiator Springs Racers is Cars Land's premier attraction. Race along the stars of Pixar's *Cars* in this "dark ride" and thrill attraction combination (must be 40"/102cm or taller).

Cozy Cone Motel serves traffic cones filled with churros, drinks, soft-serve ice cream, queso, pretzel bites, frozen drinks, and popcorn. If you're looking to sit and eat, try Flo's V8 Cafe. This diner has plenty of indoor and outdoor seating and is open for breakfast, lunch, and dinner. Kids' dining options include a roast beef or turkey sandwich, and macaroni 'n cheese.

HOLLYWOOD LAND

From glamour, film studios, and decrepit buildings, this land captures the true spirit of Hollywood. For young kids, we recommend Monsters, Inc. Mike and Sulley to the Rescue! This "dark ride" is filled with vibrant colors and follows the story of Pixar's *Monsters, Inc*.

The Disney Animation Building has something for everyone. Young kids will love the hilarious, interactive show, Turtle Talk with Crush (from *Finding Nemo*), and older kids will enjoy drawing Disney characters at the Animation Academy and creating animation at the Sorcerer's Workshop. For dining, try a smoothie at Schmoozies or a hot dog at Award Wieners.

PACIFIC WHARF

A land reminiscent of San Francisco wharfs. This area is filled with food mainly aimed at adults, but most have great options for kids. We also like Pacific Wharf because it has ample seating for large families.

The Cocina Cucamonga Mexican Grill serves a chicken and rice toddler meal plus kids' meals with a bean and cheese burrito or chicken quesadilla. The Pacific Wharf Distribution Co. serves a toddler meal of cheesy macaroni, and a kids' meal of a turkey sandwich.

GRIZZLY PEAK

Venture into California's wilderness, complete with redwoods and roaring rapids, all surrounding a bear-shaped mountain. The Redwood Creek Challenge Trail allows kids to climb, play, and earn badges by completing tasks. This is a great way to burn off some of their pent up energy!

Older kids will like Soarin' Around the World, a hang glider simulation for the entire family. However, this ride is not recommended for those who don't enjoy heights or brief periods of darkness (must be 40"/ 102cm or taller). On hot days, get on board the Grizzly River Run. This raft-based rapids adventure ends in a giant splash (must be 40"/ 102cm or taller to ride)! The Smokejumpers Grill is an ideal choice for kids. Try their chicken nuggets!

MORE FUN FOR KIDS

DISNEY PRINCESS BREAKFAST ADVENTURES (when available)
If your kids love Disney Princesses, you may want to treat them to a special breakfast experience. The Disney Princess Breakfast Adventures series takes place on select dates at Napa Rose in the Grand Californian Hotel. This exclusive dining event comes with a 3-

course meal followed by an up-close experience with one of Disney's princesses.

Though this event comes with a hefty price tag of $125 per person, you're paying for more than just dinner and a show. This is a unique picture moment with special memories and keepsakes. Children receive an autograph book, pen, games, and plenty of delicious treats. Princesses including Tiana, Belle, Mulan, Jasmine, Aurora, Snow White, Rapunzel, Pocahontas, Ariel, and more might show up for the event! There's also a unique story time with a princess that's perfect for photo opportunities.

The food is delicious and appealing to adults, too. Items feel more like a gourmet brunch than breakfast and include fruit, pastries, mac & cheese, chicken and waffles, sliders, shepherd's pie, short ribs, and pork belly. Specialty cocktails called "Royal Morning Libations" are available starting at $15 each. These are concoctions themed after Disney Princess animated films (non-alcoholic options are available as well).

If you're still wincing at the price of this dining event, it's completely understandable. After all, the cost is around the same as a 1-day ticket to Disneyland. Think of this as a special occasion if you're looking for something extra memorable for young kids ages 3-8. The package also includes up to five hours of complimentary valet parking at the Grand Californian Hotel, which is plenty of time for this experience.

The Disney Princess Breakfast Adventures runs from 8am-12pm on select dates (usually Thursday through Monday). Tax and gratuity are extra, and prices are subject to change. Reservations can be made online at disneyland.com or by calling (714) 781-3463.

ADULT GUIDE

INTRODUCTION

The Disneyland Resort may be family-friendly but that doesn't mean it can't also be an adult retreat. From luxury hotels and fine-dining to thrill rides and a dive bar, the Disneyland Resort has plenty to entertain adults! In this section we outline grown-up activities from the best places to drink to avoiding families with children. Outside of a few restaurants, Disneyland Park does not serve alcohol. Disney California Adventure and Downtown Disney have many options for wine, beer, and cocktails (must be 21 years of age or older with a valid ID to consume alcoholic beverages).

THINGS FOR ADULTS

BARS AND DRINKS

Would it surprise you to hear that there is a Disney-themed dive bar at the Disneyland Hotel and that it's *awesome*? Check out our recommendations of the best places to drink while at the Disneyland Resort.

TRADER SAM'S ENCHANTED TIKI BAR – *Top Choice!*
Location: Disneyland Hotel (pool area)
Description: Island-themed dive bar.
Price: $$

Why We Recommend It: Dim lighting, air conditioning, and scraggly bartenders serve excellent drinks and bar food in this unique setting. Try a specialty cocktail or order a beer on draft. Certain drinks cause the room's volcanoes to erupt or a storm to brew!

· Magic Tips ·
Bring the kids in the daytime if you'd like! After 8pm, Trader Sam's is 21 and older only. There also is a secret menu including a delicious alcoholic Dole Whip!

LAMPLIGHT LOUNGE – *Top Choice!*
Location: Disney California Adventure, Pixar Pier
Description: Casual lounge with a full bar and extensive wine selection.
Price: $$
Why We Recommend It: A great place to take it easy and enjoy a specialty cocktail or glass of wine while inside of the park. The Lamplight Lounge is outdoors but covered, and has excellent views of the Pier. Get there early to avoid lines. The Lamplight Lounge is a popular destination, but before 11:30am, you can have a great snack of Lobster Nachos or other bar food and start drinking without the lines.

NAPA ROSE LOUNGE
Location: Disney's Grand California Hotel and Spa
Description: Casual lounge with a full bar and extensive wine selection.
Price: $$
Why We Recommend It: A wine-lover's Disneyland dream! The Napa Rose Lounge is perfect for taking a break from the rides as you sit back and relax while you sip wine or nibble on excellent appetizers.

NAPLES RISTORANTE E PIZZERIA OUTDOOR LOUNGE
Location: Downtown Disney
Description: Casual lounge.
Price: $$
Why We Recommend It: This open-seating lounge has delicious cocktails, wines, and beers with easy access from the Disneyland theme parks. Find the outdoor lounge just past the World of Disney Store in Downtown Disney.

CARTHAY CIRCLE ALFRESCO DINING
Location: Disney California Adventure, Buena Vista Street
Description: Casual lounge with a full bar and extensive wine selection.
Price: $$-$$$
Why We Recommend It: Enjoy a cocktail or a gourmet bit in this outdoor lounge.

RITA'S BAJA BLENDERS
Location: Disney California Adventure, Pacific Wharf
Description: A stand with delicious margaritas and sangria.
Price: $
Why We Recommend It: Order a Grand Margarita that you can carry with you around the park.

> · **Magic Tips** ·
> If you're carrying an alcoholic drink, you must finish or discard it before you ride an attraction. However, Disney allows you to drink while you're waiting in the queue.

WINE COUNTRY TRATTORIA
Location: Disney California Adventure, Pacific Wharf
Description: Wine and wine flights on a terrace.
Price: $$
Why We Recommend It: Excellent wine and magnificent views of Pacific Wharf.
Dining Package: Book a World of Color package and drink wine before watching the show from reserved seating (book at Disneyland.com or call 714-781-3463).

RESTAURANTS WITH ALCOHOL

DISNEYLAND PARK

- **Blue Bayou** – A small selection of beer, wine, and some specialty cocktails. You may only drink while inside the restaurant and may be limited on the number of adult beverages you order.

- **Carnation Cafe, River Belle Terrace, & Cafe Orleans** – Each have selections of wine, beer, and limited specialty cocktails
- **Oga's Cantina** – Located in Galaxy's Edge, Oga's has everything from beer to cocktails. We also highly encourage reservations, especially for midday visits.

DISNEY CALIFORNIA ADVENTURE

- **Bayside Brews** – Craft beer on draft and wine.
- **Carthay Circle Lounge** – Full bar with specialty cocktails.
- **Carthay Circle Restaurant** – Disney Family of Wines and
- cocktails.
- **Lamplight Lounge** – Full bar, cocktails, beer, and wine.
- **Mendocino Terrace** – Large selections of wines and beer.
- **Port of San Fransokyo Cervecería** – Find a variety of Karl Strauss beer
- **Pym Tasting Lab** – Avengers-themed cocktails and draft pours
- **Sonoma Terrace** – Wine and craft beer selection.
- **Wine Country Trattoria** – Wine and wine flights, cocktails, sangria, and domestic beer.

DOWNTOWN DISNEY

- **Ballast Point** – The ultimate adult hangout. Grab a beer that's been brewed on site or one of their delicious burgers.
- **Black Tap Craft Burgers & Shakes** – Specialty burgers and giant, shareable shakes.
- **Naples Ristorante e Pizzeria** – Specialty cocktails, wines, and domestic beer.
- **Jazz Kitchen** – Specialty cocktails.
- **Splitsville** – Known for its "cocktails on tap" and other spirits, Splitsville has a wide variety of beer, wine, and mixed drinks to try.
- **Tortilla Jo's** – Specialty Margaritas, beer, cocktails, and wines.

HOW TO AVOID CHILDREN

It's impossible to see absolutely no children at the Disneyland Resort, but you can avoid being around the bulk of them. We've noticed that children 10 and older are generally very well-behaved at Disneyland. You also may not notice them as they are excited and stimulated by the sights just like you will be. We've listed some great tips on how to stay clear of families with small children at the park:

1. **Visit Trader Sam's Enchanted Tiki Bar after 8pm.** No one under 21 is allowed in Trader Sam's at that time. You can drink from a full bar, eat, and lounge in this dive bar located in the Disneyland Hotel pool area (non-guests are allowed).
2. **Stay Away from Fantasyland and Mickey's Toontown.** These kid-friendly lands are typically filled with small children. If you'd like to avoid them, we recommend staying away at all costs. The Matterhorn Bobsleds are a great option as the height restriction keeps the tiny children at bay.
3. **Avoid Parades** as these attractions are like magnets for small children. You've been warned! Instead, ride an attraction during a parade. This is the best time to experience the Fantasyland attractions without the hoards of families with small children. Check the park map for parade times.
4. **Reserve a table at the Blue Bayou** in Disneyland. This restaurant is generally quiet and kid-free. The low, ambient lighting also makes it one of Disneyland's most adult-friendly atmospheres. Adults 21 and older can purchase drinks with alcohol here.
5. **Dine at a bar instead of a restaurant.** The Lamplight Lounge in California and Carthay Circle Lounge are two of many places in Disney California Adventure that are generally kid-free (or have far fewer children than other places).
6. **Stay away from Alien Pizza Planet** in Tomorrowland. This place is typically filled with kids eager to run around tables while they devour pizza.
7. **Pay attention to height requirements** because these restrictions instantly weed out small children. Rides like Indiana Jones Adventure, Space Mountain, Tiana's Bayou Adventure, and Guardians of the Galaxy are generally free of kids under 10.

8. **Visit the parks late.** Kids tend to get tired around sunset, so head to the parks in the late afternoon and watch them drop like flies. Some days,

Disneyland is also open until midnight!

DOWNTOWN DISNEY FOR ADULTS

There are many things to do in Downtown Disney that adults will love, from movies to shopping and even seeing a rock concert or a live DJ!

1. **Go Bowling** – Splitsville is a swanky and fun bowling alley that serves some very delicious dining options!
2. **Go Shopping** – Buy quality sandals at California Sole or makeup at Sephora.
3. **Lounge at Starbucks** – With free Wi-Fi and plenty of coffee, you can spend time on their massive patio as people stroll by.
4. **See a Free Concert** – Musicians love performing in Downtown Disney. They rent the stages and booths to perform nightly concerts. Check one out—dancing is encouraged!
5. **Fine Dine** – Book a reservation for Napa Rose at the Grand Californian for some elegant, fine dining. The menu here is exquisite—and so is the wine list!

MORE FUN

WALT'S MAIN STREET STORY TOUR

Take a walking tour through Main Street and make a special visit inside Walt's apartment above the Fire Station! This fascinating tour tells the story of how Main Street, U.S.A. came to be and gives some insight to how Walt saw his park. Pricing starts at $160 per guest.
Booking: https://disneyland.disney.go.com/events-tours/disneyland/walts-main-street-story-tour/

NON-RIDER TIPS

Since its inception, Disneyland's greatest guest pull has come from its rides. From roller coasters to kid-friendly dark rides, there are plenty of reasons one might enjoy visiting the park.

But what if you or your guest don't enjoy the drops, turns, and twists that come along with the rides? Are there things for you to do? Would you enjoy yourself at a theme park? Would a visit be worth the money? In short, is the Disneyland Resort for you?

Our answer is: YES! Most of Disney's attractions aren't rides at all. They are shows, sights to see, activities, character meets, dining, and more! Disneyland and Disney California Adventure are something to behold.

TOP SHOWS AND PARADES

1. Mickey's Mix Magic (Disneyland)
2. World of Color (Disney California Adventure)
3. Magic Happens Parade (Disneyland)
4. Fantasmic! (Disneyland)
5. Great Moments with Mr. Lincoln (Disneyland)
6. Laughing Stock Co. (Disneyland)
7. Fantasy Faire (Disneyland)
8. The Amazing Spider-Man! (Disney California Adventure)

THE BEST SLOW RIDES

These attractions don't have drops or move quickly at all. Here are some you may enjoy (in order):

1. **Explore the Disney Animation Building** (*California Adventure*)
2. **Peter Pan's Flight** (*Disneyland*) – See the story of *Peter Pan* while flying in a slow-moving pirate ship.
3. **Jungle Cruise** (*Disneyland*) – A humorous tour guide takes you on a riverboat through the Amazon and Africa.
4. **Alice in Wonderland** (*Disneyland*) – A classic "dark ride" through the story of Disney's *Alice in Wonderland*.
5. **The Little Mermaid ~ Ariel's Undersea Adventure** (*Disney California Adventure*) – A slow-moving "dark ride" that explores the story of Disney's *The Little Mermaid*.
6. **Haunted Mansion** (*Disneyland*) – A slow-moving "dark ride" through a haunted house.
7. **"it's a small world"** (*Disneyland*) – The classic, slow-paced boat ride around the world.
8. **Mr. Toad's Wild Ride** (*Disneyland*) – A slow-moving classic Disney dark ride.

SPECIAL EVENTS & MORE

INTRODUCTION

Throughout its history, Disneyland has hosted various special events to entertain guests in all-new ways. In 1957, Disneyland debuted a Date Nite that hosted fun experiences in the later park hours. There was dancing, live music, snacks, and of course, rides for visitors to enjoy.

Since then, Disneyland has hosted several more events, both day and night. Some of these experiences occur during regular park hours, while others, like Halloween parties, are separately ticketed events after the theme parks close.

DISNEYLAND AFTER DARK

In 2018, Disneyland returned its "Date Nite" concept with Disneyland After Dark. These separately ticketed after-hours parties are usually hosted during the off-season, January through May. During Disneyland After Dark, guests can meet rare characters, see special shows (sometimes fireworks), dance to live DJs or bands, pose in photo ops, order specialty snacks, and more! Some attractions may not be available during the evening, like Star Wars: Rise of the Resistance (the ride is usually open during Star Wars Nite). In addition, those who attend may dress in costume!

Though Disneyland After Dark events rotate from year to year, some have become increasingly popular. For example, the Valentine's Day party, Sweethearts' Nite, started off with a couple of dates in February and grew to seven nights in 2023. Though

Disneyland may not host the same After Dark events annually, here are a couple of repeated ones:

SWEETHEART'S NITE
Sweethearts' Nite is a romantic time at Disneyland Park from the end of January through mid-February. See projections on Main Street U.S.A., watch fireworks, try Valentine's Day snacks, dance with Disney Princesses, and more! While entertainment may be available each year, this event always sells out. Expect ticket sales to drop in November or December the year before.

STAR WARS NITE – Celebrate "May the 4th" with memorable Star Wars experiences at Disneyland Park in May. Meet rare characters, pose in photo ops, and watch fireworks based on the Star Wars franchise. For example, in 2023, guests could pose with Queen Amidala and Anakin Skywalker. While experiences change yearly, expect tickets to open up early in 2024.

· Magic Tips ·
If you're attending an After Dark event, we recommend placing a mobile order earlier to secure your snacks, as lines can get long. However, if there are fireworks, you only have to arrive 20 minutes beforehand to snag a great spot.

OOGIE BOOGIE BASH

Celebrate Halloween at Disney California Adventure during this separately ticketed event! Meet rare characters, get free candy, chat with villains, see the Halloween-style Frightfully Fun Parade, and more. Disney California Adventure comes to life with spooky villains, including Oogie Boogie from the Nightmare Before Christmas! One of the best surprises of the night is an enchanted garden walkthrough, Villains Grove. Disneyland describes it as a stroll through the dreams of Disney villains using lighting effects, fog, projections, sounds, and even scents!

Oogie Boogie Bash tickets sell out quickly! There are usually over two dozen dates, and tickets are gone in just a few hours because each night has limited crowds. Disneyland usually begins ticket sales around the end of June and will announce these dates on its social media channels.

· **Magic Tips** ·
All after hours events usually have limited crowds. Though you may pay $120 or more for a ticket, its worth paying more for a lot of folks to have shorter ride wait times. Some of the popular rides have longer lines earlier in the event but become much shorter later on.

FESTIVALS

Throughout the year, Disney California Adventure throws several festivals. These events usually have limited-time entertainment, food, and unique attractions. The celebrations also occur during regular park hours, so no extra ticket is needed to enjoy them.

LUNAR NEW YEAR CELEBRATION

Running from January through February, this event hosts special character meets, Asian cuisine, arts and crafts, decor, and more! In 2024, Disneyland will celebrate the Year of the Dragon with special character ambassadors. You'll find several marketplace kiosks around the park selling tasty Asian-inspired food. In addition, guests can watch Mulan's Lunar New Year processional, a short parade that runs through Disney California Adventure.

FOOD & WINE FESTIVAL

In the spring, try delicious bites and pours inspired by California cuisine! Several restaurants and kiosks throughout Disney California Adventure serve new takes on favorite dishes. The menu changes annually, but the original Soarin' Over California usually returns for the event.

DISNEY FESTIVAL OF HOLIDAYS

During the holiday season from mid-November through early January, see the festive decor and snacks at Disney California Adventure. Guests can enjoy new takes on holiday food at marketplace kiosks. In addition, the Holiday Toy Drummers and Disney Viva Navidad! street party entertains guests in Paradise Gardens Park.

GUESTS WITH DISABILITIES

The Disneyland Resort is constantly improving to make itself better accessible to all visitors. Though their accessibility isn't perfect, there are several ways that guests with disabilities can experience the attractions with ease.

RESOURCES

All accessibility resources can be found at Disneyland Guest Relations located outside and to the right of Disneyland Park's main gate. For more information about Guest Services for those with disabilities, visit: **https://disneyland.disney.go.com/guest-services/guests-with-disabilities**.

MOBILITY

Guests with mobility challenges may want to bring their own wheelchair or Electronic Conveyance Vehicle (ECV). In 2019, the Disneyland Resort underwent project Pixie Dust which widened pathways thus making moving around via ECV easier. For those wishing to rent a transport, manual wheelchairs are $12 per day and ECVs are $50 at Guest Services.

Disneyland also provides accessible parking for those with disabilities. Parking structures and lots will have signage directing guests to these locations.

DISNEYLAND DISABILITY PASS

Disneyland has its own dedicated Disability Access Service simply known as DAS. Disney designed this system for guests who cannot wait in conventional queues or stand in the lines. DAS works similarly to Genie+, allowing guests and their traveling party to return at a different time for riding within the Disneyland app. Disneyland Cast

Members determine which guests get the DAS pass. Simply having a wheelchair will not automatically grant you access to the DAS.

To register for the DAS pass, check in with Guest Relations (booths found at City Hall at Disneyland and the Chamber of Commerce in Disney California Adventure, as well as other spots around the park that sometimes change). They may ask for specifics about your needs to determine if DAS is right for you. If selected, you may need the tickets of each member of your party to list them in your traveling group. Since many Disneyland attractions accommodate guests with wheelchairs and other accessibility vehicles, not everyone will be granted the DAS pass. Each pass expires about two months after the first use, but guests can reregister on a later date.

Using DAS is easy and uses the Disneyland app! You'll be able to scan your mobile device to access rides, similarly to how Genie+ works. Instead of waiting in line, you'll be offered a return time that essentially holds your place in the queue for your party. Restrictions may only allow guests to experience one line at a time.

· Magic Tips ·

Guests with DAS can also use products like Genie+ and Lightning Lane. At times, DAS return times can be longer than the Lightning Lane system, so you may want to use both, depending on your ability to wait in a queue. Some rides like those found in Fantasyland will not have DAS return times. Instead, you'll likely be granted quick access onto the ride without the wait.

HEARING ACCESSIBILITY

For those with difficulties hearing, Disneyland's Guest Relations distributes Assistive Listening Systems for a $25 deposit, refundable upon return. Select attractions and shows will work with these devices in both theme parks.

For those in need of a sign language interpreter, select shows at both theme parks will have these during certain showtimes. A display of dates and times for interpreters can be found at the following link: https://disneyland.disney.go.com/guest-services/hearing-disabilities.

GUESTS WITH LIGHT AND OTHER STIMULUS SENSITIVITIES

The Disneyland Resort is a vibrant place with sunny skies, brightly colored buildings, and dazzling shows. Most of the stage shows and rides use theatrical production effects to bring storylines to life. The environments within the parks often contain flashing lights and special effects, especially at night. Keep these in mind if someone in your traveling party has these sensitivities. Children with disorders and syndromes with light and stimulus sensitivities may need special caution before entering the theme parks.

SERVICE ANIMALS

Disneyland welcomes guests and their trained service animals. However, the guest must be in charge of their service animal at all times. Cast Members are not permitted to assist with your animal regardless of the situation. Most rides don't allow for service animals. Guest Relations has an updated list of attractions that restrict service animals. Animals are permitted for potty breaks around the Resort, but Disneyland asks that the owners clean up afterward

HOTELS

The Disney on-property hotels have accessible rooms for those who need them. During the booking process, check the box for "accessible rooms" before searching. These rooms detail wheelchair and hearing accessibility depending on your selection.

· **Magic Tips** ·

If you're traveling with a guest who has a disability, we highly recommend pre-planning your trip based on proximity. Instead of carefully following our touring list, plan to experience rides closer together. This will prevent moving through many crowds and ultimately improve your over all experience. Even if you're granted a DAS pass, creating a list of rides and attractions based on proximity will help better complete your day.

CHAPTER SEVENTEEN

HIDDEN MICKEY LOCATIONS

INTRODUCTION

It's no secret that Walt Disney loved his cartoon mouse, Mickey. Ever since he created the character in the 1920s, Mickey has found his way into nearly every piece of Walt Disney's creations from films to logos to theme parks. Now, you may not have noticed Mickey Mouse in Disney's *Cinderella* or *Aladdin* animated films, but his image shows up in brief, hidden ways. You know that famous logo of the Mickey ears? It's just three circles, a large one for the face and two smaller ones for the ears. Well, these show up *everywhere*, from the bubbles while Cinderella scrubs the floors to a quick scene where Jasmine's pet tiger, Raja, changes briefly into a Mickey-like head. Even Disney's smash-hit *Frozen* has a Mickey doll in a bookcase in one of the scenes. But like we said, Mickey doesn't just show up in the films—he's also all over the parks. These often hard-to-spot images of him are called "Hidden Mickeys" because, well, they're hidden!

But why? Think of Hidden Mickeys as a nod to Walt, the creator and spirit of Disneyland. They also act as a secret and special treat for the guests. Finding Hidden Mickeys is a fun way to pass the time while waiting in lines or exploring the theme parks. Downtown Disney also has Hidden Mickeys!

In this exciting chapter, we reveal dozens of Hidden Mickeys all around the Disneyland Resort. From Disneyland to California Adventure, they are everywhere! How many can you spot?

DISNEYLAND

1. **Adventureland** – On the Jungle Cruise, check out a cast iron pan with a familiar shape inside of it.
2. **Adventureland** – The Adventureland Bazaar is home to a Hidden Mickey. Look for a Mickey head on a wall inside of a wooden circle.
3. **Adventureland** – The Indiana Jones Adventure has a Mickey hidden in its hieroglyphs on the well cover. This one is hard to spot!

4. **Critter Country** – In the Many Adventures of Winnie the Pooh ride, look for a Mickey hat near Pooh's honey bottles as he falls asleep in his room.

5. **Fantasyland** – While riding "it's a small world" look for a character in a hot air balloon. A hidden Mickey is painted on the fabric of the balloon.
6. **Fantasyland** – On the Alice in Wonderland ride, keep your eyes open for a hidden Mickey in red paint splashed on one of the Queen's hedges.
7. **Fantasyland** – While climbing aboard the Storybook Land Canal Boats, look for Hidden Mickeys painted on the floral designs.
8. **Fantasyland** – When starting the wait for Peter Pan's Flight, look up to a window with toys. A Hidden Mickey is located in the teddy bear's paw.
9. **Fantasyland** – On King Arthur's Carrousel, a horse named Jingles has three jewels in the shape of a Mickey head.
10. **Fantasyland** – When waiting in line to meet Tinker Bell in Pixie Hollow, look for the "Fairies Welcome" sign. On the post, you'll see a Mickey head carving.
11. **Fantasyland** – Mr. Toad's Wild Ride has a Hidden Mickey in the corner of the stained glass window. You'll see this door right after the suit of armor falls.
12. **Fantasyland** – Look for a wooden Mickey head at the top of the pirate ship in Pinocchio's Daring Journey toward the end of the ride.

13. **Frontierland** – The Golden Horseshoe stage has a Hidden Mickey in one of the vents at the bottom of the stage.
14. **Frontierland** – At the top of the Mark Twain Riverboat, look for a Mickey head in the iron bars next to the smokestacks.

15. **Frontierland** – In the Rancho del Zocalo Restaurante, look for a Hidden Mickey near the condiments.
16. **Frontierland** – On Big Thunder Mountain, look for three large gears that are shaped like a Mickey head.

17. **Main Street, U.S.A.** – In City Hall, look for a painting with Mickey Mouse holding a child's hand. On the other side is a man in a white t-shirt. On the back of his shirt is a Hidden Mickey.
18. **Main Street, U.S.A.** – In the Main Street Magic Shop, a Hidden Mickey is made out of white trick rope in a display case.
19. **Main Street, U.S.A.** – Just after you enter the Main Street Magic Shop, look on the ceiling for a card with a Hidden Mickey in the center!
20. **Main Street, U.S.A.** – If you wander the corners of Main Street, you'll see the Disneyland Casting Agency. The sign for the agency has two Hidden Mickeys at the top and one at the bottom, made of gold leaf.
21. **Main Street, U.S.A.** – The Market House has an iron decoration with Mickeys around the rim.

22. **New Orleans Square** – The famous Blue Bayou restaurant has stained glass in its lobby. Look to the top and spot three circles of glass in the shape of a Mickey head.
23. **New Orleans Square** – During the Haunted Mansion, look for the ballroom scene with the ghosts. On a table, there are three plates together in the shape of Mickey's head.
24. **New Orleans Square** – When you first splash down in Pirates of the Caribbean, look for a beach with crabs. You'll spot three shells in the sand in the shape of a Mickey head.
25. **New Orleans Square** – Pirates of the Caribbean has a difficult-to-spot Hidden Mickey in the final area. As the pirates fire shots at one another, look to the left for gold armor hanging on the walls behind the barrels of explosives. In the center of the gold armor chest plate is a Hidden Mickey.

26. **Tomorrowland** – Buzz Lightyear's Astro Blasters has a hidden Mickey on the Scrabble-like wooden blocks in the first room.
27. **Tomorrowland** – Little Green Men Store Command, when you exit Buzz Lightyear's Astro Blasters, has a Hidden Mickey surrounded by rings at the top of the displays.
28. **Tomorrowland** – The speakers for Space Mountain on the seats are in the shape of a Hidden Mickey.

29. **Tomorrowland** – When in line for Star Tours – The Adventures Continue, look for a Hidden Mickey on C-3PO's top display monitor.

30. **Star Wars: Galaxy's Edge** – The back of Docking Bay 7 Food & Cargo has a Hidden Mickey blasted onto the wall. Look for three laser hits in the shape of the famous mouse!
31. **Star Wars: Galaxy's Edge** – In the queue for the Millennium Falcon: Smugglers Run ride, look for a monitor with Hondo Onaka giving you flight instructions. On the side of the monitor are bolts in the shape of a Hidden Mickey!
32. **Star Wars: Galaxy's Edge** – In the Millennium Falcon: Smugglers Run ride, look at the top of the cockpit in the center of the space to see a Hidden Mickey!
33. **Star Wars: Galaxy's Edge** – In Oga's Cantina, look directly at DJ R-3X's face and you'll see that his mouth and eyes look like a Hidden Mickey!

CALIFORNIA ADVENTURE

34. **Buena Vista Street** – The black alarm bell in Oswald's Filling Station has Mickey ears.
35. **Buena Vista Street** – The Five & Dime Band's car has Hidden Mickeys on the tire rubber.
36. **Buena Vista Street** – Elias & Company's men's department has iron bars in the shape of Mickey heads.
37. **Buena Vista Street** – Julius Katz & Sons' display window has Mickey-shaped watch parts.

38. **Cars Land** – Look at the power lines in the land and you might see a cable in the shape of Mickey!
39. **Cars Land** – In the line for Radiator Springs Racers, look for three circular cacti in the shape of Mickey's head.
40. **Cars Land** – The Radiator Springs Racers have a Hidden Mickey in the projections on the walls when the tractors tip.
41. **Cars Land** – Look for a Mickey in the paint on the red tool shed with wheels right after Guido's Casa Della Tires.
42. **Cars Land** – Mater's Junkyard Jamboree has a Hidden Mickey made of hubcaps in the top corner of the queue.
43. **Cars Land** – Look for three barrels at the edge of Mater's Junkyard Jamboree. They are placed to look like a Mickey Head (the red barrel is his face).
44. **Cars Land** – When taking a photo with Mater, check out the shape of the screw on his hood!
45. **Cars Land** – At the back of Cars Land, look for the power line just above the "Spark Plugs" sign. You'll notice that the down swinging line is looped like a Mickey head.
46. **Cars Land** – In the windows of Ramone's Body Shop, look for car hoods with tiny Hidden Mickeys painted on them!

47. **Grizzly Peak** – During Soarin' Around the World, look for three hot air balloons to make a Hidden Mickey.

48. **Hollywood Land** – Outside of the Animation Building, look for a Mickey Head at the top of the flagpole.
49. **Hollywood Land** – If you're looking for an easy-to-spot Mickey, go into the Sorcerer's Workshop in the Animation Building. There, you'll spot Mickey-shaped balloons at the drawing station.
50. **Hollywood Land** – In the line for Monsters Inc. Mike & Sulley to the Rescue! look for the yellow cabs in the artwork on the televisions that have upside-down Hidden Mickeys near the grill.

51. **Hollywood Land** – The Monsters Inc. ride also has a furry Sulley animatronic that has a purple spot in the shape of Mickey's head on his bottom.

52. **Avengers Campus** – Some of the spatter marks around the Guardians of the Galaxy tower create the shape of a Mickey.
53. **Avengers Campus** – In the queue for WEB Slingers, look for a spider-bot crawling behind a vent. Occasionally, its blue lights will illuminate a Hidden Mickey.

54. **Paradise Gardens Park** – The Little Mermaid ~ Ariel's Undersea Adventure has a Hidden Mickey in the shape of barnacles on the mural when loading into the clam shells.
55. **Paradise Gardens Park** – The pole of the Jumpin' Jellyfish has a Hidden Mickey painted on it.
56. **Paradise Gardens Park** – Goofy's Sky School has a Hidden Mickey on the wrench toward the exit.

57. **Pixar Pier** – Toy Story Midway Mania has Jessie and friends in three circles that make up a Hidden Mickey. Spot this when you're loading for the ride.

58. **San Fransokyo Square** – Some of the street art (graffiti) in the land have hidden Mickeys sprayed into the lettering.

DOWNTOWN DISNEY

59. **Kiosks** – Almost all of the kiosks have Hidden Mickeys in the metalwork!
60. **Marceline's Confectionary** – The swirling "M" and "C" of the logo form a mouse head.
61. **World of Disney** – This store is a gold mine of Hidden Mickeys! Scan the murals, statues, and railings for Hidden Mickeys. To start, look for the blue Mickey head at the top of the World of Disney sign.

CHAPTER EIGHTEEN

DISNEYLAND SECRETS

INTRODUCTION

Over the past 60 years, The Disneyland Resort has garnered its share of legends and myths. Some speak of cats roaming the grounds at night while others worry about ghosts that come out after dark. Could any of these legends be true? You may be surprised to know that many of these myths are heavily based on reality. In fact, some of the craziest myths of them all could be completely real! While many of the rumors might just be material of the imagination, we'll pick them apart and tell you the facts. This section contains a list of some of the most popular myths surrounding the Disneyland Resort.

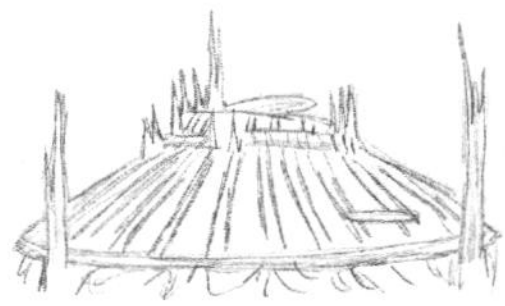

DISNEYLAND LEGENDS

JUNGLE CRUISE MAPS

The Legend: At the end of the Jungle Cruise ride you can ask for a free map.

Reality: Fact!

Notes: Unlike the "death certificate," this one is real! After unloading from the Jungle Cruise boat, you can ask a Cast Member for a free map. These, however, are a bit difficult to get. If you desire a free map of the Jungle Cruise river, head to the ride at the start of the day.

As soon as you leave the ride, ask a Cast Member at the exit for a map. Many times, they run out of these in the early morning.

PIRATES OF THE CARIBBEAN SKULL

The Legend: Inside the ride, on the headboard of the treasures room is a real skull and bones. Some of these bones were taken from the UCLA Medical Center.

Reality: Likely fiction

Notes: While it's crazy to think that a real person's bones could be buried inside of the ride, it appears that this is a work of fiction. We believe if there is any fact in it, the bones may have been cast from actual ones, but they are not real. Disneyland hasn't confirmed this, so we may never truly know!

DISNEYLAND BIRTH

The Legend: If a child is born in the park, he or she will get a lifetime membership to Disneyland.

Reality: Fiction

Notes: In 1979, a baby girl was accidentally born at Disneyland (the first person ever born at the park). Today, it remains just a myth that she was ever given a free lifetime membership to the park. She did get her photo taken with Mickey and his friends! Expectant mothers are advised to induce labor elsewhere.

Fact: Since its opening, four babies have been born at the Disneyland Resort. All of them have been girls!

THE MATTERHORN BASKETBALL COURT

The Legend: Inside of the Matterhorn is a half basketball court.

Reality: Fact!

Notes: In the early days of Disneyland, the Matterhorn had mountain climbers that would scale it to entertain guests. A basketball hoop was placed inside of the mountain to keep the the climbers busy when they weren't working. Unfortunately, this cool piece of Disney memorabilia is not open to guests.

TOMORROWLAND EDIBLE PLANTS

The Legend: All of the plants are edible.

Reality: Fact!

Notes: Look for beautiful cabbages, herbs, cornstalks, and fruit trees all over Tomorrowland. The area's theme is a "space colony," which is why the plants might need to be edible for the future. While not every part of these plants are edible (they could be trees that bear fruit), Disneyland recommends that you please admire them without touching.

DISNEYLAND CATS

The Legend: Disneyland is home to dozens of cats that roam the grounds at night.

Reality: Fact!

Notes: Cats indeed run about the park and sometimes you can see them wandering at night! The cats are well-fed and encouraged to stay there to keep down the population of rats that might otherwise infiltrate the park. During the day, the cats go behind the scenes to rest up before starting their late-night prowling.

"ANDY'S COMING!"

The Legend: If you yell "Andy's coming!" to the costumed characters of Pixar's *Toy Story*, they will all instantly drop and freeze.

Reality: No longer fact

Notes: Videos on the internet suggest that this was once true, but they don't do this anymore. It's not recommended to yell "Andy's coming" at the characters as it won't work.

WALT'S APARTMENT

The Legend: Walt Disney kept a private apartment in the Disneyland Park.

Reality: Fact!

Notes: You can see it on Main Street, U.S.A., just above the firehouse. These seasonal backstage tours take guests inside of this space that is now a small museum dedicated to the visionary.
To book a tour, call (714) 781-8687.

TATTOOS ARE BANNED FROM DISNEYLAND

The Legend: Guests must cover up all tattoos before entering the park.

Reality: Fiction

Notes: Though magazines have published that Disneyland bans tattoos, this is completely false. In fact, you'll see many, many guests with tattoos from head to toe—many of them Disney related! The only rule is that tattoos that are offensive or contain nudity must be concealed. Cast Members are also allowed to show certain tattoos.

WALT DISNEY IS FROZEN

The Legend: Walt Disney is cryogenically frozen at the Disneyland Park and will be reanimated in the future when he can be cured.

Reality: Fiction
Notes: Walt Disney was a private man, so the public wasn't privy to the details surrounding his death. Walt's grave is located in Glendale, California at the Forest Lawn Memorial Park, right across from the studio where many of Disney's most famous movies have been filmed or animated.

$1 TICKETS
The Legend: When Disneyland first opened, an adult ticket was just a buck!
Reality: Fact!
Notes: It's true that when the Disneyland Park first opened in 1955, admission for an adult was only a buck—and 50 cents for kids! Now, you might argue that with inflation that's not a big variance. However, it is! $1 in 1955 works out to about $8.85 in today's money. Considering that an average Disneyland ticket is over $100, that's a huge pricing difference (also keep in mind that there are many more attractions these days).

DISNEYLAND GHOSTS
The Legend: Close to a dozen ghosts haunt the grounds of Disneyland after the guests have gone home.
Reality: Unconfirmed
Notes: It depends what you believe, but many Cast Members have reported seeing strange apparitions late at night after the guests have gone. Disneyland attempts to keep these ghost stories alive to entertain guests. For instance, they posted a video on YouTube showing a Cast Member in the former Twilight Zone Tower of Terror ride and a ghostly figure flickering in an empty seat. It was later discovered to be a thing of Disney magic. Someone also supposedly died of fright when Disney first opened The Haunted Mansion in the 1960s, so the designers had to reimagine the ride to make it a lot less frightening. To this day, that deceased guest's ghost is said to live within the walls of the attraction.

FAMOUS PIRATES
The Legend: Johnny Depp has dressed as Captain Jack Sparrow and greeted guests riding on Pirates of the Caribbean.
Reality: Fact!
Notes: After Disney installed life-like animatronic Jack Sparrow in the ride, rumors swirled that sometimes Johnny Depp was actually there when he felt like strolling down to Disneyland and sneaking into the ride. This previous legend soon became a reality. A month before the

release of the film, *Pirates of the Caribbean: Dead Men Tell No Tales*, Johnny Depp dressed as Jack Sparrow and surprised guests riding Pirates at Disneyland. If you want to see this, there are several videos of him in character on the ride circulating YouTube.

DISNEYLAND
SECRETS & FAST FACTS

1. **Great Towns Look Alike**
   Main Street, U.S.A. pulls its American charm from the real-life town of Marceline, Missouri—Walt Disney's hometown!

2. **What's That Heavenly Smell?**
   Disneyland pumps the scent of baking sweets onto Main Street, U.S.A. This helps bring to life the small town vibe as well as make your mouth water for some Disney delicacies!

3. **Lucky Numbers**
   Disneyland is located at 1313 Harbor Blvd. Why 13? Well, "M" is the thirteenth letter in the alphabet, so two 13s make "M M" as in Mickey Mouse!

4. **Churro King**
   Disneyland sells about 3.8 million churros a year! That's more than 10,000 every day!

5. **Famous Cast**
   Before becoming an international celebrity, actor Steve Martin worked at the Magic Shop on Main Street!

6. **The Real Draw**
   The Sleeping Beauty Castle's drawbridge is real and it works! It's only been lowered twice in the park's history: once on opening day in 1955 and a second time when New Fantasyland debuted in 1983!

7. **Forced Fireworks**
   The famous Disney fireworks always launch from behind Sleeping Beauty Castle in order to make the castle look larger!

8. **Heavy Celebration**
During Disneyland's 60th anniversary celebration, giant diamond decorations were placed on Sleeping Beauty Castle. These diamonds were so heavy that it actually made the castle sink a little into the ground!

9. **Horsing Around in Style**
Of the many horses on the King Arthur's Carrousel, one stands out the most. "Jingles" is the leading horse of the ride and she can be identified by her white coat, golden beads and saddle, and the crown on top of her head!

10. **A Golden Year**
During Disneyland's 50th Anniversary, "Jingles" was painted completely gold to celebrate the occasion!

11. **Cruise Zoo**
During the planning stages of Disneyland, Walt wanted to use real animals in the Jungle Cruise. After talking with wildlife experts who warned Walt that most of the animals would sleep during the day, he opted for animatronics.

12. **Not So Deep**
Attractions like Rivers of America and Jungle Cruise display deep-looking rivers. The water is shallower than it seems as special dye makes it appear deeper!

13. **Mouse Island**
Tom Sawyer Island was originally planned to be Mickey Mouse Club Island! However, Tom Sawyer fit better with the Frontierland theme.

14. **What's Poppin?**
The various snack carts around Disneyland have small figurines that appear to churn popcorn. These figurines are called Roasty-Toasties and are different in each land. Which ones can you spot?

15. **Name That Tune**
The Sherman Brothers wrote "The Tiki, Tiki, Tiki Room," the official theme song to the Enchanted Tiki Room!

16. **Eeyore the Adventurer**
When the Indiana Jones Adventure ride was being constructed,

the former Eeyore parking lot was closed to make room. A parking lot sign with the gloomy donkey from Winnie the Pooh can still be spotted in the queue for Indiana Jones. Just look near the projector in the projection room to see it (you may need to ask a Cast Member for help)!

17. **Tiny Visitor**
One of the trees in Adventureland (near Indiana Jones Adventure) has a little door, window, and chimney at its base. This is the home of Patrick Begorra, the Little Man of Disneyland, a leprechaun from the 1955 book of the same name!

18. **Real Relics**
Most of the corroded artifacts found around Big Thunder Mountain Railroad are real! These items were crated in from actual mines by Disney to give the ride a more authentic look and feel!

19. **How'd They Do That?**
The special effect that brings Haunted Mansion's residents to "life" is called a "Pepper's Ghost." This simple, but eerily staged illusion uses angled mirrors, a sheet of plastic, and dim lights!

20. **A Gardener's Nightmare**
The Haunted Mansion's lawn isn't tended to very often. This is on purpose to suspend the illusion of a creepy, weathered old house!

21. **The Death Count**
The Haunted Mansion is said to be haunted by 999 ghosts—spooky!

22. **Namesake Ghoul**
Madame Leota's name came from Walt Disney Imagineer, Leota Toombs, who worked on attractions like Pirates of the Caribbean and, of course, Haunted Mansion!

23. **You're Sinking!**
The effect of the stretching room in the Haunted Mansion is created by lowering guests in a giant elevator before boarding the ride!

24. **Talking on Circles**
In Tomorrowland, head to the Star Wars Launch Bay building. Just outside of the entrance there are a couple of circles on the ground. Step on one of those circles and say something for a surprise!

25. **Give Them Props!**
In the queue for Star Tours, guests see C-3PO and R2-D2 interacting with one another. These stunning life-size animatronics were made from actual props used in the original *Star Wars* film series!

26. **Golden Age**
To have C-3PO keep his iconic golden gleam, Imagineers coated the animatronic in thousands of dollars of actual gold!

27. **Disappearing Paint**
The Disneyland Resort is always changing, so construction zones often border some popular areas. In order to make guests feel immersed in the parks, Disney paints construction walls "go away green" (also known as "no see um green"), a flat color that blends into the background!

28. **No-Chew Zone**
To keep areas clean, Disney does not sell gum at any of its parks, but you can bring your own!

29. **After Hours**
Disneyland allows guests to wait in line up until the very last minute. For example, if the park closes at 9pm, but you get in line for a ride at 8:59pm, Cast Members will still allow you entry.

30. **Till the Towering Spire!**
There are several petrified trees—or spires —around Star Wars: Galaxy's Edge, and the tallest one measures 135 feet (41 m)!

31. **Watery Surprise**
The drinking fountain found in Galaxy's Edge's marketplace is also home to an alien creature called a dianoga. This creature was first seen in the original *Star Wars* film's trash compactor

scene. The dianoga's name is "Tiny" and can be seen every few seconds when it pops up in the water tanks!

32. **Out of This World Playlist**
DJ R-3X—the resident music droid in Oga's Cantina—plays a 3-hour setlist, so you won't hear a repeat during your visit.

33. **Linking Worlds**
At the finale of Millennium Falcon: Smugglers Run, look for a Star Tours ship leaving Black Spire Outpost! This story directly connects to the events of Star Tours where ships drop passengers off in Batuu.

34. **No Wasting Food**
The Disneyland Resort donates unserved food to the Second Harvest Food Bank of Orange County. In 2019, over 20,000 meals were served!

CALIFORNIA ADVENTURE
SECRETS & FAST FACTS

35. **Permanent Parking**
Disneyland had to close and relocate its parking lot to make room for Disney California Adventure Park!

36. **Eastern Influence**
Original concepts for Disney California Adventure were part of a project called WestCot. This was a futuristic and stylish take on Epcot at Walt Disney World. WestCot was also supposed to feature a giant golden ball! The City of Anaheim and several other factors vetoed this possibly gaudy design and California Adventure came to life years later.

37. **Mickey's Mark**
Walt originally wanted to name his iconic mouse, Mortimer. However, his wife, Lily, insisted for a friendlier sounding name. The name wasn't lost forever as you can visit Mortimer's Market on Buena Vista Street!

38. **California Natives**
Disney takes its plants very seriously! In fact, they spent over

half a million dollars planting trees around Grizzly Peak to give it an authentic California feel!

39. **On Patrol**
    A Buena Vista "Police Officer" patrols the street in the morning, greeting guests. However, if he sees you "acting up," you might get a playful citation. To speed up this process, you can always pose for a photo with the officer and tell him that your friend or family member has been grumpy or misbehaving.

40. **Sun Power**
    Cars Land is home to 40,000 square feet of solar paneling. The energy harnessed there is used to help power the park!

41. **Toy Invader**
    When looking through the glass of the Cozy Cone Motel office, look for a lifting traffic cone to spot Buzz Lightyear sneaking by!

42. **Incredibly Long**
    At over a mile in track length, the Incredicoaster is one of the top ten longest steel roller coasters in the world!

43. **Staged Landmark**
    Since Disney couldn't get permission to film while flying over the Taj Mahal, *Soarin's* version is mostly computer animated!

44. **Timed Launch**
    When *Soarin'* was revamped in 2016, it debuted along with Epcot's (in Walt Disney World) on June 17, 2016—one day after Shanghai Disneyland opened! This was done for unity amongst the three parks as they welcomed their new sister park in China!

45. **A New Location**
    There are several *Soarin'* attractions around the world at different Disney theme parks. Though much is the same during the ride, the endings are different at each park. For example, at Disney California Adventure park the final scene takes guests back to Disneyland, at the Walt Disney World Resort the flight lands at Epcot, and at Shanghai Disneyland the ride flies over buildings in Shanghai!

46. **Missing Rodent**
    When the Rocket the Raccoon animatronic isn't working in the

Guardians of the Galaxy—Mission: Breakout ride, Disney plays a video of him talking instead!

47. **Hidden Office**
    There's a hidden "office" dining spot in the back of Lamplight Lounge. To enter, you'll have to crank open a safe and enter the vault! The room is spacious and has views of Pixar Pier. There are also board games and other things to do inside the space. However, it's rarely given to daytime guests though VIP tours can request it. Still worth asking about if you have a large party of 10 or more!

SECRET MENU ITEMS

While the Disneyland Resort is filled with famous treats options like the Dole Whip and warm churros, there are several secret off-menu items to enjoy! These secret treats are little known and are spread by word of mouth only. Discover them here and give them a shot when ordering at Disneyland during your visit!

DISNEYLAND

Mac-n-Chili Bread Bowl
Main Street Refreshment Corner — Main Street, U.S.A.
Chili with creamy mac 'n' cheese served in a delicious bread bowl!

"Alien Style" Galactic Burger and Fries
Galactic Grill — Tomorrowland
Taking this idea from In-N-Out Burger's "animal style" favorites, the Galactic Grill in Tomorrowland spreads thousand island dressing, grilled onions, and extra cheese over their Galactic burger and french fries!

The Hidden Burrito
Rancho del Zocalo — Frontierland
An enormous combination burrito with chicken, beef, pork, rice, cheese, chilis, sauces, and beans!

Ice Cream "Nachos"
Golden Horseshoe — Frontierland

Chips made of ice cream cone with Neapolitan ice cream (strawberry, vanilla, and chocolate scoops), hot fudge, and whipped cream topped with chocolate chips and cherries!

Dole Whip with Tajin
Tiki Juice Bar — Adventureland
The Tiki Juice bar has packets of spicy Tajin pepper to try with your Dole whip for a delicious mix of sweet, spicy, and salty flavors! Just ask for the packets!

Dole Whip with Bacon
Tropical Hideaway — Adventureland
Ask for bacon as a free topping for your Loaded Dole Whip!

DISNEY CALIFORNIA ADVENTURE

Make Mine Mocha Smoothie
Schmoozies — Hollywood Land
A coffee blended shake with chocolate and vanilla ice cream!

Mac 'n Cheese Bread Bowl
Pacific Wharf — Pacific Wharf Cafe
A Boudin sourdough bread bowl filled with mac n cheese!

Flo's Neapolitan Shake
Flo's V8 Cafe — Cars Land
Flo's famous vanilla, chocolate, and strawberry shakes can be layered on top of each other for a delicious, flavor-changing treat!

The Funwheel Drink
Lamplight Lounge — Pixar Pier
An alcoholic beverage with three "layers" of multicolored liquids: pineapple juice (yellow), passion fruit vodka (red), and Blue Curaçao (blue). It's all topped with creamy soda water!

DOWNTOWN DISNEY

Dole Whip Drink
Trader Sam's — Disneyland Hotel
A blend of pineapple juice and rum. Not every bartender knows how to make this drink—but it's worth asking!

FREE STUFF

While technically nothing at Disneyland is free (you are paying to enter, after all), it still feels great to score something special without spending extra money on it. We've composed a list of these cool souvenirs you should grab during your visit.

FREE STUFF IN BOTH PARKS

1. **Free Special Occasion Buttons**
   Celebrate your birthday, anniversary, and more with a free pin-on button at the park. Just visit Disneyland's City Hall (Main Street, U.S.A.) or California Adventure's Chamber of Commerce (Buena Vista Street) or a Disneyland Resort Hotel (if you're staying on property) and ask a Cast Member for a special occasion button!

· **Magic Tips** ·
Buttons are often in a rack outside of City Hall, so there's no need to wait for one! Pins are also available at the Emporium shop on Main Street, U.S.A.

2. **City Hall Menus**
   Disneyland's City Hall once distributed free recipes, but most of those have moved online. However, you can often get brochures with plant-based and seasonal items here.

3. **Free Stickers**
   When entering and leaving the parks, you may see Cast Members with tablets. Take their guest survey and ask for a free sticker upon completing the questionnaire.

4. **Free Maps**
   This might be a no-brainer, but maps are great souvenirs, especially since they have the surrounding dates of your arrival. These are located at the entrances to Disneyland and California Adventure.

5. **Free Professional Photos**
We've mentioned this before, but it's worth repeating. Stop at any of the photo booths scattered around the parks and ask the Disney photographer to take a photo with your camera. They are happy to do so and typically they do a great job!

FREE AT DISNEYLAND

6. **Free Fortunes**
The Play Disney app accesses free collectable fortune cards in a couple of locations. The Esmeralda the Fortune Teller box on Main Street is where guests use Play Disney for a free fortune printout. The Tall Tales of Fortune Red is a Pirates of the Caribbean version of Esmeralda and is located in the Pieces of Eight store in New Orleans Square.

7. **Bina's Guide to the Creatures of Batuu**
Designed for kids ages 10 and younger, this short guidebook reviews the creatures found on the planet of Batuu. It's a fun and free book that you can pick up at the Creature Stall in Star Wars: Galaxy's Edge.

FREE AT CALIFORNIA ADVENTURE

8. **Free Boudin Bread**
During the Boudin Factory Tour in Pacific Wharf, each guest receives a free piece of sample bread.

9. **Free Disney Art**
Learn to draw your favorite Disney characters at the Animation Academy in Hollywood Land and keep the paper drawing you created!

10. **Free Buttons & Pins**
If you attend an opening day event for a Disneyland attraction, restaurant, or special appearance, you may receive a commemorative button or pin. For example, when Tiana's Palace opened, guests were given buttons during opening day.

CHAPTER NINETEEN

UNIVERSAL STUDIOS HOLLYWOOD, LOS ANGELES, AND SAN DIEGO

UNIVERSAL STUDIOS

INTRODUCTION

If you're planning an extended stay at the Disneyland Resort, we'd highly recommend getting out and experiencing other attractions in Southern California. Both Los Angeles and San Diego are filled with world-class sights and amusements to make your trip even more magical! The Disneyland Resort is about 35 miles from Hollywood and 95 miles from San Diego. That means that they are so close that you could leave in the morning and return the same day! Here, we've outlined tips and travel advice for visiting Universal Studios Hollywood, attractions in Los Angeles, and San Diego highlights.

HOLLYWOOD

The world famous Universal Studios Hollywood is dubbed "the entertainment capital of the world" for some very good reasons! With thrilling rides based on famous films like *Harry Potter* and *Jurassic World*, this amusement park studio is the real deal. The tram tour is a 50-minute ride into actual Hollywood film sets and sound stages where you can see everything from props to famous landmarks (like Wisteria Lane from *Desperate Housewives* and the house from Alfred Hitchcock's *Psycho*). Not only will you see *how* Hollywood magic is made, but you'll also *experience* it, firsthand, as you enter immersive spaces like The Wizarding World of Harry Potter!

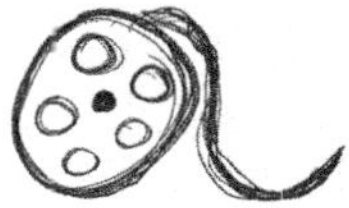

TIPS BEFORE YOU GO

Universal Studios Hollywood is a much smaller area than the Disneyland Resort and it's split into two levels: the upper lot and the lower lot. The lower lot only has three rides: a Jurassic World water ride, a 3-D Transformers ride, and a Revenge of the Mummy indoor rollercoaster. The upper level has the entire Hogsmeade Village from Harry Potter (which includes two rides, Harry Potter and the Forbidden Journey and a family-friendly rollercoaster, Flight of the Hippogriff), The Simpsons ride, and a Despicable Me ride. The real bulk of the attractions are located in the World-Famous Studio Tour tram which guides you around the

backlots of Universal Studios and includes simulation rides like Fast & Furious - Supercharged and King Kong 360.

While Disney is loaded with attractions for people of all ages, Universal mostly hits well with tweens to adults—especially those who love Harry Potter. Depending on how adventurous your young kid is (6 and under), he or she may not enjoy the experiences at Universal Studios Hollywood. It's also common for Universal Studios guests not to get to the park until around 11am, so getting there about 20-30 minutes before opening will allow you to experience all of the attractions quickly by avoiding the lines that form later in the day.

For an even speedier method of riding, Universal offers Universal Express passes for an additional cost (between $70-$150 extra per guest). This pass allows you to cut the line for most rides and attractions. While Universal Express does get you on the rides faster, it won't be necessary unless you are there on very crowded days (like in July or around Christmas).

Since Universal Studios Hollywood takes aim at pulling its visitors into the movies, many of its attractions are based around motion simulation. This means the ride chair or vehicle moves along with a screen to simulate you driving, flying, crashing, and escaping action sequences (think *Star Tour*s at Disneyland). In fact, of Universal's nine rides, five of them use motion simulation, including its Studio Tour tram. So, if attractions like this make you feel ill, you may want to consider this before heading to Universal Studios.

Many guests visit Universal Studios to experience the magic of Harry Potter. You'll step into Hogsmeade Village as a Muggle and leave a wizard! Buy a school robe and wand at Ollivanders and cast spells that interact with the area. See magical creatures, escape a dragon, sip Butterbeer, and ride a Hippogriff in this unique and fascinating world!

If you're visiting in September or October, you may be able to experience one of the coolest Halloween theme parks ever! Universal Studios Hollywood hosts its annual ghoulfest, Halloween Horror Nights. This terrifying and unforgettable experience immerses guests in horror movie magic. The park transforms its sound stages and backlots into terrifying thrills as lunatics with chainsaws and blood-spewing monsters chase you down real Hollywood sets! You'll also experience horrific terrors in twisted mazes themed after movies like *The Shining* and TV series like *American Horror Story*. The

Hollywood actors and special gore effects really make this one terrifying and fun experience! Needless to say, we don't recommend this experience for the kids. Horror film-loving teens and adults will find these attractions a lot of fun!

The earlier you buy your Halloween Horror Nights ticket, the better. Weekends tend to sell out, especially in October. Also be sure to get to Horror Nights early to avoid the crazy lines—near Halloween, the lines can be 5 hours long! Also, Horror Nights is the one time that Universal Express makes the most sense. You'll likely pay about $100-$150 more for it, but it will ensure that you experience every maze and chill that evening. For tickets, visit: http://www.halloweenhorrornights.com Save money on your regular Universal Studios Hollywood ticket by purchasing online beforehand: www.universalstudioshollywood.com. Regular adult ticket prices range from $109-$119 ($103-$113 child), depending on the day. Weekends and holidays tend to be more expensive. Buying directly at the gate will cost up to an additional $30 per ticket.

· Magic Tips ·

Discount tickets are often sold through AAA, military bases and nearby college campuses, Costco (annual pass), and travel websites like Expedia. We usually see a $5-$10 per ticket difference in cost from the website.

GETTING THERE

BY CAR

From the Disneyland Resort, we recommend traveling by car. Whether you are driving your own car or renting one, traveling there is easy.

Directions from the Disneyland Area:

1. I-5 North Freeway to 101 Hollywood Freeway North
2. Exit Universal Studios Blvd
3. Follow the signs to Universal Studios Hollywood

PARKING

Universal Studios charges $30 for General Parking in one of their garages. You can also select Preferred Parking for $40, which will get you closer to the theme park. However, if you are looking for extra-close parking, we would recommend Front Gate Parking instead for $60. If you don't mind walking through Universal's CityWalk mall, we recommend saving the money and paying for general parking.

RIDES – UPPER LOT

WORLD-FAMOUS STUDIO TOUR

Description: Hop aboard a large tram and visit actual Hollywood sets! The tram also gets attacked by Jaws, King Kong, gangsters from Fast & Furious, and faces the wrath of many elements including massive earthquakes and floods! Fast & Furious – Supercharged and King Kong 360 are part of this tram tour.
Level: Everyone
Recommendation: An unforgettable hour-long ride for everyone.

· **Magic Tips** ·
To better spot celebrities and live tapings, plan your tram tour on a weekday and in the late morning before lunchtime.

THE SECRET LIFE OF PETS: OFF THE LEASH

Description: Based on the popular animated film series, this dark ride takes guests through a hilarious and family-friendly journey. Max, Snowball, Gidget, and many other characters show up on the ride!
Level: Young Kids, Kids, Families
Recommendation: We recommend this attraction for families with children 12 and under as the experience is tailored for them. Access a Virtual Line Pass for this ride using the Universal Studios Hollywood mobile app.

KUNG FU PANDA: THE EMPEROR'S QUEST

Description: Follow Po and his friends as they complete a fantastic quest using stunning visual effects. This theatre-in-the-round show has moving seats but is gentle enough for young kids to experience.

Level: Young Kids, Kids, Tweens

Recommendation: This attraction has whimsical action, humor, and beautiful special effects. Children will not be permitted to sit on the laps of adults in the moving seats. If you have a young child, ask a Universal Team Member to direct you to a stationary seat.

THE SIMPSONS RIDE

Description: The world's favorite cartoon family brings their crazy antics to this hilarious motion simulation ride.

Level: Tweens, Teens, Adults, Thrill Riders

Recommendation: The humor might be a little crude for young kids (or it may go over their heads entirely), but The Simpsons Ride is a hilarious adventure that we highly recommend.

HARRY POTTER AND THE FORBIDDEN JOURNEY

Description: Walk through Hogwarts Castle to meet Harry, Hermione, and Ron before boarding a 3-D motion simulation ride like nothing you've ever experienced! The queue for this ride is an amazing journey through Hogwarts castle!

Level: Kids, Teens, Adults, Thrill Riders

Recommendation: Harry Potter fans 7 and up will love this unique thrill ride. It does get a bit spooky, but is a smile-inducing spectacular!

FLIGHT OF THE HIPPOGRIFF

Description: A family-friendly outdoor roller coaster designed after a flying hippogriff from Harry Potter.

Level: Families

Recommendation: A short and fun coaster for families with kids. The seats to this ride are very small, so taller and larger adults may not find them comfortable.

DESPICABLE ME MINION MAYHEM

Description: Ride with Gru, his kids, and of course, dozens of yellow minions in this motion simulator.

Level: Families

Recommendation: Perfect for families and fans of Despicable Me, but thrill riders might be okay with skipping this one.

SILLY SWIRLY FUN RIDE

Description: A Dumbo-like ride themed after *Despicable Me*.

Level: Young Kids, Kids

Recommendation: A rotating ride perfect for young kids.

SUPER SILLY FUN LAND
Description: A water soak zone playground.
Level: Young Kids, Kids
Recommendation: A mini-water park intended for young kids. Be sure to bring a change of clothes!

> **· Magic Tips ·**
> Easily check wait times on the free Universal Hollywood mobile app available for Apple and Android devices. We recommend downloading this ahead of your visit to prevent slow installation.

RIDES – LOWER LOT

JURASSIC WORLD—THE RIDE
Description: Enter Jurassic World on a gentle river ride that ends with an 80-foot plunge! You'll see dinosaurs brought to life with stunning animatronics and digital effects.
Level: Thrill Riders
Recommendation: Jurassic World is Universal Hollywood's best thrill ride! If you love thrilling water rides, you'll enjoy Jurassic World.

Child Swap: If a young one in your party doesn't want to ride, enter the child swap line in the queue. One adult will wait with the child and then switch when the other person finishes. Look for signs before you enter the queue.

TRANSFORMERS: THE RIDE-3D
Description: Help the Autobots keep the Allspark away from the deadly Decepticons in this explosive 3-D motion simulation ride.
Level: Kids, Teens, Adults, Thrill Riders
Recommendation: A heart-pumping ride perfect for most thrill riders.

REVENGE OF THE MUMMY
Description: An indoor rollercoaster themed after *The Mummy*.
Level: Thrill Riders

Recommendation: A high-speed roller coaster that lags a bit at the end, but has some pretty cool special effects. Thrill riders will appreciate this indoor coaster.

MARIO KART: BOWSER'S CHALLENGE

Description: There is one ride-through attraction in Super Nintendo World and it's based on the Mario Kart video game series. Guests ride together through massive scenes and wear augmented reality headsets shaped like Mario's signature red cap The AR technology brings to life digital characters that race through physical sets. However, guests are not racing each other, rather they are to outpace the villain Bowser and his many minions. Rather than a fast-paced rather (the karts move rather slowly) guests can pick up and toss digital koopa shells at enemies.

Level: Kids, Teens, Adults, Thrill Riders

Recommendation: Mario Kart: Bowser's Challenge is an attraction is great for those who love interactive gameplay within rides. Guests collect and shoot koopa shells, aiming with their headset and firing with a steering wheel. So you'll see both physical set pieces and digital characters racing around your during the ride. We find that this attraction is more fun with each ride through. However, lines can get very long, so we recommend visiting early in the day and riding it first.

· **Magic Tips** ·

Super Nintendo World has many interactive elements throughout the land. Guests can collect digital coins by purchasing Power-Up Bands for around $40. These bands are available at stores in Super Nintendo World and other parts of the park. To collect coin, bop the bottom of coin boxes and other spots within the land.

Virtual Line – Super Nintendo World may use a virtual queue to access the land. To use this, open the Universal Studios app once you are inside the park and join. We recommend getting to the park at opening as spots can fill up.

BOWSER JUNIOR SHADOW SHOWDOWN

If you have a Power-Up Band, you can take on four different bad guys within Super Nintendo World and unlock the Bowser Junior boss battle. Really, you only need to defeat three of the four baddies but but once you've collected enough coins, head to Bower Jr.'s lair to the left of the Mario Kart ride entrance to battle him!

SHOWS AND OTHER ATTRACTIONS

WATERWORLD (Upper Lot) – An explosive stunt show on the water starring characters and themes from the film *Waterworld*. The explosions and stunts are fantastic and really like nothing you'll see anywhere else. The closer you sit to the water, the better chances you have of getting wet. To stay dry, keep out of the labeled soak zones. Guests can also get a Virtual Line Pass for this attraction using the Universal Studios Hollywood app!

OLLIVANDERS (*The Wizarding World of Harry Potter*, Upper Lot) – A short show where one lucky guest has a wand choose her or him. For hardcore Harry Potter fans, this is a must. Others may not find it worth the wait in line.

⋆ **Magic Tips** ⋆
There isn't a sure-fire way to get chosen for Ollivanders, but those standing near the front and who are making good eye contact with Ollivander may have a better chance.

THE NIGHTTIME LIGHTS AT HOGWARTS CASTLE (Seasonal at *The Wizarding World of Harry Potter*, Upper Lot) – See magnificent lights and projections illuminate the Hogwarts Castle. Each of the four houses are represented by the magic of their animal from Gryffindor to Slytherin!

DARK ARTS AT HOGWARTS CASTLE (Seasonal at *The Wizarding World of Harry Potter*, Upper Lot) – Similar to the Nighttime Lights at Hogwarts Castle, this seasonal projection show covers the dark side of the Wizarding World. Projections display wicked curses, creatures, and even fantastic magic brought to life in mind-blowing ways!

⋆ **Magic Tips** ⋆
The Hogwarts light shows last around 5 minutes and run every 20 minutes or so. We recommend waiting until a later show to avoid the initial rush.

DINING RECOMMENDATIONS

TOADSTOOL CAFE (*Super Nintendo World*, Lower Lot) – Try Italian and American-style food prepared by Chef Toad! This spot is very popular so you may need to book a reservation at the entrance of the cafe once you're there.

BUTTERBEER (Butterbeer Cart – *The Wizarding World of Harry Potter*, Upper Lot) – A creamy non-alcoholic soda or slushy with an unforgettable flavor. If you like butterscotch or cream soda, we highly recommend this. The soda version is sweeter than the slushy version, and most seem to enjoy the slushy better.

BIG PINK DONUT (Lard Lads – Simpsons Area, Upper Lot) – An enormous pink, sprinkled donut perfect for sharing. If Lard Lads has a long line, head to the Kwik-E-Mart where these donuts are in prepackaged boxes.

HOG'S HEAD PUB (*The Wizarding World of Harry Potter*, Upper Lot) – Adults can try a lager while there is non-alcoholic pumpkin juice for kids (it tastes like nutmeg and cinnamon!). If you like cocktails, try the delightful Pear Dazzle—a mix of vodka, lemonade, and pear cider.

JURASSIC CAFE (Lower Lot) – Dine on Costa Rica-inspired dishes from fish and grains to burgers and fries.

THREE BROOMSTICKS (*The Wizarding World of Harry Potter*, Upper Lot) – Try some delicious British favorites in a *Harry Potter*-themed restaurant! We recommend the Cornish Pasties or the Fish and Chips!

UNIVERSAL CITYWALK RESTAURANTS – Just outside of Universal Studios Hollywood's gates is a mall filled with dining. Try fun chains like Bubba Gump Shrimp Co., the Hard Rock Hotel, and Jimmy Buffett's Margaritaville.

LOS ANGELES

HOLLYWOOD

Visit the Hollywood Walk of Fame, the famous Grauman's Chinese Theatre, and the Hollywood Highland Center where the Academy Awards are filmed. On the way, you'll see the Hollywood Sign high up on the hills. We will warn you that while Hollywood is a cool sight-seeing and photo-op place, it's not the fanciest. It's an authentic downtown location and the streets can feel dirty. For something posher, shop on Rodeo Drive or head to Beverly Hills nearby.

GETTY CENTER

1200 Getty Center Dr, Los Angeles, CA 90049

See an exquisite art museum in a state-of-the-art building near Hollywood. There's also a tram that transports you to the museum! Admission is free, but parking is $20.

EL CAPITAN THEATRE

Located in the heart of Hollywood, this magnificent, Disney-owned cinema hosts many of the Disney film premiers. When watching a movie here, you can often see exclusive props and promotional material before and after the screening. Also look for special events for classic Disney film screenings.
Tickets: elcapitantheatre.com

DISNEY'S CAROLWOOD BARN

5202 Zoo Dr., Los Angeles, CA 90027

Visit the miniature barn influenced by Walt Disney's love of trains and the American Midwest. See inspirations for the Disneyland Park including miniature trains and tracks. The museum is only open every third Sunday and admission is free.

SAN DIEGO

SAN DIEGO ZOO

2920 Zoo Dr, San Diego, CA 92101

Tickets: $52 Adults (12 and up) / $42 Children (3-11)

An enormous landscape filled with exotic animals that the whole family will love. See everything from splashing penguins to graceful elephants on your visit. It's about a 90-minute drive (120 minutes with traffic) and located in downtown San Diego. We recommend dining at the beautiful and delicious Albert's Restaurant in the zoo.

SAN DIEGO ZOO'S SAFARI PARK

15500 San Pasqual Valley Rd, Escondido, CA 92027

Tickets: $52 Adults (12 and up) / $42 Children (3-11)

This remotely located wildlife preserve (87 miles from Disneyland) is home to even more exotic animals that roam massive fields. In fact, for an extra cost (starting at $111 per person) you can hand feed giraffes and rhinos in the Caravan Safari as you travel through the amazing enclosures during this two-hour tour.

LEGOLAND, CALIFORNIA

1 Legoland Dr, Carlsbad, CA 92008

Tickets: Starting at $95 Adults (13 and up) / $89 Children (3-12)

Legoland is a unique park themed after the world's most famous building bricks and is specifically designed for families with kids. The weekdays are generally slow, even during the summer and holiday times. Weekends can get packed with locals, but the lines rarely reach atrocious lengths. Kids ages 3-12 will love the small roller coasters and Lego-themed attractions. Teenagers and solo adults will find that Legoland is missing experiences designed for them. However, the park is clean, well-kept, and fun for families. Discount tickets are available through CITYPass, Costco, and AAA.

CHAPTER TWENTY

TOP 10 LISTS: THE BEST OF DISNEYLAND

OUR LISTS

The Disneyland Resort has seemingly endless attractions, sights, and food to enjoy. We can understand if you feel overwhelmed deciding what to do! Don't worry because we're coming to the rescue with our most recommended things to do during your stay at Disneyland!

We've compiled this list in order with 1 being the most-recommended:

Note: Disneyland is marked (DL) and Disney California Adventure is marked (DCA).

BEST THRILL RIDES

1. Star Wars: Rise of the Resistance (DL)
2. Indiana Jones Adventure (DL)
3. Guardians of the Galaxy – Mission: Breakout! (DCA)
4. Incredicoaster (DCA)
5. Space Mountain (DL)
6. Tiana's Bayou Adventure (DL)
7. Radiator Springs Racers (DCA)
8. Big Thunder Mountain Railroad (DL)
9. Millennium Falcon: Smugglers Run (DL)
10. Grizzly River Run (DCA)

BEST FAMILY RIDES

1. Mickey & Minnie's Runaway Railway (DL)
2. Star Wars: Rise of the Resistance (DL)
3. Pirates of the Caribbean (DL)
4. Peter Pan's Flight (DL)
5. Haunted Mansion (DL)
6. Star Tours – The Adventures Continue (DL)
7. Jungle Cruise (DL)
8. "it's a small world" (DL)
9. Toy Story Midway Mania! (DCA)
10. The Mad Tea Party (DL)

BEST RIDES FOR YOUNG KIDS (3-5)

1. Mickey & Minnie's Runaway Railway (DL)
2. Peter Pan's Flight (DL)
3. The Little Mermaid (DCA)
4. Dumbo the Flying Elephant (DL)
5. Alice in Wonderland (DL)
6. Mad Tea Party (DL)
7. The Many Adventures of Winnie the Pooh (DL)
8. Storybook Land Canal Boats (DL)
9. Inside Out Emotional Whirlwind (DCA)
10. Toy Story Midway Mania! (DCA)

BEST NON-RIDE ATTRACTIONS

1. Wondrous Journeys (DL)
2. World of Color (DCA)
3. Fantasmic! (DL)
4. Magic Happens Parade (DL or DCA)
5. Mickey's PhilharMagic (DCA)
6. Animation Academy (DCA)
7. Sorcerer's Workshop (DCA)
8. Sleeping Beauty Castle Walkthrough (DL)
9. The Amazing Spider-Man! (DCA)
10. Enchanted Tiki Room (DL)

BEST SWEET SNACKS

1. Dole Whip Float (DL – Tiki Juice Bar and Tropical Hideaway)
2. Churros (various churro carts in DL and DCA)
3. Raspberry Rose Mickey Macaron (DL – Jolly Holiday)
4. Mickey Premium Ice Cream Bars (ice cream carts in DL and DCA)
5. Dessert Lumpia (DL – Tropical Hideaway)
6. Celestial-Sized Choco-Smash Candy Bar (DCA – Pym Test Kitchen)

7. Beignets (DTD – Beignets Xpressed)
8. Cheshire Cat Tails (DL – Candy Palace)
9. Mickey Beignets (DL – Mint Julep Bar)
10. Blue Milk (DL – Star Wars: Galaxy's Edge)

BEST SAVORY SNACKS

1. Barbacoa Nachos (DCA – Lamplight Lounge)
2. Ronto-Less Garden Wrap (DL – Ronto Roasters)
3. House Gumbo (DL – Tiana's Palace)
4. New York's Tastiest (DCA – Shawarma Palace)
5. Safari Skewer Bacon-Wrapped Asparagus (DL – Bengal Barbecue)
6. Corn Dog (DL – Little Red Wagon / DCA – Corn Dog Castle)
7. Traditional Pork Lumpia (DL – Tropical Hideaway)
8. Bacon Mac 'n' Cheese Cone (DCA – Cozy Cone Motel)
9. Popcorn (popcorn carts in DL and DCA)
10. Breakfast Chimichanga (DL – Frontierland snack cart)

BEST TABLE SERVICE RESTAURANTS

1. Carthay Circle Restaurant (DCA)
2. Napa Rose (Grand Californian Hotel)
3. Cafe Orleans (DL)
4. Blue Bayou (DL)
5. Splitsville Luxury Lanes (Downtown Disney)
6. Storytellers Cafe (Grand Californian Hotel)
7. Carthay Circle Alfresco Dining (DCA)
8. Lamplight Lounge (DCA)
9. Jazz Kitchen (Downtown Disney)
10. River Belle Terrace (Disneyland)

BEST QUICK-SERVICE RESTAURANTS

1. Tropical Hideaway (DL)
2. Docking Bay 7 Food and Cargo (DL)
3. Tiana's Palace
4. Bangal Barbecue (DL)
5. Tangaroa Terrace Tropical Bar & Grill (Disneyland Hotel)
6. Pym Test Kitchen (DCA)
7. Award Wieners (DCA)
8. Shawarma Palace (DCA)
9. GCH Craftsman Bar and Grill (Grand Californian Hotel)
10. Corn Dog Castle (DCA)

CHAPTER TWENTY-ONE

PRE-PLANNED ATTRACTION LISTS

INTRODUCTION

While you can plan a Disneyland trip in any order you'd like, there are ideal ways to maximize your time and have a lot of fun! Our pre-planned ride guides are tested and proven to help avoid long lines and make the day more relaxing. Whether you are there for days on end or trying to get to both parks in one day, we have you covered.

TIME-SAVING TIPS:

1. Get to the park early and grab a map at the entrance.
2. Take a photo of the ride list you've chosen with your phone or cut it out to take with you.
3. Reserve all table-service dining before arrival.
4. Take a break when you need to in between rides.
5. Keep calm, enjoy the sights, and take in the magical feelings of The Happiest Place on Earth!

Note: For the best results, get to the parks at least 20-30 minutes before opening. You'll be able to experience more rides within the first 90 minutes on busier days.

DISNEYLAND

MUST-SEE ATTRACTIONS PLAN

1. **Star Wars: Rise of the Resistance** (Disneyland)
2. **Haunted Mansion** (New Orleans Square)
3. **Indiana Jones Adventure** (Adventureland)
4. **Pirates of the Caribbean** (New Orleans Square)
5. **Jungle Cruise** (Adventureland)
6. **Tiana's Bayou Adventure** (Critter Country)* ∞
7. **Big Thunder Mountain Railroad** (Frontierland)
8. **Millennium Falcon: Smugglers Run** (Galaxy's Edge)
9. **Peter Pan's Flight** (Fantasyland)
10. **Snow White's Enchanted Wish** (Fantasyland)
11. **Alice in Wonderland** (Fantasyland)
12. **"it's a small world"** (Fantasyland)
13. **Matterhorn Bobsleds** (Fantasyland)
14. **Space Mountain** (Tomorrowland)
15. **Star Tours** (Tomorrowland)
16. **Disneyland Fireworks** (Main Street, U.S.A.)

FOR THRILL RIDERS PLAN

1. **Star Wars: Rise of the Resistance** (Disneyland)
2. **Space Mountain** (Tomorrowland)
3. **Indiana Jones Adventure** (Adventureland)
4. **Pirates of the Caribbean** (New Orleans Square)
5. **Tiana's Bayou Adventure** (Critter Country)* ∞
6. **Millennium Falcon: Smugglers Run** (Galaxy's Edge)
7. **Big Thunder Mountain Railroad** (Frontierland)
8. **Matterhorn Bobsleds** (Fantasyland)
9. **Star Tours** (Tomorrowland)
10. **Disneyland Fireworks** (Main Street, U.S.A.)

BONUS:

11. **Jungle Cruise** (Adventureland)
12. **Peter Pan's Flight** (Fantasyland)
13. **The Haunted Mansion** (New Orleans Square)

**May use a Virtual Queue*
∞ Opens later in 2024

DISNEYLAND

WITH KIDS AGES 2-5 PLAN

We recommend spacing out rides with most preschool-aged kids. If you can manage two rides back to back, allow them some roaming time in Fantasyland to check out the shops or grab a snack. When they're ready for the next ride, hop in line.

1. **Peter Pan's Flight** (Fantasyland)
2. **Snow White's Enchanted Wish** (Fantasyland)
3. **Pinocchio's Daring Journey** Ω (Fantasyland)
4. **Dumbo the Flying Elephant** (Fantasyland)
5. **Storybook Land Canal Boats** (Fantasyland)
6. **Fantasy Faire** (Fantasyland)
7. **Magic Happens Parade** (Fantasyland)
8. **Alice in Wonderland** (Fantasyland)
9. **"it's a small world"** Ω (Tomorrowland)
10. Explore Mickey's Toontown
11. **The Many Adventures of Winnie the Pooh** Ω (Critter Country)
12. **Disneyland Fireworks** (Main Street, U.S.A.)

Ω *Attractions with typically short wait times.*

WITH KIDS AGES 6-9 PLAN

1. **Star Wars: Rise of the Resistance** (Disneyland)
2. **Peter Pan's Flight** (Fantasyland)
3. **Snow White's Enchanted Wish** (Fantasyland)
4. **Millennium Falcon: Smugglers Run** (Galaxy's Edge)
5. Explore Star Wars: Galaxy's Edge
6. **Roger Rabbit's Car Toon Spin** (Mickey's Toontown)
7. **Mad Tea Party** (Fantasyland)
8. **Alice in Wonderland** (Fantasyland)
9. **Autopia** (Adventureland)
10. **Star Tours** (Tomorrowland)
11. **The Haunted Mansion** (New Orleans Square)
12. **Pirates of the Caribbean** (New Orleans Square)
13. **Disneyland Fireworks** (Main Street, U.S.A.)

**May use a Virtual Queue*

∞ Opens later in 2024

CALIFORNIA ADVENTURE
MUST-SEE ATTRACTIONS PLAN

1. **Radiator Springs Racers** (Cars Land)
2. **WEB Slingers: A Spider-Man Adventure** (Avengers Campus)*
3. **Guardians of the Galaxy** (Hollywood Land)**
4. **Monsters Inc.*** (Hollywood Land)
5. **Soarin'** (Grizzly Peak)
6. **Grizzly River Rapids** (Grizzly Peak)
7. **The Little Mermaid** (Paradise Gardens Park)
8. **The Amazing Spider-Man! mini show** (Avengers Campus)
9. **Incredicoaster** (Pixar Pier)**
10. **Toy Story Midway Mania** (Pixar Pier)
11. **Pixar Pal-A-Round** (Pixar Pier)
12. **Animation Academy** (Hollywood Land)
13. **World of Color** (Paradise Gardens Park)

BONUS:

14. **Mater's Junkyard Jamboree** (Cars Land)
15. **Luigi's Rollickin' Roadsters** (Cars Land)

FOR THRILL RIDERS PLAN

1. **Radiator Springs Racers** (Cars Land)
2. **Guardians of the Galaxy** (Hollywood Land)
3. **WEB Slingers: A Spider-Man Adventure** (Avengers Campus)*
4. **Soarin'** (Grizzly Peak)
5. **Grizzly River Rapids** (Grizzly Peak)
6. **Goofy's Sky School** (Paradise Gardens Park)
7. **Silly Symphony Swings** (Paradise Gardens Park)
8. **Pixar Pal-A-Round: Swinging Gondolas** (Pixar Pier)
9. **Toy Story Midway Mania** (Pixar Pier)
10. **Incredicoaster** (Pixar Pier)
11. **Mater's Junkyard Jamboree** (Cars Land)
12. **World of Color** (Paradise Gardens Park)

BONUS:

13. **Ride Guardians again** for a different drop sequence!

* If this attraction uses a Virtual Queue, get it first.

** These are extreme thrill rides not suitable for every guest.

CALIFORNIA ADVENTURE

WITH KIDS AGES 2-5 PLAN

We recommend spacing out rides with most preschool-aged kids. If you can manage two rides back to back, allow them some roaming time in Pixar Pier to meet characters. When they're ready for the next ride, hop in line. Kids in this age group may also enjoy WEB Slingers: A Spider-Man Adventure.

1. **Toy Story Midway Mania!** (Pixar Pier)
2. **Inside Out Emotional Whirlwind** (Pixar Pier)
3. **Jessie's Critter Carousel** Ω (Pixar Pier)
4. **The Little Mermaid** Ω (Paradise Gardens Park)
5. **Luigi's Rollickin' Roadsters*** (Cars Land)
6. **Mater's Junkyard Jamboree** (Cars Land)
7. **Mickey's PhilharMagic*** Ω (Hollywood Land)
8. **Monsters, Inc.** (Hollywood Land)

Ω Attractions with typically short wait times.

WITH KIDS AGES 6-10 PLAN

We also recommend the "Must-See Attractions Plan" for kids these ages.

1. **Radiator Springs Racers** (Cars Land)
2. **Toy Story Midway Mania** (Pixar Pier)
3. **Pixar Pal-A-Round** (Pixar Pier)
4. **Silly Symphony Swings** (Paradise Gardens Park)
5. **Jumpin' Jellyfish** (Paradise Gardens Park)
6. **Goofy's Sky School** (Paradise Gardens Park)
7. **The Little Mermaid** (Paradise Gardens Park)
8. **Grizzly River Rapids** (Grizzly Peak)
9. **Soarin'** (Grizzly Peak)
10. **Animation Academy** (Hollywood Land)
11. **Monsters, Inc.** (Hollywood Land)
12. **WEB Slingers: A Spider-Man Adventure** (Avengers Campus)
13. **The Amazing Spider-Man!** mini show (Avengers Campus)
14. **Doctor Strange Sanctum** mini show (Avengers Campus)
15. **Mater's Junkyard Jamboree** (Cars Land)
16. **Luigi's Rollickin' Roadsters** (Cars Land)
17. **World of Color** (Paradise Gardens Park)

BOTH PARKS IN ONE DAY

MUST-SEE ATTRACTIONS PLAN

Note: We highly recommend purchasing Genie+ for best results.

Start at Disneyland

1. Join the Virtual Queue for an attraction (if applicable)
2. **Indiana Jones Adventure** (Adventureland)
3. **Jungle Cruise** (Adventureland)
4. **Pirates of the Caribbean** (New Orleans Square)
5. **Haunted Mansion** (New Orleans Square)
6. **Tiana's Bayou Adventure** (Critter Country)* ∞
7. **Millennium Falcon: Smugglers Run** (Galaxy's Edge)
8. **Space Mountain** (Tomorrowland)
9. **Star Tours** (Tomorrowland)

Move to Disney California Adventure

10. **WEB Slingers: A Spider-Man Adventure** (Avengers Campus)
11. **The Little Mermaid** (Paradise Gardens Park) *OR* **Guardians of the Galaxy** (Hollywood Land)
12. **Radiator Springs Racers** (Cars Land)
13. **Maters Junkyard Jamboree** (Cars Land) OR **Incredicoaster** (Pixar Pier)
14. **Toy Story Midway Mania** (Pixar Pier)
15. **Soarin'** (Grizzly Peak)

Move Back to Disneyland

16. **Matterhorn Bobsleds** (Fantasyland)
17. **Peter Pan's Flight** (Fantasyland)
18. **Snow White's Enchanted Wish** (Fantasyland)
19. **Big Thunder Mountain Railroad** (Frontierland)
20. **Disneyland Fireworks** (Main Street, U.S.A.)

**May use a Virtual Queue*

∞ Opens later in 2024

BOTH PARKS IN ONE DAY
FOR THRILL RIDERS PLAN

This plan has Thrill Riders bouncing around each park a bit. However, it's the most efficient when it comes to cutting down wait times.

Start at Disneyland

1. Join the Virtual Queue for an attraction (if applicable)*
2. **Space Mountain** (Tomorrowland)
3. **Indiana Jones Adventure** (Adventureland)
4. **Pirates of the Caribbean** (New Orleans Square)
5. **Tiana's Bayou Adventure** (Critter Country)* ∞
6. **Millennium Falcon: Smugglers Run** (Galaxy's Edge)
7. **Big Thunder Mountain Railroad** (Frontierland)
8. **Mad Tea Party** (Fantasyland)
9. **Matterhorn Bobsleds** (Fantasyland)

Move to Disney California Adventure

10. **Radiator Springs Racers** (Cars Land)
11. **Guardians of the Galaxy** (Hollywood Land)
12. **WEB Slingers: A Spider-Man Adventure** (Avengers Campus)
13. **Soarin'** (Grizzly Peak)
14. **Grizzly River Rapids** (Grizzly Peak)
15. **Goofy's Sky School** (Paradise Gardens Park)
16. **Toy Story Midway Mania** (Pixar Pier)
17. **Incredicoaster** (Pixar Pier)

Move Back to Disneyland

18. **Star Tours** (Tomorrowland)
19. **Big Thunder Mountain Railroad** (Frontierland)
20. **Disneyland Fireworks** (Main Street, U.S.A.)

**May use a Virtual Queue*

∞ Opens later in 2024

UNIVERSAL STUDIOS HOLLYWOOD
ONE-DAY PLAN

1. **Mario Kart: Bowser's Challenge*** (Lower Lot)
2. **Explore Super Nintendo World***
3. **Jurassic World—The Ride** (Lower Lot)
   Join the virtual queue for The Secret Life of Pets
4. **Revenge of the Mummy** (Lower Lot)
5. **Transformers: The Ride—3D** (Lower Lot)
6. **The Simpsons Ride** (Upper Lot)
7. **The World-Famous Studio Tour** (Upper Lot)
8. **The Secret Life of Pets: Off the Leash*** (Upper Lot)
9. **Despicable Me: Minion Mayhem** (Upper Lot)
10. **WaterWorld** (Upper Lot)
11. **Special Effects Show** (Upper Lot)
12. **Ollivanders** (Upper Lot)
13. **Harry Potter and the Forbidden Journey** (Upper Lot)
14. **Flight of the Hippogriff** (Upper Lot)
15. **Explore Hogsmeade Village** (Upper Lot)
16. **DreamWorks Theatre: Kung Fu Panda** (Upper Lot)

**Check the Universal Studios Hollywood mobile app to to see if the Virtual Line is required.*

CUSTOM RIDE LIST

Names: ____________________ ____________________

____________________ ____________________

____________________ ____________________

1. ____
2. ____
3. ____
4. ____
5. ____
6. ____
7. ____
8. ____
9. ____
10. ____
11. ____
12. ____
13. ____
14. ____
15. ____
16. ____
17. ____
18. ____
19. ____
20. ____
21. ____
22. ____
23. ____
24. ____
25. ____

CUSTOM RIDE LIST

Names: ______________________ ______________________

______________________ ______________________

______________________ ______________________

1. ____
2. ____
3. ____
4. ____
5. ____
6. ____
7. ____
8. ____
9. ____
10. ____
11. ____
12. ____
13. ____
14. ____
15. ____
16. ____
17. ____
18. ____
19. ____
20. ____
21. ____
22. ____
23. ____
24. ____
25. ____

VACATION CHECKLIST

- ❑ Park tickets
- ❑ Ride list
- ❑ ID
- ❑ Credit card / cash
- ❑ Hotel address
- ❑ Phone (and charging cable)
- ❑ Sunscreen
- ❑ Toiletries: toothbrush, toothpaste, etc.
- ❑ Swimsuit
- ❑ Jacket
- ❑ Comfortable shoes
- ❑ Plastic bag for cellphone (water rides)
- ❑ Snacks
- ❑ Water bottles (if you aren't flying)
- ❑ Backpack or bag
- ❑ Restaurant reservations
- ❑ This Disneyland Guidebook
- ❑ ______________________________
- ❑ ______________________________
- ❑ ______________________________
- ❑ ______________________________
- ❑ ______________________________
- ❑ ______________________________
- ❑ ______________________________
- ❑ ______________________________
- ❑ ______________________________
- ❑ ______________________________

CONCLUSION
AND DISNEYLAND'S FUTURE

When Disneyland first opened in 1955, the theme park looked drastically different from today. Only a handful of the original attractions still remain and those—like Dumbo the Flying Elephant and Jungle Cruise—don't have the same appearance as their early days. Nearly seventy years later, Disneyland is still a place of constant change with new attractions, updated experiences, and innovative ways to experience imaginative worlds.

Disneyland has confirmed a few new attractions debuting in the coming years. An all-new *Avatar* experience is heading to the Disneyland Resort. In addition, there are future plans for another Avengers-themed ride set in the multiverse. In this attraction, guests battle King Thanos! Disneyland has yet to set a opening dates for these future attraction.

In 2021, Disneyland also announced plans for a massive expansion that would add new attractions, hotels, and shopping experiences. The DisneylandForward project presents some interesting ideas that would increase the footprint of the existing two parks as they take over some spaces around Downtown Disney. The Toy Story Parking Lot is also proposed to offer more retail and accommodations for guests. Though these projects will need approval from the City of Anaheim, it's great to see that Disneyland has its eye on the future.

Whatever Disney has in sore for us, we only expect that the fun is only just beginning!

Happy and safe travels!
Magic Guidebooks

INDEX

A

B

C

D

E

F

G

H

I

J

K

L

M

N

O

P

Q

R

S

T

U

W

Z

Was this book helpful?

★★★★★

If so, can you please leave us a quick review on Amazon.com?

Your reviews GREATLY help us out!
THANK YOU!

Wishing you a magical vacation!
Magic Guidebooks

Printed in Great Britain
by Amazon

47464840R00159

YOUR FAST AND INFORMATIVE GUIDE TO A MAGICAL VACATION!

Plan your vacation right! Magic Guidebooks presents a detailed look at the dazzling Disneyland Resort! Discover invaluable tips for dining, where to stay, and even how to save money. This is your easy, one-stop guide to all of the excitement at Disneyland !

- **Covers the entire Disneyland Resort** including Disneyland park, Disney California Adventure park, Downtown Disney, and beyond
- Dedicated chapters to **Star Wars: Galaxy's Edge guide** and **Avengers Campus** with reviews, tips, and secrets for exploring the lands
- **Covers New Attractions** including the upcoming Tiana's Bayou Adventure Star Tours updates, and more!
- **Virtual Queue hacks** for best ways to secure an attraction boarding pass
- **Money and time-saving tactics** for worry-free planning
- **Disney Genie+ explanation and tips**—and line-skipping strategies so tha you don't need to purchase Genie+!
- **Discover the best food** with unbiased restaurant reviews & recommendati
- **Need-to-know tips for visiting with kids**, tweens, teens, and adults!
- **Explore secrets**, histories, and magical details found around the Disneyland Resort—including lists of **Hidden Mickeys**!
- **BONUS: Guides to Universal Studios Hollywood**, Los Angeles attractions, the San Diego Zoo, and Legoland!

www.magicguidebooks.com

ISBN 9798988976837

90000

9 798988 976837